IFIP Advances in Information and Communication Technology 613

IFIP – The International Federation for Information Processing

IFIP was founded in 1960 under the auspices of UNESCO, following the first World Computer Congress held in Paris the previous year. A federation for societies working in information processing, IFIP's aim is two-fold: to support information processing in the countries of its members and to encourage technology transfer to developing nations. As its mission statement clearly states:

IFIP is the global non-profit federation of societies of ICT professionals that aims at achieving a worldwide professional and socially responsible development and application of information and communication technologies.

IFIP is a non-profit-making organization, run almost solely by 2500 volunteers. It operates through a number of technical committees and working groups, which organize events and publications. IFIP's events range from large international open conferences to working conferences and local seminars.

The flagship event is the IFIP World Computer Congress, at which both invited and contributed papers are presented. Contributed papers are rigorously refereed and the rejection rate is high.

As with the Congress, participation in the open conferences is open to all and papers may be invited or submitted. Again, submitted papers are stringently refereed.

The working conferences are structured differently. They are usually run by a working group and attendance is generally smaller and occasionally by invitation only. Their purpose is to create an atmosphere conducive to innovation and development. Refereeing is also rigorous and papers are subjected to extensive group discussion.

Publications arising from IFIP events vary. The papers presented at the IFIP World Computer Congress and at open conferences are published as conference proceedings, while the results of the working conferences are often published as collections of selected and edited papers.

IFIP distinguishes three types of institutional membership: Country Representative Members, Members at Large, and Associate Members. The type of organization that can apply for membership is a wide variety and includes national or international societies of individual computer scientists/ICT professionals, associations or federations of such societies, government institutions/government related organizations, national or international research institutes or consortia, universities, academies of sciences, companies, national or international associations or federations of companies.

More information about this series at http://www.springer.com/series/6102

Steven Furnell · Nathan Clarke (Eds.)

Human Aspects of Information Security and Assurance

15th IFIP WG 11.12 International Symposium, HAISA 2021
Virtual Event, July 7–9, 2021
Proceedings

 Springer

Editors
Steven Furnell ⓘ
University of Nottingham
Nottingham, UK

Nathan Clarke ⓘ
University of Plymouth
Plymouth, UK

ISSN 1868-4238   ISSN 1868-422X (electronic)
IFIP Advances in Information and Communication Technology
ISBN 978-3-030-81113-6   ISBN 978-3-030-81111-2 (eBook)
https://doi.org/10.1007/978-3-030-81111-2

This Springer imprint is published by the registered company Springer Nature Switzerland AG
The registered company address is: Gewerbestrasse 11, 6330 Cham, Switzerland

Preface

It is now widely recognized that technology alone cannot provide the answer to cyber security problems. A significant aspect of protection comes down to the attitudes, awareness, behavior, and capabilities of the people involved, and they often need support in order to get it right. Factors such as lack of awareness and understanding, combined with unreasonable demands from security technologies, can dramatically impede the ability to act securely and comply with policies. Ensuring appropriate attention to the needs of users is therefore a vital element of a successful security strategy, and users need to understand how the issues may apply to them and how to use the available technology to protect their systems.

With all of the above in mind, the Human Aspects of Information Security and Assurance (HAISA) symposium series specifically addresses information security issues that relate to people. It concerns the methods that inform and guide users' understanding of security, and the technologies that can benefit and support them in achieving protection.

This book presents the proceedings from the fifteenth event in the series, held virtually, due to the COVID-19 pandemic, during July 7–9, 2021. A total of 18 reviewed papers are included, spanning a range of topics including security management, cyber security education, and people and technology. All of the papers were subject to double-blind peer review, with each being reviewed by at least two members of the International Program Committee. We are grateful to all of the authors for submitting their work and sharing their findings. We are also grateful to David Emm, from Kaspersky, UK, for being the keynote speaker for this year's event.

The HAISA symposium is the official event of IFIP Working Group 11.12 on Human Aspects of Information Security and Assurance, and we would like to thank Prof. Kerry-Lynn Thomson for supporting the event as Working Group chair. We would also like to acknowledge the significant work undertaken by our International Program Committee, and recognize their efforts in reviewing the submissions and ensuring the quality of the resulting event and proceedings. Finally, we would like to thank Dr. Christos Kalloniatis and the organizing team for making all the necessary arrangements to enable this symposium to take place.

July 2021

Steven Furnell
Nathan Clarke

Organization

General Chairs

Steven Furnell   University of Nottingham, UK
Nathan Clarke   University of Plymouth, UK

IFIP TC11.12 Conference Chair

Kerry-Lynn Thomson   Nelson Mandela University, South Africa

Local Organizing Chair

Christos Kalloniatis   University of the Aegean, Greece

Publicity Chair

Fudong Li   University of the Portsmouth, UK

International Program Committee

Sal Aurigemma   University of Tulsa, USA
Maria Bada   University of Cambridge, UK
Peter Bednar   University of Portsmouth, UK
Matt Bishop   UC Davis, USA
Patrick Bours   Norwegian University of Science and Technology, Norway
William Buchanan   Edinburgh Napier University, UK
Mauro Cherubini   University of Lausanne, Switzerland
Jeff Crume   IBM, USA
Adele Da Veiga   University of South Africa, South Africa
Dionysios Demetis   University of Hull, UK
Ronald Dodge   Palo Alto Networks, USA
Paul Dowland   Edith Cowan University, Australia
Jan Eloff   University of Pretoria, South Africa
Simone Fischer-Huebner   Karlstad University, Sweden
Stephen Flowerday   Rhodes University, South Africa
Lynn Futcher   Nelson Mandela University, South Africa
Stefanos Gritzalis   University of Piraeus, Greece
Julie Haney   NIST, USA
Karen Hedström   Örebro University, Sweden
Kiris Helkala   Norwegian Defence University College, Norway
Joanne Hinds   University of Bath, UK

Contents

People and Technology

Attitudes and Perspectives

Cyber Security in Healthcare Organisations

Dhrisya Ravidas[1], Malcolm R. Pattinson[1(✉)], and Paula Oliver[2]

[1] Adelaide Business School, University of Adelaide, Adelaide, South Australia, Australia
`{dhrisya.ravidas,malcolm.pattinson}@adelaide.edu.au`
[2] Department of Innovation and Skills, AustCyber SA Node, Adelaide, South Australia, Australia
`paula.oliver@sa.gov.au`

Abstract. The aim of the research described in this paper was to develop a cyber security survey for the purpose of assessing the state of cyber security controls in a selection of healthcare organisations in South Australia. To achieve this aim, a gap analysis was conducted, using the collected data, that identified cyber security controls which had not been implemented satisfactorily, according to management. An acceptable level of cyber security is dependent on a specific set of controls that should have been implemented in order to maintain the Confidentiality, Integrity and Availability (CIA) of digital healthcare data and the risk appetite of the organisations. Specifically, in this case, healthcare management was concerned about the increasing number of cyber threats to Patient Health Information (PHI). In this era of a connected world, information is highly sought after and vulnerable to cyber security breaches. In this context, cyber security can be seen to be very similar to personal hygiene, such that, personal hygiene is only achieved if the appropriate practices, routines, actions, and behaviours are in place.

Keywords: Digital Information Systems (DIS) · Goal Attainment Scaling (GAS) · Cyber security · Healthcare sector · Confidentiality · Integrity and Availability (CIA) · Gap analysis · Patient Health Information (PHI) · Notifiable Data Breaches (NDB)

1 Introduction

Cyber security has become a critical issue for most organisations today, particularly those with a significant investment in Digital Information Systems (DIS). However, management and internal auditors still ask, 'is our information secure?' or 'do we have the necessary blend of controls in place to withstand the various threats to our information?'. These questions are still tough to answer. In the past, management has sought answers by having both internal and external specialists conduct information security reviews and risk analysis on a regular basis. These projects were typically costly, time-consuming, and resource-intensive, because they were originally designed for large organisations with extensive information systems (Love 1991). The Healthcare Sector (hospitals, clinics and other healthcare facilities) has become globally dependent on digital technology to

© IFIP International Federation for Information Processing 2021
Published by Springer Nature Switzerland AG 2021
S. Furnell and N. Clarke (Eds.): HAISA 2021, IFIP AICT 613, pp. 3–11, 2021.
https://doi.org/10.1007/978-3-030-81111-2_1

monitor, send, retrieve, store and share healthcare data. It is clear that cyber security threats are more common due to the rising value of sensitive health information and the increased dependency on digital systems. Cyber security breaches in the Healthcare Sector will negatively impact both patients and healthcare organisations, potentially life-threatening consequences such as PHI being compromised (Andre 2017). Healthcare organisations are vulnerable due to the historic lack of investment in cyber security and vulnerabilities in existing hardware and software. However, employee actions, processes, routines or behaviour (Coventry and Branley 2018) continue to be the primary source of risk. As we move forward, cyber security must be an integral part of healthcare organisations' responsibilities. Although the management of cyber security risks and their mitigation is the responsibility of individual organisations, the government should also enact laws and regulations to secure the general public from such cyber threats.

Cyber security plays an integral role in making Australia a safer and highly trusted place to do business. The rapid and widespread uptake of digital technology by households and businesses following the COVID-19 pandemic underscores the importance of digital technology as an economic enabler (Offner et al. 2020). Millions of Australians are working from home, staying connected through software apps and using essential digital services such as telehealth (Jalali et al. 2019). Consequently, there is an urgent need to put in place a framework of controls to ensure a level of cyber security that is acceptable to management. Evolving government policies and fast technological advancement are exposing the vulnerabilities of the healthcare sector to cyber security breaches. While other sectors, like finance and defense, have invested in securing their data and systems, healthcare organisations still fall behind in adapting to the newer regulations, security protocols and the pace at which it adopts more modern technology (Andre 2017). This is identified as the reason that the healthcare sector is a prime target for PHI security breaches. Furthermore, it is essential that cyber security is paid its due attention to ensure the protection of personal health information of healthcare stakeholders (Australian Cyber Security Centre 2020). It does this by ensuring that the Confidentiality, Integrity and Availability (CIA) of PHI is achieved and maintained.

1.1 Research Aim

The research described in this paper aims to develop a cyber security survey to assess the state of cyber security controls within selected South Australian healthcare organisations. A gap analysis methodology known as Goal Attainment Scaling (GAS) was used to achieve this aim.

2 Literature Review

As part of the literature review, various types of cyber security breaches were investigated together with their associated threats and risks. There have been multiple cyber incidents, including the WannaCry (Ehrenfeld 2017) other, which are indicative of poor cyber security in healthcare organisations.

In September 2016, the Health Minister of Australia disclosed that the data of 3 million patients had been accessed due to vulnerability of the Medicare system. This gave perpetrators access to doctors' prescriptions and PHI (Spooner and Towell 2016).

Recently the Australian Cyber Security Centre (ACSC) reported that there is a significant increase in malicious cyber activity in healthcare or COVID-19 environments such as aged-care facilities and other healthcare sectors. For example, some financially motivated perpetrators used the 'Maze' ransomware attack to lock an organisation's valuable information so that they could steal important business information and threaten to post this information online unless a ransom was paid (Australian Cyber Security Centre 2020).

The Office of the Australian Information Commissioner (OAIC) compared notifications made under the Notifiable Data Breaches (NDB) scheme across the top five industry sectors. It stated that during the reporting period from January to June 2020, the health service sector recorded 115 data breaches. These statistics imply that the healthcare industry has become a prime target for cyber adversaries (Notifiable Data Breaches Report: January–June 2020 2021).

Furthermore, the OAIC report found that the leading cause of the data breaches during the 12 months was phishing, causing 153 violations. Still, over a third of all notifiable data breaches were directly due to human error (52 per cent). It is to be noted that other leading sources of human error are the unintended release or publication of PHI (20 per cent) and the loss of paperwork or data storage devices (23 per cent) (Eddy 2019).

According to recently released data compiled by the Centre for Strategic and International Systems (CSIS), Australia is in the top six most hacked countries in the world, with 16 significant cyber-attacks reported in the period between May 2006 and June 2020 (Livingstone 2020).

3 Research Method

This research used an email-distributed questionnaire that utilised the Goal Attainment Scaling (GAS) methodology to identify the potential cyber security vulnerabilities in selected organisations within the healthcare sector in South Australia. This research was conducted in three phases. In the first phase, the cyber security controls were identified as the essential eight cyber security practices, together with five implementation levels of the controls and the GAS-based instrument was developed using the Qualtrics online survey. In the second phase, data collection was done using this online survey to conduct the assessment. In the third phase, the results were calculated, analysed, and reported to the selected management.

3.1 Description of Goal Attainment Scaling (GAS)

The GAS methodology is a program evaluation methodology used to evaluate the effectiveness of a program or project (Kiresuk et al. 2014). A program evaluation methodology is a process of determining how well a particular program is achieving or has achieved its stated aims and expectations. Kiresuk and Lund (1982) state that program evaluation is a process of establishing "…the degree to which an organisation is doing what it is supposed to do and achieving what it is supposed to achieve." (p. 227). Goal Attainment

Scaling (GAS) has been in use for 35 years as a means of measuring outcomes from different contexts and enabling these measures to be represented by a quantitative measure (Pattinson 2001).

One of the essential components of the GAS methodology is the evaluation instrument. This is primarily a table or matrix whereby the columns represent objectives to be assessed and the rows represent levels of attainment of those objectives. Kiresuk *et al.* (2014) refer to these objectives as goals or scales within a GAS Follow-up Guide. The rows represent contiguous descriptions of the degree of expected goal outcomes. These can range from the best-case level of goal attainment to the worst case, with the middle row being the most preferred level of goal attainment.

It is "a flexible tool for internal evaluation" (Love 1991, p. 93), enabling different organisations to set their own objectives and measurement criteria. This is in contrast to most other evaluation techniques that have pre-set standards that cannot be readily modified by stakeholders. This is primarily a table or matrix whereby the columns represent objectives to be assessed, and the rows represent levels of attainment of those objectives. These can range from the best-case level of goal attainment to the worst case, with the middle row being the most likely level of goal attainment. Goal attainment scaling is rated using the standard 5-point scale (-2 to $+2$) and formula to derive aggregated T-scores, as recommended by its originators (Kiresuk et al. 2014).

The sample GAS Follow-up Guide in Fig. 1 below is one of the eight follow-up guides that comprised the complete evaluation tool in this study.

PASSWORD USE

Please click on only ONE box in each of the three CONTROL columns

LEVEL OF IMPLEMENTATION	CONTROL 1 Password complexity	CONTROL 2 Multi-factor authentication (MFA)	CONTROL 3 Passwords for different accounts
Much less than expected	• Passwords are NOT used or have less than 12-characters • Does NOT use a combination of uppercase, lowercase letters, numbers or special characters	• MFA is NOT used to access networks and applications	• Use the SAME passwords for ALL accounts
Somewhat less than expected	• Passwords have a minimum 12-characters • Does NOT use a combination of uppercase, lowercase letters, numbers or special characters	• MFA is used to access MOST networks and applications	• Use DIFFERENT passwords for MOST accounts
Expected	• Passwords have a minimum 12-characters • Use AT LEAST one uppercase, lowercase letters, numbers or special characters	• MFA is used to access ALL networks and applications	• Use DIFFERENT passwords for all IMPORTANT accounts
Somewhat more than expected	• Passwords have a greater than 12-characters • Use MORE than one uppercase, lowercase letters, numbers or special characters	+ Use of swipe card or biometrics identification	• Use COMPLEX passwords for SOME accounts
Much more than expected	+ Forced to change the password every month + Re-use of passwords not allowed	+ Reviewed and audited at least 3-MONTHLY	• Use COMPLEX passwords or passphrase for all IMPORTANT accounts

Fig. 1. Password use GAS chart

3.2 Phase 1: Development of the GAS Evaluation Instrument

This phase utilises the eight essential controls referenced by the Cyber Check me document (Edith Cowan University 2020) on the information assets and the security CIA that applies across the South Australian healthcare sector (CyberCheckMe 2020).

A GAS follow-up guide for each of the eight essential practices was developed by identifying three of the most highly critical cyber security controls as per Fig. 2 below. This gave a total of twenty-four controls to be evaluated within the selected healthcare systems. The specific implementation of the controls may differ according to the technology choice and security needs of the respective organisation.

Essential Practices	Control No. 1	Control No. 2	Control No. 3
PASSWORD USE	Password complexity	Multi-factor authentication (MFA)	Passwords for different accounts
INTERNET USE	Using public Wi-Fi	Using virtual private network (VPN)	Using HTTPS website addresses
EMAIL USE	Suspicious files & links	Report suspicious emails	Encrypt confidential emails
SOFTWARE UPDATES	Anti-virus software	Application patches	Operating system patches
PHYSICAL DEVICE PROTECTION	Physical entry controls	Working in secure areas	Clean desk & clear screen policy
DATA BACKUPS	Identify the data to be backed up	Backup stored in a safe location	Data backup frequency
INCIDENT REPORTING	Reporting cyber security incidents	Follow up from incidents	Disciplinary process
EMPLOYEE TRAINING	Cyber security training	Frequency of training	Type of training

Fig. 2. Practices and controls used

3.3 Phase 2: Use the GAS Evaluation Instrument

This phase of the research relates to the distribution of the survey by email to the ICT authority of the five selected SA healthcare organisations. The GAS charts are interpreted to evaluate the essential controls. This is to encourage readability and positive engagement of the user. The principal objective of obtaining valuable data through an online survey is to develop a survey questionnaire specifically designed for the selected participants. Each respondent will select one appropriate level of implementation for each of the 24 controls within the eight essential practices. The chosen level of implementation should be the one that best describes their current situation.

The research described in this paper is a preliminary study only and will be extended to many more healthcare organisations and respondents. This will provide more validity of the GAS methodology and, therefore, a more accurate assessment of an organisation's level of cyber security.

3.4   Phase 3: Analyse the Evaluation Results and Report to Management

This phase involves the analysis of the data collected after all responses had been received. Raw scores were converted into GAS T-scores for each of the eight Follow-up Guides in accordance with the Kiresuk *et al.* (2014) methodology. The data from each survey response consisted of 24 scores within the range values of $-2, -1, 0, +1$ and $+2$ as per the GAS methodology. All responses for any one organisation would then be combined and converted to into one non-weighted T-score for each of the 8 follow-up guides.

A GAS T-score is a linear transformation of the average of the raw scores in each follow-up guide using the formulae documented by Kiresuk et al. (2014) and is presented below:

$$T - score = 50 + \frac{10 \sum w_i x_i}{\sqrt{(1-p) \sum w_i^2 + p\left(\sum w_i\right)^2}}$$

where x_i is the outcome score for he i^{th} scale with a weight of w_i, and p is the weighted average inter-correlation of the scale scores and commonly set at 0.3. Scores on the individual scales between -2 and $+2$ each are assumed to have a theoretical distribution with a mean of zero and a standard deviation of 1. This formula then produces T-scores with a mean of 50 and a standard deviation of 10 when each scaled control is scored using the -2 to $+2$ scale by Kiresuk *et al.* (2014). The five-point range of levels for cyber security controls is shown in Fig. 3 below.

Fig. 3.   Goal attainment scaling score

The GAS T-scores were calculated for each of the 8 follow-up guides, and a non-weighted T-score graph is depicted in the results, as shown in Fig. 4 below.

4   Results

A GAS T-score of 50 or more indicates that, on average, the controls specified within a GAS follow-up guide for a particular cyber security practice are considered acceptable to management. This assumes that management is aware of the levels of management expectations and compliance requirements with the specific cyber security policies and guidelines. If these controls are representative of all controls specified for this cyber security practice, then it can be contended that the controls in place are generally acceptable to management.

The extent of management expectations is reflected in the amount that the score is greater than 50. Conversely, a GAS T-score of less than 50 for a particular cyber security practice indicates that, in general, the cyber security controls in place are not acceptable to management. Therefore, the organisation is at risk of being breached through exploitation of that weak control. Figure 4 below is indicative of the eventual data analysis results. For example, Employee Training appears to be satisfactory whereas Password Use and Physical Device Protection are seriously inadequate and need to be addressed by the organisations management.

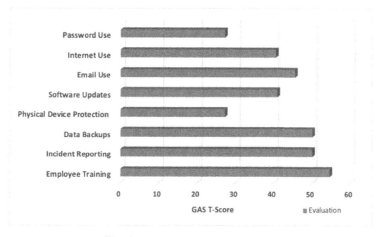

Fig. 4. Non-weighted GAS T-scores

5 Limitations and Future Research

The research outlined in this paper needs to be replicated in several private South Australian healthcare organisations and with many ICT managers' responses before the methodology is considered to be validated. This research was only intended to be a preliminary study prior to a full-scale study.

An evaluation of controls in this way, is not considered an audit of cyber security controls. In other words, it does not test inputs, processes, outputs, and business operations for conformance against a Standard. Instead, it measures stakeholder perceptions of the current state of play. Hence, it is recommended that the results be validated by conducting an independent audit of the controls. Further research is guaranteed to address the following research questions:

- Is the GAS methodology suitable for different sized organisations?
- Is the GAS methodology suitable for different organisations other than Healthcare?
- Is the GAS methodology suitable in organisations with multiple digital platforms?
- Could this GAS methodology be used to compare the state of cyber security controls within different organisations?

6 Conclusions

This research demonstrated that the GAS methodology, combined with a specific set of cyber security controls, is a feasible methodology to evaluate cyber security effectively and enable management to address the state of cyber security controls. Some attributes that contribute to this claim are:

- It is "a flexible tool for internal evaluation" (Love 1991, p. 93), enabling different organisations to set their own objectives and measurement criteria. This is in contrast to most other evaluation techniques that have pre-set criteria that stakeholders cannot readily modify.
- It is particularly suitable for assessing management controls because it involves both summative and formative evaluations (Love 1991, p. 93). The summative evaluation equates to assessing the level of attainment of cyber security controls after they have been implemented. The formative evaluation relates to on-going assessments of how well the cyber security controls are being maintained.
- It differs from many traditional evaluation approaches in that the assessment of a single control can result in one of five possible outcomes. Most other methods rely on dichotomous outcomes. For example, the approaches such as "Management by Objectives and Goal Monitoring", measure whether a goal was attained or not (Love 1991).
- It is one of the few evaluation techniques that converts a qualitative assessment of an area or issue into a quantitative result. More specifically, the GAS methodology generates a number for each Follow-up Guide by averaging evaluator raw scores. These numbers facilitate the comparison between evaluations at different times.

References

Andre, T.: Cybersecurity an enterprise risk issue. Healthc. Financ. Manag. **71**(2), 40–46 (2017)

Australian Cyber Security Centre (ACSC) (2020). https://www.cyber.gov.au/acsc/view-all-content/advisories/2020-013-ransomware-targeting-australian-aged-care-and-healthcare-sectors

Coventry, L., Branley, D.: Cybersecurity in healthcare: a narrative review of trends, threats and ways forward. Maturitas **113**, 48–52 (2018)

CyberCheck.me (2020). Cyber Guides. https://www.cybercheck.me/cyber-guides.html

Edith Cowan University (2020). Cyber Hints and Tips. https://www.ecu.edu.au/schools/science/research-activity/ecu-security-research-institute/cybercheckme/cyber-hints-and-tips.

Eddy, N.: Healthcare IT news (2019). https://www.healthcareit.com.au/article/healthcare-leads-data-breaches-security-issues-report-finds

Ehrenfeld, J.M.: Wannacry, cybersecurity and health information technology: a time to act. J. Med. Syst. **41**(7), 104 (2017)

Jalali, M.S., Razak, S., Gordon, W., Perakslis, E., Madnick, S.: Health care and cybersecurity: bibliometric analysis of the literature. J. Med. Internet Res. **21**(2), e12644 (2019)

Kiresuk, T.J., Lund, S.H.: Goal attainment scaling: a medical-correctional application. Med. L. **1**, 227 (1982)

Kiresuk, T.J., Smith, A., Cardillo, J.E. (eds.): Goal Attainment Scaling: Applications, Theory, and Measurement. Psychology Press, London (2014)

Livingstone, T.: 9News (2020). https://www.9news.com.au/national/cyber-attacks-australia-sixth-most-hacked-country-in-world-new-data-reveals/4a762e06-9342-4c8a-a7af-1632a1d1042a

Love, A.J.: Internal Evaluation: Building Organizations from Within. Sage Publications, Newbury Park (1991)

OAIC. Notifiable Data Breaches Report: January–June 2020 (2021). https://www.oaic.gov.au/privacy/notifiable-data-breaches/notifiable-data-breaches-statistics/notifiable-data-breaches-report-january-june-2020/#malicious-or-criminal-attack-breaches-top-five-industry-sectors

Offner, K.L., Sitnikova, E., Joiner, K., MacIntyre, C.R.: Towards understanding cybersecurity capability in Australian healthcare organisations: a systematic review of recent trends, threats and mitigation. Intell. Natl. Secur. **35**(4), 556–585 (2020)

Pattinson, M.R.: *Evaluating* Information System Security: An Application of Goal Attainment Scaling. Doctoral dissertation, Flinders University of South Australia, School of Commerce (2001)

Towell, R.: Fears that patients' personal medical information has been leaked in Medicare data breach. The Sydney Morning Herald (2016). https://www.smh.com.au/public-service/privacy-watchdog-called-after-health-department-data-breach-20160929-grr2m1.html

Cybersecurity and Digital Exclusion of Seniors: What Do They Fear?

Jesper Holgersson⬤, Joakim Kävrestad(✉)⬤, and Marcus Nohlberg⬤

University of Skövde, Skövde, Sweden
{jesper.holgersson,joakim.kavrestad,marcus.nohlberg}@his.se

Abstract. The rapid development of digitalization has led to a more or less endless variety of ways for individuals to communicate and interact with the outside world. However, in order to take advantage of all the benefits of digitalization, individuals need to have the necessary skills. Seniors represent a group that, compared to other groups, lives in a digital exclusion to an excessive extent, mainly due to the fact that they lack the necessary knowledge to use digital technology and digital services. Based on empirical data collected from seniors partaking in digital training, we have analyzed their perceptions of why they and other seniors are digitally excluded. Our findings point out that a major barrier for seniors to be more digitally included is different variants of fear of using digital technology and digital services. The common denominator can be traced down the possibilities to be exposed to frauds, scams, viruses, and faulty handling, which in turn cause undesired consequences. Consequently, we propose a research agenda where digital training and digital inclusion measurements should be studied side by side with cybersecurity behavior. Thus, making cybersecurity a fundamental part of digital inclusion has the potential to minimize the fears identified in this research as inhibitors to technology adoption.

Keywords: Digital exclusion · Cybersecurity · Digital divide · Fear

1 Introduction

The digital divide first and foremost refers to "the gap between those who do and those who do not have access to new forms of information technology" [7, pp 221–222]. The digital divide may refer either to a lack of possibilities to use access to the internet or absent availability to digital equipment, such as computers, tablets, or smartphones [5]. Although, in developed countries where there is an extensive digital infrastructure present, the digital divide is discussed in terms of access to knowledge and skills regarding how to make use of digital technology and services [8].

© IFIP International Federation for Information Processing 2021
Published by Springer Nature Switzerland AG 2021
S. Furnell and N. Clarke (Eds.): HAISA 2021, IFIP AICT 613, pp. 12–21, 2021.
https://doi.org/10.1007/978-3-030-81111-2_2

Among digitally excluded, seniors constitute a large demographic in many developed countries [6]. This situation is problematic due to several reasons. As pointed out by [13], seniors represent a group of citizens with a major need for digital service, for example, with respect to health-related services where the need often increases with age. At the same time, seniors use digital versions of such services the least. They are in many cases skeptical to start using digital alternatives to services that so far, in many cases, have been offered in more traditional ways [18].

In general, thanks to the increased digitalization of society, public service providers on both a national as well as on a local level have got great opportunities to generate efficiency gains and thereby save taxpayers' money. Moreover, digitalization can bring environmental gains in the form of reduced paper consumption and the ability to provide increased service for citizens through increased accessibility, faster processes, and so on. However, some groups risk being left out, not least seniors. An example from Sweden, which is considered to be one of the leading countries in OECD[1] when it comes to using digital technologies [19], seniors are underrepresented when it comes to using basic digital services, such as healthcare, public transportation, and taxes [10]. As a consequence, this group has limited possibilities to take part in modern society, including making use of digital services provided by governments [22,24]. To book a doctor's appointment, to pay bills, or to have the opportunity to participate in democratic processes is today cumbersome for digitally excluded elderly. Without the possibility to use electronic IDs and similar commonly used services for identification, it can be assumed that everyday life as a digitally excluded elderly citizen is unnecessarily complicated. Hence, the digital divide is still very much present for many seniors.

Research suggests several, often interrelated, arguments for why seniors are digitally excluded, e.g., negative attitudes and a lack of interest [17], high age and literacy problems [11], and linguistic problems [9]. However, as pointed out by [12]), the main barrier that prevents seniors from embracing the digitalization of society is a general lack of knowledge which in many cases results in a fear of using digital technology and services. [12] concludes that seniors fear what might happen if they push the wrong buttons or when it is safe or not to give out personal information. In addition, research on cybersecurity points out that anxiety and fear of online threats are inhibitors of technology adoption amongst elders [15]. This suggests a low perceived security self-efficacy. Security self-efficacy has been found to be an important factor in information security where a correlation between a high level of security self-efficacy and secure behavior has been identified [23]. Interestingly, research also suggests that seniors and users with low experience with technology are prone to exhibit a less risk-taking behavior [20]. However, it is well known that lack of knowledge, in turn, leads to increased susceptibility of online risks [2,3]. In addition, [24] emphasize the importance of raising seniors' skills regarding safety when being online and suggest further training of seniors in these matters.

---

[1] Organisation for Economic Co-operation and Development : https://www.oecd.org/.

We argue that digital inclusion and security self-efficacy must be studied side by side to enable not only digital inclusion but also secure digital inclusion. This paper aims to explore how fear of using digital technology and services is manifested and perceived among Swedish seniors. The study is carried out as a survey of over 1000 respondents as part of a series of training workshops intended to increase the digital self-efficacy of the participants. The result is an outline of what fears the respondents perceive as inhibitors to technology adoption, which provides a better understanding of how seniors perceive online threats and what effect that has on technology, their adoption, and self-efficacy of digital technology. As such, this study can serve as a starting point for future efforts in how to promote secure digital inclusion of seniors.

2   Research Approach

The research presented is based on qualitative empirical data collected from Swedish seniors. As pointed out in the introduction, Sweden is considered as one of the world's most developed countries when it comes to digitalization, and 98% of households have Internet access. Data was collected from a series of training sessions organized jointly by Telia Sweden AB[2] and six Swedish municipalities as a part of the "More Digital" training program. Each training session followed the same basic pattern. Invitations to the training sessions were sent out over a month in advance to all seniors, defined as citizens of at least 65 years of age, in the municipality of interest. No other requirements for participation were stated, such as digital literacy level, but seats were allocated on a first-come, first-served-principle. As a result, all seniors had an equal chance of participating in the workshop which enables a probability sample. It should, however, be acknowledged that the study does only include participants that opted to participate and risk of participation bias cannot be completely mitigated.

The invitations asked the participants to bring any questions they might have and invited the participants to bring their own digital devices. In each session, the participants were distributed over a set of tables. Each table had computers and two supervisors available. One supervisor was a senior provided by the arranging municipality, and the other was a high school student. The intention was to enable the younger generation to teach the seniors about digitalization, and they did so in response to the senior's questions.

Data was collected using qualitative inquiry [21], based on free text questions handed out as a short open-question questionnaire, and collected on-site. Each inquiry was then transcribed to the digital format by the research team. A small sample of the inquiries was collected online instead of with physical questionnaires, but exactly the same questions were used in the digital variant of the questionnaires. In total, 1099 transcripts were analyzed, collected from workshops distributed over six regionally distributed municipalities. The inquiries

---

[2] Telia Sweden AB is Sweden's largest telecom operator. Telia Sweden AB sells connections in fixed telephony, data communications, Internet, digital TV, IP telephony, and mobile telephony to private individuals, companies and organizations.

covered a wide range of aspects regarding the participants' experiences of and attitudes towards digital technology. However, in the research presented here, we have been explicitly addressing the participants' arguments and motives for why they perceive themselves and other seniors as digitally excluded.

Data analysis was conducted using content analysis [4,14,25]. In its essence, content analysis yields "a relatively systematic and comprehensive summary or overview of the data set as a whole" [25, p. 182], by observing repeating themes and categorizing them using a coding system that is developed inductively during the coding process. As a starting point, one of the researchers (researcher 1) read through the transcripts and documented each theme to get an overall general picture of the content. Second, researcher 1 used the initial set of codes and put those into a spreadsheet. For each unique statement made by the respondents, the researcher marked which of the themes were applicable. As an example, the statement "Uncertainty about how the technology works. Fear of account hijacking or data loss, spam? Hidden costs for e.g., download" is a statement which was interpreted as first and foremost a general fear of using digital technology and what that might bring in terms of exposure for threats. Moreover, the statement also was interpreted as a fear of doing things wrong, which might result in unpleasant consequences for the respondent. In addition, the statement was also interpreted as an explicit fear of being conned or fooled which is based on the respondent's uncertainty. For each of the statements, researcher 1 tried to interpret the inherent meaning in order to associate the statement to the corresponding themes initially identified.

In order to ensure coding consistency and intercoder reliability, the remaining members of the research team (two researchers) individually reanalyzed the initial coding and noted any misconceptions and uncertainties. Thereafter, the research team met and completed the coding process in consensus.

3   Results and Analysis

As pointed out, the participants were asked about their perceptions as to why they and/or other seniors are digitally excluded. In doing so, out of the 1099 participants answering the question, 423 of the participants express a general fear of what digitization and the use of digital technology may bring. A general fear of being forced to change behavior where you as an individual do not feel that you have full control over what you can and cannot do and what consequences any actions may have in a longer perspective is something that frightens these participants. As such, a general fear of technology limits the elderly from taking full advantage of digitization and therefore is a major contributor to the digital divide. The participants describe that computers are something new, and learning something new on your own is both difficult and scary, as shown by some of the collected quotes (translated from Swedish):

– We "chicken out" from the news we do not really understand without help (Woman, 74)

– Because it has not been natural for us to use the computer from childhood. It becomes more frightening (Woman, 72)
– Fear of feeling unknowing, fear of doing wrong and not taking the consequences of one's actions (woman, 86)
– Lack of contact with the younger generation, fear of doing wrong, lack of information from the society (Man, 69)

Further analysis of the data revealed four types of fear addressed by the participants: 1) Fear of doing things wrong and what consequences doing things wrong might bring to the participants. 2) Fear of new technology advancements which acts as an inhibitor towards using digital technology. 3) Fear of being conned or tricked by impostors as well as being exposed to, e.g., Trojans and viruses. 4) Fear of letting others understand how little the participants know about how to use digital technology and digital services, i.e., a sense of shame or embarrassment. Obviously, these types overlap to various degrees, but we have chosen to present each category individually. The fear types identified, and the number of participants specifically addressing each of those types is presented in Table 1. These types of fears are presented and discussed in the remainder of this section.

Table 1. Identified types of fear

Label	Prevalence
Fear	423 participants
Fear of doing wrong	131 participants
Fear of new technology	79 participants
Fear of being conned	65 participants
Shame	18 participants

3.1   Fear of Doing Wrong

The most prevalent type of fear was fear of doing wrong, expressed by 131 (12%) of the participants. Fear of doing wrong includes many different aspects. Still, in its essence, it seems to be about fear of not knowing what to do when using digital technology and what negative consequences might be the result of poorly performed actions, or as two of the participants state: "You are scared of "destroying" and do not dare to test (Man, no age)," "Not as brave as younger, believe hat something can break if you push the wrong button (Woman, 70)". In addition, several respondents mention not daring to test in fear of what that might result in, and not knowing the result of a certain action leads to not daring to perform that action at all. This fear is highlighted by quotes from some of the participants as follows: "Because the belief that the computer can break off the press to mush, and that is not the case (Man, 76)", "Believe they can make mistakes, afraid to try (Woman, 78)".

3.2   Fear of New Technology

Rather than a fear of doing something wrong, fear of new technology highlight insecurity connected to using new technology that is unknown and a feeling of being left alone with no one to turn to for help. When analyzing the data, we found in total 79 participants (7%) who express a lack of interest and low self-esteem as well as lack of knowledge as specific inhibitors of technology adoptions. As can be seen in the following quotes, fear of the technology component itself may act as an inhibitor for digital inclusion of seniors: "The starting point" is unknown and scary (Woman, 74)", "Fear of new technology. Bad self-esteem and unenterprising (Woman, 89)", "Not used to handle a computer, afraid of trying (Man, 83)", and "Fear of the computer, hard to learn, hard to get help (Man, 70)".

3.3   Fear of Being Conned

This theme explicitly addresses the fear of being conned and subjected to various types of fraud online. 65 participants (6%) of the participants mention a fear of being victimized in this way. They mention having read about fraudsters, viruses, account hijacking, and similar. This leads to suspicion and a fear of losing accounts or money when using digital technology and the internet. As highlighted by quotes from four of the participants, fear of being conned is often expressed together with a general fear or perceived lack of knowledge, i.e., in many cases, they are afraid to push a button or following a link due to the possibility of being tricked in some way. This might be hard for any user of digital technology, but it seems a lot harder for a user who is not familiar with the digital equipment being used.

- Insecurity about how technology works. Fear of account hijacking or loss of information, spam? Hidden costs when, for instance, downloading (Woman, 65)
- Feeling of insecurity, fear of pressing buttons. Fear of costs, Afraid that someone will access your account (Woman, 68)
- You do not want to get drawn in. It is easy to be conned (Man, 80)
- We did not learn in school. Are scared because you read so much in the papers about trickery and hoaxes (Woman, 72)

3.4   Shame

The final category of fears identified in the data was shame, present in 18 of the responses (2%). Shame was described by the participants as feeling insecure about asking for help: "Fear, does not want to be of trouble (Man, 69)" and not wanting to show that they do not understand or know what to do since admitting such a lack of digital knowledge is embarrassing to admit for others: "Fear, does not want to be of trouble (Man, 69)", "Raised in a different way, no making mistakes! Got no one to ask (Woman, 75)". Also, handling digital components poorly or faulty, thus possibly causing them to malfunction, is seen as an embarrassment that is avoided if possible: "Breaking the computer, fear of not succeeding (Man, 76)".

4   Discussion and Conclusion

This paper aims to explore how fear of using digital technology and services is manifested and perceived among Swedish seniors. The study is carried out as a survey of over 1000 respondents as part of a series of training workshops intended to increase the digital self-efficacy of the participants. The result is an outline of what fears the respondents perceive as inhibitors to technology adoption, which provides a better understanding of how seniors perceive online threats and what effect that has on technology, their adoption, and self-efficacy of digital technology.

The aim of this research was to explore how fear of using digital technology and services is manifested and perceived among Swedish seniors. The study was carried out as a survey distributed to participants of a workshop series intending to increase the digital self-efficacy of the elderly. This paper reports on the results of an open question where the participants were asked about their explanations for why seniors are digitally excluded. The gathered data was analyzed using content analysis, where one researcher coded the majority of the data, and the rest of the research team checked the coding for consistency. First, the data was analysed to identify the prevalence of fear as an explanation for digital exclusion. The analysis showed that about 38% of the respondents explained digital exclusion amongst seniors with a general sense of fear. A general pattern was that a lack of knowledge or understanding of the digital world leads to fear that has a paralyzing effect on seniors' motivation to become active members of the digital society.

A deeper analysis intended to identify the types of fears perceived by the participants. Four distinct types of fears were identified. *Fear of doing wrong* was described by the participants as a general fear stemming from not knowing what may happen if you try, leading to not trying at all. *Fear of new technology* was expressed as a general fear of the digital world which is perceived as fear of the unknown. *Fear of being conned* speaks to a perceived risk of being victimized by, for instance, account hijacking or online fraud and *shame* is a feeling of not wanting to disclose your ignorance or ask for help. While the types of fear are different, they are often overlapping, expressed in combination with a perceived lack of knowledge and lack of information source. This suggests that the underlying factor is a lack of understanding of digital technology. On this note, several participants mentioned that they feel like there is a lack of support and that they are just expected to know what to do from the start. This, in turn, leads to a lack of interest or fear of testing new technology, which can explain why seniors do not engage with the digital society to the same extent as the remaining members of the society. A consequence is, of course, that the digital divide is cemented.

In the context of cybersecurity, previous research has suggested that anxiety and fear of being conned are indeed inhibitors to technology adoption [15]. The results of this research emphasize that notion. Interestingly, research into cybersecurity awareness suggests that anxiety and fear can lead to higher awareness of cyber-threats which, in turn, leads to more secure behavior [20]. The main conclusion that can be drawn from our research is that fear stemming from a lack of knowledge is an inhibitor to technology adoption among seniors, i.e. if using digital technology is avoided, the risk of being exposed to threats and frauds are severely limited, but the prize that has to be paid is to be left out of all the positive aspects that can be associated with the usage of digital technology. As such, this problem should be addressed with efforts into training seniors to increase their digital self-efficacy. As pointed out by [24], one major competence that should be included when designing training programs for seniors is how to use digital technology and digital services in a safe manner. In addition, [12] points in the same direction when highlighting the fear of being exposed to threats and frauds as one major component that should be included in training programs for seniors where the goal is to enhance digital inclusion. Likewise, training is described in scientific literature as the go-to solution for increasing cybersecurity awareness and thus, decreasing the risk of victimization for online frauds, account hijacking and so on [1]. Given the fears perceived by the participants in this research, the suggestion of training to improve cybersecurity behavior, and the possibility for higher awareness stemming from fear and anxiety, we argue that digital inclusion and cybersecurity behavior should be studied side by side. We argue that secure digital inclusion makes for a promising research domain and suggest that future research should focus not only on how to include seniors in the digital world but on how to do so securely. Making cybersecurity a fundamental part of digital inclusion has the potential to minimize the fears identified in this research as inhibitors to technology adoption.

This research took place in a Swedish environment using a qualitative approach. While the dataset was gathered from 1099 respondents, a statistical analysis measuring the generalizability of the results was not possible to obtain in this study. Instead, it intends to provide insights into how fear of technology works as an inhibitor to technology adoption. Further, the Swedish context may present limitations as to how the results of this study are applicable in other nations. On that note, national culture is known to impact, for instance, cybersecurity behavior [16]. As such, a possible direction for future work is to research the same topic as this study but in other nations.

References

1. Al-Alosi, H.: Cyber-violence: digital abuse in the context of domestic violence. UNSWLJ **40**, 1573 (2017)
2. Bada, M., Sasse, A.M., Nurse, J.R.: Cyber security awareness campaigns: Why do they fail to change behaviour? arXiv preprint arXiv:1901.02672 (2019)
3. Bagga, T., Sodhi, J., Shukla, B., Qazi, M.: Smartphone security behaviour of the Indian smartphone user. Man In India **97**(24), 333–344 (2017)

4. Berelson, B.: Content Analysis in Communication Research. Content Analysis in Communication Research, Free Press, New York (1952)

5. Bélanger, F., Carter, L.: Trust and risk in e-government adoption. J. Strateg. Inf. Syst. **17**(2), 165–176 (2008)., https://www.sciencedirect.com/science/article/B6VG3-4RN4892-1/2/af26a5d6a3b53b9cf437a405625045d4, https://doi.org/10.1016/j.jsis.2007.12.002

6. van Deursen, A., Helsper, E.: A nuanced understanding of internet use and non-use among the elderly. Eur. J. Commun. **30**(2), 171–187 (2015). https://doi.org/10.1177/0267323115578059

7. van Dijk, J.: Digital divide research, achievements and shortcomings. Poetics **34**(4), 221–235 (2006)

8. Ebbers, W.E., Jansen, M.G.M., van Deursen, A.J.A.M.: Impact of the digital divide on e-government: Expanding from channel choice to channel usage. Gov. Inf. Q. **33**(4), 685–692 (2016). https://doi.org/10.1016/j.giq.2016.08.007, https://www.sciencedirect.com/science/article/pii/S0740624X16301460

9. Fortes, R.P.M., Martins, G.A., Castro, P.C.: A review of senescent's motivation in the use of tactile devices. Procedia Comput. Sci. **67**, 376–387 (2015). https://doi.org/10.1016/j.procs.2015.09.282, https://www.sciencedirect.com/science/article/pii/S1877050915031282

10. The Sweden Internet Foundation: The swedes and the internet. Report (2019). www.svenskarnaochinternet

11. Hill, R., Betts, L.R., Gardner, S.E.: Older adults' experiences and perceptions of digital technology: (dis) empowerment, wellbeing, and inclusion. Comput. Hum. Behav. **48**, 415–423 (2015). https://doi.org/10.1016/j.chb.2015.01.062, https://www.sciencedirect.com/science/article/pii/S0747563215000904

12. Holgersson, J., Söderström, E.: Bridging the gap: Exploring elderly citizens' perceptions of digital exclusion. In: 27th European Conference on Information Systems (ECIS), Stockholm & Uppsala, Sweden, June 8–14, 2019. Association for Information Systems (2019)

13. Jarke, J.: Co-creating Digital Public Services for an Ageing Society. PAIT, vol. 6. Springer, Cham (2021). https://doi.org/10.1007/978-3-030-52873-7

14. Krippendorff, K.: Reliability in content analysis: Some common misconceptions and recommendations. Human Commun. Res. **30**(3), 411–433 (2006). https://doi.org/10.1111/j.1468-2958.2004.tb00738.x

15. Kumar, S., Ureel, L.C., King, H., Wallace, C.: Lessons from our elders: identifying obstacles to digital literacy through direct engagement. In: Proceedings of the 6th International Conference on PErvasive Technologies Related to Assistive Environments, pp. 1–8 (2013)

16. Ndibwile, J.D., Luhanga, E.T., Fall, D., Kadobayashi, Y.: A demographic perspective of smartphone security and its redesigned notifications. J. Inf. Process. **27**, 773–786 (2019)

17. Niehaves, B., Plattfaut, R.: Internet adoption by the elderly: employing is technology acceptance theories for understanding the age-related digital divide. Eur. J. Inf. Syst. **23**(6), 708–726 (2014). https://doi.org/10.1057/ejis.2013.19

18. Nishijima, M., Ivanauskas, T.M., Sarti, F.M.: Evolution and determinants of digital divide in brazil (2005–2013). Telecommun. Policy **41**(1), 12–24 (2017). https://doi.org/10.1016/j.telpol.2016.10.004, https://www.sciencedirect.com/science/article/pii/S0308596116301835

19. OECD: Going digital in sweden - oecd reviews of digital transformation. Report (2018). https://www.oecd.org/sweden/going-digital-in-sweden.pdf

20. Pattinson, M., Butavicius, M., Parsons, K., McCormac, A., Calic, D.: Factors that influence information security behavior: an Australian web-based study. In: Tryfonas, T., Askoxylakis, I. (eds.) HAS 2015. LNCS, vol. 9190, pp. 231–241. Springer, Cham (2015). https://doi.org/10.1007/978-3-319-20376-8_21
21. Patton, M.Q.: Qualitative Research & Evaluation Methods. Sage, London (2002)
22. Polat, R.K.: Digital exclusion in turkey: a policy perspective. Gov. Inf. Q. **29**(4), 589–596 (2012). https://doi.org/10.1016/j.giq.2012.03.002, https://www.sciencedirect.com/science/article/pii/S0740624X12000950
23. Rhee, H.S., Kim, C., Ryu, Y.U.: Self-efficacy in information security: its influence on end users' information security practice behavior. Comput. Secur. **28**(8), 816–826 (2009)
24. Rose, J., Holgersson, J., Söderström, E.: Digital inclusion competences for senior citizens: the survival basics. In: Viale Pereira, G., et al. (eds.) EGOV 2020. LNCS, vol. 12219, pp. 151–163. Springer, Cham (2020). https://doi.org/10.1007/978-3-030-57599-1_12
25. Silverman, D.: Interpreting Qualitative Data: Methods for Analysing Talk, Text and Interaction, vol. 2nd edn. Sage, London (2001)

Exploring Experiences of Using SETA in Nordic Municipalities

Aous Al Salek, Joakim Kävrestad(✉), and Marcus Nohlberg

University of Skövde, Skövde, Sweden
aous.al.salek@gmail.se, {joakim.kavrestad,marcus.nohlberg}@his.se

Abstract. User behavior is a key aspect of cybersecurity and it is well documented that insecure user behavior is the root cause of the majority of all cybersecurity incidents. Security Education, Training, and Awareness (SETA) is described by practitioners and researchers as the most important tool for improving cybersecurity behavior and has been for several decades. Further, there are several ways to work with SETA found in academic literature and a lot of research into various aspects of SETA effectiveness. However, the problem of insecure user behavior remains revealing a need for further research in the domain. While previous research have looked at the users' experience of SETA, this study looks at SETA adoption from the perspective of the adopting organization. For this purpose, a survey was sent out to all Nordic municipalities with the intent of measuring if and how SETA is conducted, and how the respondents would ideally like to conduct SETA. The results show that a majority of the participating organizations use SETA and that e-learning is the most common delivery method. However, the results also show that gamification and embedded training is seldom used in practice nor a part of the participants' picture of ideal SETA.

Keywords: SETA · Awareness training · User awareness · Adoption · Organizations

1 Introduction

Cybersecurity is a domain that is socio-technical by its nature [18]. While the technical part of cybersecurity is certainly important it has been made evident that human behavior is a key factor in the majority of security incidents today [6,7]. In essence, attackers have realized that exploiting user behavior is a feasible way to launch attacks against individuals as well as against organizations [13]. Improving user behavior, with regards to security, is one of the most pressing matters in cybersecurity [10]. The most commonly suggested, and adopted, means to this ends is SETA, Security Education, Training and Awareness, which

© IFIP International Federation for Information Processing 2021
Published by Springer Nature Switzerland AG 2021
S. Furnell and N. Clarke (Eds.): HAISA 2021, IFIP AICT 613, pp. 22–31, 2021.
https://doi.org/10.1007/978-3-030-81111-2_3

commonly attempts to educate users on correct behavior and make them aware of the risks associated with insecure behavior [17].

SETA has been discussed in scientific literature for at least two decades [20]. Further, there is a multitude of methods by which SETA can be delivered discussed in previous research, with different benefits and drawbacks. Current methods of SETA delivery include:

- *Instructor led training* where participants are thought in the format of a lecture [22,24]. This method is often appreciated by participants but the participants may not retain the acquired knowledge over time.
- *E-learning* where participants are sent, or given access to, digital training material [21]. A benefit of this training is that participants are able to access the SETA on-demand, but a consequence of that is that some users in the organization may not use the training.
- *Gamified training* is similar to e-learning but the learning modules are delivered as games [9,12]. Gamified training is often motivated by the use of game mechanics to improve the learning process and has been shown to be appreciated by its users but suffer from the same potential shortcomings as e-learning.
- *Embedded training* where SETA is delivered to users in a situation where the training is of direct relevance [14,16]. This is argued to add an awareness increasing mechanism and make the users more likely to participate in the training since it is presented to the user in a situation where it is of relevance. A potential drawback is that it may be seen as bothering by the users and that it is inherently more complex to deploy than the other described methods.

While neither the importance of user behavior nor the need for SETA is unknown, and while organizations do spend time and money on SETA efforts, the problem of insecure user behavior persists suggesting a need for continued research into the domain [2,5]. A lot of previous research have studied SETA from a user perspective and there are several promising methods for SETA delivery discussed in scientific literature. However, how organizations procuring or developing SETA methods select and perceive different SETA methods is an underresearshed perspective. This paper addresses that perspective through a survey targeting Nordic municipalities. The survey intends to measure to what degree the participating municipalities employ SETA, and how they do it. The study will also investigate the participants' perception of ideal SETA with the intent of analyzing if there is a gap between the current and ideal practice. The study will complement existing research into SETA with an organizational perspective that can help researchers and practitioners understand the organizational effects of various SETA methods and the driving factors behind a decision to implement a certain SETA method.

2   Research Approach

The intent of this study it to generate results representative for the municipalities in the Nordic countries; Sweden, Denmark, Norway, Finland and Iceland. There are 1123 municipalities in total in these countries and a survey was considered a feasible way to give all of them a chance to participate in the study. Furthermore, surveys are often considered to make it easier for the respondents to provide information on sensitive topics, such as cybersecurity [8]. A survey with two question blocks was developed by the research team. The first block of questions intended to measure the proportion of municipalities that use SETA, what type of SETA they use and the perceived effect of SETA. The questions in this block were quantitative and designed to capture the proportion of the respondents that selected a certain option. As such, the results from the first block are reported as frequencies with corresponding margins of error, given a confidence level of 95%, as suggested by [26]. The second block intended to capture data about the participants' perception of ideal SETA including how SETA should be delivered and what content it should cover. To ensure that the participants were not biased by pre-decided answers, those questions were designed as free-texts answers. The data collected was therefore qualitative in nature, and analyzed using content analysis with the aim of summarizing the general opinions of the respondents [3,15]. The answers were analyzed by one researcher with the intent of identifying themes discussed under each question, and the prevalence of each theme. During this process, each answer was coded as one or more themes. the coding was then reviewed by the rest of the research team and differences of opinions were discussed to form a common view.

3   Results and Analysis

One of the major concerns of a web based survey methodology is to ensure that the participants correctly understand the questions [4]. In this case, the survey was sent to respondents in several countries, and a multilingual survey was developed to ensure that the respondents could answer the survey in their native language. The survey was developed in English and translated to the languages of the Nordic countries after development, by the company TransPerfect. Further, the survey was subjected to pretesting before and after translation in order to ensure its quality, as follows:

1. The survey was developed by the research team.
2. The survey was reviewed by two persons who were not IT-professionals, one of whom was an expert in statistics.
3. The survey was answered by an IT-professional during a think-aloud session.
4. The survey was translated and sent to 7 respondents from the various Nordic countries with additional questions requesting feedback on the survey itself.

The survey was distributed using e-mail and the tool Limesurvey. E-mail addresses to the Nordic municipalities were acquired from public list, except for the Norwegian municipalities were a list had to be procured. The survey was open for three weeks and a reminder was sent out after a period of two weeks. The survey was completed by 96 participants. Several municipalities have joint IT-department. Therefore, the 96 participants are representing 136 municipalities. Table 1 reflects the number of participants per country.

Table 1. Participants per country.

Country	Municipalities	Participants	Municipalities covered
Sweden	290	70	89
Norway	356	10	23
Iceland	69	3	3
Denmark	98	7	7
Finland	310	6	14
Total	1123	96	136

The first question in block one intended to measure how many municipalities that currently use, or previously used SETA. The respondents were asked "Does your organization currently offer information security awareness training for users?" and respodents who answered "no" were also asked "Has your organization had information security awareness training for users in the past?". The responses are presented in Table 2.

Table 2. Prevalence of SETA

Answer	Proportion	Margin of error
Yes - now	71%	8.7%
Yes - in the past	14.6%	
No	14.6%	

Table 2 shows that a vast majority of the participants' municipalities are offering SETA, or has offered SETA to users in the past. The next question asked the participants that currently used SETA what type of SETA they used. The answer options and proportion of respondents picking each option is presented in Table 3, note that the participants were asked to select all answers that applied to them. Table 3 shows that online training is the most common type of SETA used by the participating municipalities followed by written or oral information. Gamified or embedded training is only used by a small proportion of the respondents.

The third question intended to analyze how frequently the users in the municipalities were subjected to SETA and was "How often do users receive information security awareness training?". The answer options and proportion of respondents selecting each answer are shown in Table 4, which demonstrates that while the frequency of SETA varies quite a lot, a majority of the participants report subjecting users to SETA annually or less frequently.

The final question in block one asked the participants "What is the general attitude of trainees towards information security awareness training?". 61.8% responded that the trainees are positive to the SETA while 32.6% perceived

Table 3. Use of SETA types

Answer	Proportion	Margin of error
Oral informative (lecture or personal)	54.4%	11.5%
Written information	52.9%	11.5%
Promotional	10.3%	7.3%
Online	80.9%	9%
Gamified	4.4%	5.3%
Embedded	11.8%	7.7%
Other	10.29%	7.3%

Table 4. SETA frequency

Answer	Proportion	Margin of error
Daily	2.9%	4.6%
Weekly	5.9%	5.9%
Monthly	14.7%	8.2%
Quarterly	8.8%	6.9%
Semi-annually	2.9%	4.6%
Annually	35.3%	11%
Less frequently	27.9%	10.3%

them as indifferent. Only 1.5 % of the respondents perceived the trainees as negative towards SETA.

The second block of the survey contained three open questions that intended to capture the respondents perception of how SETA should ideally be carried out and what it should result in. Those questions were answered by all respondents, regardless of their responses to the previous questions. The data was analyzed using a content analysis approach. The analysis was carried out in four steps:

1. Each answer was analyzed and the themes described in the answer were recorded by the lead researcher.
2. The coding was reviewed by the rest of the research team.
3. The themes were summarized by the lead researcher.
4. The summaries were reviewed by the rest of the research team.

The first question was *What are the most important key factors regarding the design of information security awareness training? (e.g., frequency, length, cost, users covered, being mandatory)*. The themes identified in the responses to this questions were:

- It should be mandatory - 18 mentions.
- It should be easy to consume, require little time and be easy to access - 45 mentions.

– It should be re-occurring - 25 mentions.
– It should be appreciated by users - 3 mentions.
– It should be possible to adapt the material - 8 mentions.
– It should not be costly - 10 mentions.
– Management must be openly positive towards it - 3 mentions.
– The information should be easy to understand and relevant for the users - 31 mentions.

The identified themes reveal a user centered pattern where the two most prevalent themes describe that the participants think that SETA must be easy to access for users, and not require a lot of time to consume. This is motivated both in terms of not consuming too much of the users' work-day and with the notion that users will not bother if the training is too time-consuming. The respondents also describe that the training should be relevant and at a level that is easy to consume. Some respondents explicitly mention that the material should not be too technical. A further pattern is that the respondents argue that the training should be re-occurring so that the training is reinforced and to ensure that the users are provided with up-to-date information.

The second question was *What is the information security awareness training delivery method or combination of methods that suites your organization the most?* The themes identified in the responses to this questions were:

– Instructor led training - 26 mentions.
– Training via e-mail - 5 mentions.
– Nanolearning - 12 mentions.
– E-learning - 44 mentions.
– Written guides - 1 mention.
– Tests including knowledge tests and attack simulations (such as phishing resilience tests) - 5 mentions.
– Embedded - 2 mentions.

In response to this question, the respondents mention e-learning using videos or interactive content. Some respondents also mention sending training via e-mail or using nanolearning and it is hard to differentiate between those themes and e-learning. However, the analysis clearly shows that a majority of the participants favour using a digital form of training that the users can consume in their own time. Instructor led training is also a common theme and several respondents describe that instructor led training is given during staff meetings and/or on-boarding of new employees and then combined with digital re-occurring training. It is further noticeable that embedded training is only mentioned by two respondents and gamified training is not mentioned at all. The results are also in line with what training methods that are actually used in the respondents organizations, as displayed in Table 3. Several respondents mention that a reason for using e-learning is that it is cost efficient and easy to distribute to the users continuously. However, a few participants also mention that a drawback of e-learning is that it is hard to ensure that all users are participating.

The last open question was *What are the results expected from information security awareness training?* The themes identified in the responses to this question were:

– A higher level of security - 5 mentions.
– Less security incidents - 26 mentions.
– Adherence to organizational policies - 1 mention.
– Improved security culture - 52 mentions.

The pattern that emerges in response to the last question is that improved security culture and less security incidents are expected outcomes of SETA. Those are mentioned in combination by several respondents suggesting that the respondents perceive improved security culture as a precursor to less security incidents.

4   Discussion and Conclusion

The intent of this paper is twofold. The first aim was to measure if and how Nordic municipalities provide SETA for their users. The study was carried out as a survey among Nordic municipalities and the first block of the survey contained quantitative questions aimed towards this first research aim. The results show that a majority of the participants' organizations (about 85%) used SETA now or in the past. While this is not surprising, given the impact that user behavior has on cybersecurity and how commonly SETA is described as a key factor for influencing user behavior, it suggests that the Nordic municipalities are well aware of this fact and that actions for improved user behavior are on their agenda. The results further show that e-learning, instructor led training and written information are the most common forms of SETA employed and other methods are only used in a few of the participants' organizations. E-learning is described as cost efficient and easy to distribute and its popularity is therefore not surprising. A result that was a bit more surprising was that gamification, despite its common occurrence in recent research [1, 11, 23], was used by less than 5% of the participants' municipalities. Finally, the results show that only about 40% of the participants' municipalities distribute SETA more frequently than once a year.

The second aim was to research the participants' perception of ideal SETA through the use of open ended questions. The intent was further to compare the participants' perception of ideal SETA to the current practice. The results in this part highlight that the participants perceive user behavior as a key part of cybersecurity. The participants describe that SETA should be easy to consume and relevant for the users. Several participants highlight that getting users to participate in SETA is a challenge and that could explain why they stated that SETA should be re-occurring and mandatory to participate in. On that note, it is interesting to see that a common perception is that SETA should be a natural and re-occurring part of cybersecurty practices while only about 40% of the participants' municipalities employ SETA more than once a year. The participants further describe that e-learning and instructor led training are the delivery methods best suited for their organizations. These results are well in line with the results showing that those are the most frequently used delivery methods in practice. It is, however, noticeable that embedded training is only mentioned by two respondents and gamified training is not mentioned at all. Given the pedagogical benefits attributed to gamification [12], and the re-occurring nature of embedded training [14], the low prevalence of those methods is noticeable. Whether these results reflect that the participants prefer e-learning, are unaware of embedded training and gamification, or something else is beyond the scope of this study and an interesting area for future research.

The target population of this survey was Nordic municipalities. The survey was completed by 96 participants but covered 136 municipalities since several respondents worked in IT-organizations responsible for two or more municipalities. The survey covered about 12% of the population, which is common for web based surveys [19,25]. Further, the response rate between the Nordic nations was uneven with the survey covering 31% of the Swedish municipalities but only a few percentages of the municipalities in the other Nordic countries. A possible explanation for this can be that the research team is based in Sweden and the Swedish municipalities are aware of the research institutions, whereas the other municipalities are not. The distribution of respondents could mean that the results are primarily valid for Swedish municipalities and the results should be interpreted with that in mind. A further possible limitation of this study is self-reporting bias that is always a risk with survey based studies. It is possible that respondents refrain from disclosing security sensitive data and this survey could be interpreted as such. It is further well known that respondents tend to portrait a positive image of themselves and that could lead to results that are more favourable than what is actually the case. Self-reporting bias was counteracted in this study by guaranteeing the anonymity of the respondents and by translating the survey to the respondents native language to make the respondents more comfortable with the survey. Allowing the respondents to answer the survey in the native language was also intended to increase the understandability of the survey.

This study concludes that a majority of the Nordic municipalities use SETA on a regular basis and that e-learning alone or in combination with written guides and/or instructor led training are the most common delivery methods for SETA. A second conclusion is that SETA is deployed in a multi-faceted way and it would be interesting for future studies to compare the effects of different deployment strategies. The study further concludes that the participants perceive that effective SETA should be easy for users to participate in meaning that the material should be relevant and the effort needed to participate minimized. SETA should also be a regular occurrence and the study suggests that the participants believe that SETA should be more regular than what is currently the case.

This study was limited to Nordic municipalities and the results should be interpreted in that context. A given direction for future work would be to research similar topics in the private sector and in public sector organizations outside of the Nordic region. Further, this study identifies that gamified and embedded SETA is only used by a small portion of the study's respondents. Further, those methods are not included in what the participants perceive as ideal SETA. Given the prevalence of those methods in research, and the positive aspects attributed to them, the reason for why they are not adopted should be further researched.

References

1. Aldawood, H., Skinner, G.: Educating and raising awareness on cyber security social engineering: a literature review. In: 2018 IEEE International Conference on Teaching, Assessment, and Learning for Engineering (TALE), pp. 62–68. IEEE (2018)
2. Bada, M., Sasse, A.M., Nurse, J.R.: Cyber security awareness campaigns: Why do they fail to change behaviour? arXiv preprint arXiv:1901.02672 (2019)
3. Berelson, B.: Content Analysis in Communication Research. Content Analysis in Communication Research, Free Press, New York (1952)
4. Berndtsson, M., Hansson, J., Olsson, B., Lundell, B.: Thesis Projects: a Guide for Students in Computer Science and Information Systems. Springer, London (2007)
5. de Bruijn, H., Janssen, M.: Building cybersecurity awareness: the need for evidence-based framing strategies. Gov. Inf. Q. **34**(1), 1–7 (2017)
6. Cybint: 15 alarming cyber security facts and stats (2020). https://www.cybintsolutions.com/cyber-security-facts-stats/
7. EC-Council: The top types of cybersecurity attacks of 2019, till date (2019). https://blog.eccouncil.org/the-top-types-of-cybersecurity-attacks-of-2019-till-date/
8. Fowler, F.J., Jr.: Survey Research Methods. Sage publications, Los Angeles (2013)
9. Gjertsen, E.G.B., Gjaere, E.A., Bartnes, M., Flores, W.R.: Gamification of information security awareness and training. In: ICISSP (2017)
10. Hadlington, L.: Human factors in cybersecurity; examining the link between internet addiction, impulsivity, attitudes towards cybersecurity, and risky cybersecurity behaviours. Heliyon **3**(7), e00346 (2017)
11. Handayani, V., Budiono, F.L., Rosyada, D., Amriza, R.N.S., Masruroh, S.U., et al.: Gamified learning platform analysis for designing a gamification-based ui/ux of e-learning applications: A systematic literature review. In: 2020 8th International Conference on Cyber and IT Service Management (CITSM), pp. 1–5. IEEE (2020)
12. Huynh, D., Luong, P., Iida, H., Beuran, R.: Design and evaluation of a cybersecurity awareness training game. In: Munekata, N., Kunita, I., Hoshino, J. (eds.) ICEC 2017. LNCS, vol. 10507, pp. 183–188. Springer, Cham (2017). https://doi.org/10.1007/978-3-319-66715-7_19
13. Joinson, A., van Steen, T.: Human aspects of cyber security: Behaviour or culture change? Cyber Secur. Peer-Rev. J. **1**(4), 351–360 (2018)
14. Kävrestad, J., Nohlberg, M.: Contextbased microtraining: a framework for information security training. In: Clarke, N., Furnell, S. (eds.) HAISA 2021. IAICT, vol. 593, pp. 71–81. Springer, Cham (2020). https://doi.org/10.1007/978-3-030-57404-8_6
15. Krippendorff, K.: Reliability in content analysis: some common misconceptions and recommendations. Hum. Commun. Res. **30**(3), 411–433 (2006). https://doi.org/10.1111/j.1468-2958.2004.tb00738.x

16. Lim, I.K., Park, Y.G., Lee, J.K.: Design of security training system for individual users. Wirel. Pers. Commun. **90**(3), 1105–1120 (2016) https://doi.org/10.1007/s11277-016-3380-z

17. Puhakainen, P., Siponen, M.: Improving employees' compliance through information systems security training: an action research study. MIS quarterly, pp. 757–778 (2010)

18. Safa, N.S., Von Solms, R.: An information security knowledge sharing model in organizations. Comput. Hum. Behav. **57**, 442–451 (2016)

19. Sauermann, H., Roach, M.: Increasing web survey response rates in innovation research: an experimental study of static and dynamic contact design features. Res. Policy **42**(1), 273–286 (2013)

20. Siponen, M.T.: A conceptual foundation for organizational information security awareness. Inf. Manage. Comput. Secur. **8**(1), 31–41 (2000)

21. Takata, T., Ogura, K.: IEEE: Confront phishing attacks - from a perspective of security education. In: International Conference on Awareness Science and Technology, pp. 10–13 (2019)

22. Taneski, V., Heričko, M., Brumen, B.: Impact of security education on password change, pp. 1350–1355 (2015)

23. Tchakounté, F., Wabo, L.K., Atemkeng, M.: A review of gamification applied to phishing, pp. 1–26 (2020)

24. Van Rensburg, W.J., Thomson, K.L., Futcher, L.: An Educational Intervention Towards Safe Smartphone Usage. HAISA, Dundee, vol. 2018 (2018)

25. Walston, J.T., Lissitz, R.W., Rudner, L.M.: The influence of web-based questionnaire presentation variations on survey cooperation and perceptions of survey quality. J. Official Stat. **22**(2), 271 (2006)

26. Wheelan, C.: Naked Statistics: Stripping the Dread from the Data. WW Norton & Company, New York (2013)

Cyber Security Education

SherLOCKED: A Detective-Themed Serious Game for Cyber Security Education

Alice Jaffray, Conor Finn, and Jason R. C. Nurse[✉]

University of Kent, Canterbury, UK
J.R.C.Nurse@kent.ac.uk

Abstract. Gamification and Serious Games are progressively being used over a host of fields, particularly to support education. Such games provide a new way to engage students with content and can complement more traditional approaches to learning. This article proposes Sher-LOCKED, a new serious game created in the style of a 2D top-down puzzle adventure. The game is situated in the context of an undergraduate cyber security course, and is used to consolidate students' knowledge of foundational security concepts (e.g. the CIA triad, security threats and attacks and risk management). SherLOCKED was built based on a review of existing serious games and a study of common gamification principles. It was subsequently implemented within an undergraduate course, and evaluated with 112 students. We found the game to be an effective, attractive and fun solution for allowing further engagement with content that students were introduced to during lectures. This research lends additional evidence to the use of serious games in supporting learning about cyber security.

Keywords: Cyber security · Gamification · Serious games · Education · University · Puzzle · Detective · COVID-19 · Emergency online learning

1 Introduction

Serious games are a unique opportunity for educators as they provide another, potentially more appealing, way to engage students with course content. The concept of a serious game has existed for decades and while many definitions exist, these games can be regarded as those with "an explicit and carefully thought-out educational purpose and are not intended to be played primarily for amusement" [1]. A salient point about serious games is that although amusement is not a primary objective, striking a good balance between being entertaining and educational can increase the game's appeal in learning settings. This appeal may allow educators to reach students who may be less interested in traditional forms of teaching and revision.

S. Furnell and N. Clarke (Eds.): HAISA 2021, IFIP AICT 613, pp. 35–45, 2021.
https://doi.org/10.1007/978-3-030-81111-2_4

There have been numerous research efforts exploring the development and use of games to educate individuals about cyber security. These have concentrated on game designs including table-top exercises, tower defence games, role playing games, simulations and puzzles [10,12,14]. These approaches have had varying levels of success and impact in educational and awareness settings.

This paper seeks to complement current research into gamification for cyber security education through the proposal and evaluation of a new serious game, namely SherLOCKED, targeted at undergraduate computer science university students. SherLOCKED is created in the style of a 2D top-down puzzle adventure meant to support further engagement with content delivered via lectures. We draw our primary novelty from two areas.

The first is contextual and is grounded in the fact that in-person learning has been drastically reduced due to the COVID-19 pandemic. Educators and students have had to switch suddenly to online learning (also termed, emergency online learning [2]), a reality that has impacted student motivation and cognitive engagement [2]. We sought to support students during this difficult time, and therefore developed and deployed SherLOCKED on an undergraduate course. This paper is therefore the first to our knowledge to engage in a trial and evaluation of a serious game in such a unique context.

The second key contribution of our work is in the reasonably large sample size for such an evaluation. Serious games for teaching security explored in current literature [6,10,14,17,18,21] often interact with small numbers of university students (e.g. $N<30$) which impacts the inferences that can be made. SherLOCKED is evaluated through a survey of 112 university students, where we collect feedback through quantitative and qualitative data. This therefore acts as one of the largest studies to date examining the perception and use of a serious game within an undergraduate cyber security cohort.

The remainder of this article is structured as follows. Section 2 reviews previous salient attempts at gamification. In Sect. 3, we introduce SherLOCKED and present the principles guiding its creation. The user study is outlined and discussed in Sect. 4, before concluding the report in Sect. 5.

2 Literature Review

Gamification has been explored to various extents in prior work. Serious games for general security awareness are arguably the most popular. Anti-phishing Phil [19] for instance is one of the most well-known games that has sought to educate people about detecting phishing attacks. The domain of phishing attracts a large amount of gamification research [16], likely due to the prominence of phishing and its perception as a user-oriented threat. Beyond phishing, topics such as password security and cryptography also feature. Sholefield and Shepherd [17] design a role-playing quiz application (RPG) to educate the general population about good password practices. Their evaluation highlights the importance of games as an enjoyable way to learn, but also the difficulties in such pursuits (e.g. challenges in implementing effective leader boards). Similar positive findings are found by Deeb and Hickey [6] as they explore the use of a 3D escape room game to teach students about cryptography.

Offline serious games present another way to engage individuals. Riskio is a tabletop game to raise awareness of cyber security concepts for those in business and for those studying security at university [10]. It is oriented around playing the roles of attackers and defenders within an organisational security context. Crypto Go is another physical card game proposed which can be used for educating about security, particularly cryptography [9]. Through user workshops, researchers found that the game improved motivation to study the topic and the understanding of the field.

Focusing specifically on formal teaching contexts, Jin et al. [12] situate their research on the growing need for a security workforce and use games to educate high school students. They propose and evaluate four cyber security education games (e.g. using virtual reality and tower defence) to teach topics such as security foundations, secure online behaviour, cyber-attack and defense methods and social engineering. Results were highly positive, and games were favoured by students and staff. Mostafa et al. [14] also explore multiple games for teaching security through their testing of six games and how well they were received by university students. The games spanned topics such as network attacks, key management and web security, were implemented as image puzzles, simulations, role playing and action/adventure genres. Based on a user study, they conclude that the games could contribute greatly to the educational process.

Lastly, capture the flag (CTF) games and exercises are extremely popular in cyber security. They allow participants (many of which may be students new to the field) to learn about the technical aspects of security, including finding and exploiting vulnerabilities (thus capturing 'flags'). Švábenský et al. [20] provide a recent overview of the field and highlight the various types of challenges implemented to teach security. A key finding of their work is that while CTFs clearly are an attractive proposition alongside traditional lectures, they currently predominately focus on technical knowledge but often neglect the human aspects of security; this is clearly a shortcoming given how much cybercriminals use these factors [15]. More specifically, we have seen CTFs applied for introducing new students to security [7], formative assessment [5], and as part of teaching in online universities [4]. This spread of application areas demonstrate the use of these exercises within education.

3   SherLOCKED: A Detective-Themed Serious Game for Security Education

3.1   Game Context

SherLOCKED aims to provide a game-based platform to support students in learning about cyber security. We targeted our game at consolidating content presented in undergraduate lectures. Therefore students could attend lectures and then play the game to check and refresh their understanding on certain topics. The game was conceived and deployed during the COVID-19 pandemic specifically to help address the challenges of low student motivation and poor cognitive engagement with online teaching [2]. This was a notable issue based on our own internal student consultations where there was a significant difficulty in finding the motivation to watch lecture recordings, attend live online sessions, or study more generally.

A series of in-game questions form the basis of SherLOCKED and dictate how players progress. These questions have been created using lecture content from the first half of an introductory cyber security module at the University of Kent, UK. This focus was motivated by the fact that the concepts included in these lectures form the building blocks for the remainder of the module.

There are three levels, each containing topics aligned with the lectures of the module. For the first level, the focus is placed on the Confidentiality, Integrity and Availability (CIA) triad, and understanding the meaning of key cyber security terms. The questions for the second level are centred on security attacks and their types, and related security services. The third level broadens the topic base and poses questions about the activities within the security risk management life-cycle (i.e., identify, analyse, treat and monitor). This allows students to learn more about cyber risk and the ways it can be managed and mitigated.

3.2   The Game

SherLOCKED is a multi-level, top-down 2D detective-themed game which involves the player assuming the role of a detective navigating through a house. The player controls the movement of the detective (using arrow keys or WASD) and, as they move around each level, they have to find the questions attached to objects in each room and answer them. The game was designed using various gamification principles [8] and built using the Unity game engine[1]—a decision made especially due to its cross-platform game deployment capabilities. Below we explain our motivation in support of key design decisions.

Theme. A primary decision in designing a game is the theme on which to base it. Reflecting on current literature, we found that role-playing games often performed well and were preferred by students [14,17]. We then considered various types of roles and settled on a detective theme with an animated detective as the player's character and three cases to solve, based on the three levels (and areas of content) identified earlier. This theme was also, in part, motivated by discovery and detective games, and had a retro interface given the popularity of such games of late [11].

Narrative. A strong and compelling narrative can help players become immersed in the game, which can in turn support their learning. Gamification principles point to the key value of narratives in providing meaning to actions

---

[1] https://unity.com/solutions/game.

and in building a player's commitment to the game's tasks [8]. SherLOCKED's plot follows a detective named Sherry, the player character, helping the victim of a hacking, named Ginny. Figures 1 and 2 show the opening two screens.

Fig. 1. Introducing the player to the game's narrative. Sherry (left) is currently speaking to Ginny (right) about the cases.

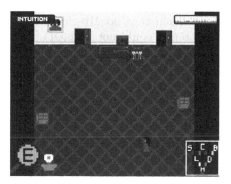

Fig. 2. The game's 2D interface. The 'E' in the bottom left highlights a clue has been found. A mini-map is depicted in the bottom right.

The narrative is told through the questions asked in the game. In the first case, the detective meets the victim and will go through the hacked home looking for clues. A clue is a question about cyber security that the player (Sherry) must answer to prove to Ginny that she's up to the task. As Sherry traverses the house, there are also various locked rooms, each room represents a new case that can only be accessed by answering enough questions correctly on the current level.

In the second case, Sherry is in the computer room. Here, she tries to learn more about the hacker's targeting of Ginny, and as such the questions are based around cyber-attacks and how they might compromise security services. The third case involves the detective walking around the various rooms with the goal of securing the house from the risk of future hacking attacks; questions therefore are about cyber risk and high-level risk treatment solutions.

Feedback. Similar to a traditional educational context, feedback within serious games is critical in supporting learning. Feedback allows students to feel responsible for achievements, and to gauge their progress towards the preset goal (e.g. solving the case or learning about certain security topics) [8]. We implemented this in various ways across SherLOCKED. For instance, when a player answers a question they are always provided with informative feedback, and we provide wider progress monitoring feedback as well, as outlined later.

More specifically, if players answer a question correctly, they are informed as such and the answer button they selected turns green (Fig. 3). If they answer incorrectly, the answer button they selected will turn red, the correct answer button will become green, and they will be given feedback on their selection (Fig. 4). This answer feedback is written to be constructive to aid learning. One study found that positive feedback was more effective than negative feedback when repair could not be made [22]. Questions can only be answered once, so positive feedback is given when a question is answered incorrectly. In Fig. 4 for instance, we gently nudge the player to reflect on the CIA triad—given their answer suggests that the student has mixed up some concepts—before playing the level again.

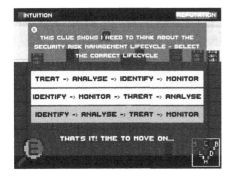 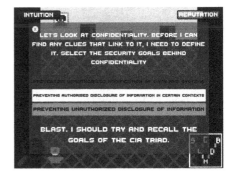

Fig. 3. Correct answer with praise and Intuition points given

Fig. 4. Incorrect answer with feedback and Reputation points lost

Progress Reporting. Studies have found that progress reporting is a powerful gamification principle to motivate students [3,8]. The game implements two progress-typed bars to support this, and the use of levels implemented via different cases. The intuition bar represents how good the player is at picking up on clues and the reputation bar represents the player's reputation as a detective. At the beginning of each level, the intuition bar is empty and the reputation bar is full. When a question is answered incorrectly, the player (Sherry's role) loses reputation experience points (XPs) and when a question is answered correctly, they gain intuition XPs (see top left and right in Fig. 3 and Fig. 4).

If all intuition XPs are gained, the player is shown their score and a notification that they have "closed" the case on that level (Fig. 5). This presents an achievement within the game and allows them to progress. If all reputation points are lost, the level is over and the player is shown their score and a notification they have been "fired" by Ginny from the case (Fig. 6).

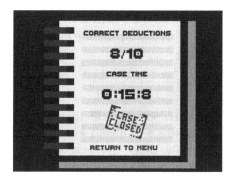

Fig. 5. Case closed as the player has answered sufficient questions correctly on that level to proceed.

Fig. 6. Player fired due to too many wrong answers on the case (and a full loss of reputation).

Competition. Competition allows players to compare their achievements and progress against others. A common way that games implement this is using leader boards [8,13]. In SherLOCKED, when a player finishes a level, they are presented with a score value (number of questions they answered correctly) and the time taken to complete a level (e.g. Fig. 5). This allows for the creation of leader boards and for players to post and compare scores, which creates competition; driving players to achieve better scores within the game and improving their learning of the covered topics.

4   User Study and Discussion

4.1   Study Design

To investigate the use of SherLOCKED at supporting student learning, we conducted a user study. The study took the form of an anonymous online survey which was disseminated to undergraduate students within an introduction to cyber security module, offered to second and final year students, at the University of Kent, UK. The study received ethical approval by the university and informed consent was sought from all participants before completing the survey.

As the game covered the first series of lectures, the study was conducted two weeks after the last of that content was delivered. Students attending the online teaching session where we launched the survey were briefed about the purpose of the game, the study and what we were aiming to achieve. They were also informed that the game would stay open for the remainder of the term if they wanted to use it to help prepare for exams.

Before playing the game, we asked students about how confident they were in their understanding of the lecture material (using a 5-point Likert scale, with 1 as not very confident and 5 as very confident), their preferred learning methods, and what features they thought were most important when playing a game. We then provided them with an online link to the game and allowed approximately

30 min of play time. After they had played the game, they were asked to conduct a post-test survey which again asked the confidence questions but also requested further feedback on the game and their experience.

4.2   Results and Discussion

A total of 112 students completed the survey, out of a potential 198 that were in the live lecture support session. While low (57%), this was already encouraging given response rates for such optional, anonymous university surveys is often 20–30% (pre-COVID-19). Considering that a main aim of the game was to support learning, we first assessed their perceptions on whether the game had an impact on how much they understood about lecture material and how confident they were about syllabus content after playing it.

We found that 87.5% (98) of students felt that the game helped improve their understanding of lecture content and as depicted in Fig. 7, student's confidence levels increased after they played SherLOCKED. It was also encouraging to find that 65.2% (73) stated that they would return to SherLOCKED to help revise for the exam and more generally, that 84.8% (95) saw playing serious games as a good way to help them to learn. These positive points align well with other existing research about the current and future value of gamification when applied to higher education learning [14].

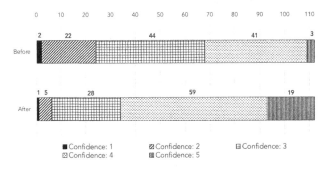

Fig. 7. Confidence levels of students before and after playing SherLOCKED. This presents results on a 5-point Likert scale, with 1 as not very confident and 5 as very confident.

When asked about their most liked part of the game, students reported enjoying its simplicity and 'retro' feel. One participant stated the game was "more engaging than reading notes" and that it "reinforced knowledge that I had, [and] helped to show areas that I was unsure about". Another commented that it was particularly "helpful where some of the definitions are similar and makes you think about which is the right one". This highlights the importance of the game to be interesting and simple but still focused on adequately engaging students with content. To further note the fun nature of the game, we had included a small number of obviously incorrect answers. A participant picked up on this expressing, "I like how sometimes the answer is obvious as other options are hilarious. It helps me when I'm unsure about the answer and acts as a revision". Again, this is a useful point for future research in this domain as it ensures that games keep a good balance between being serious and enjoyable.

Students also valued the instantaneous feedback after answering questions. As was hinted at in the quotes above, these helped direct them to relevant materials and to discover areas where their understanding or knowledge may be lacking. We also noted the significant importance of the game's theme and narrative to students. To summarise with one student's comment, "The setting fits the theme of the game. It makes sense to teach cyber sec concepts in a detective setting so it doesn't feel completely out of place like some learning games". A key takeaway point therefore is that serious games may be better tailored to the subject context instead of being generic.

Some other general findings were of note as well. Firstly, students reported that their preferred learning styles were primarily attending lectures (33% of respondents, i.e., 37 students) and engaging in question-answer sessions (46%, 52). Reading notes and textbooks (11%, 13) or writing notes (9%, 10) were not favoured. For serious games in university contexts therefore, this may be an opportunity to pair games (or levels) with individual (or groups of) lectures. We also found that when playing a game, if students had to choose one feature to represent the most important feature, feedback on actions (27% of respondents, i.e., 30 students), competition (24%, 27) and narrative (23%, 26) were key. Less so were character customisation (2%, 2), a consistent theme (e.g. RPG) (4%, 5), an informative tutorial (8%, 9) and progress reporting (12%, 13). While all of these are ideal in a game and we would certainly encourage educators to strive for them, this can help prioritise features/principles if time or resources are low.

There were some areas for improvement in our work that were identified by participants. This arose through a query where we asked what they liked least about the game. The main theme which emerged from a few participants was about the simplicity of the game; a notable point given its simplicity was praised by others. Here, a participant stated "the gameplay was quite boring, being just walk to object, interact, answer quiz, go to next object, with not much reward (apart from not losing)". This links to another participant comments on how it "would be cool with gold coins to collect". These are clearly valid points and ones that could make the game more engaging. We are currently exploring the feasibility of different interface designs (e.g. integrating the ability to track a hacker), different style questions (e.g. a puzzle instead of multiple choice), and how badges or coins may be used (e.g. a badge for fastest time, or receiving in-game Bitcoin for successfully finding out information about the hacker).

5   Conclusion and Future Work

While serious games have been discussed for decades, their uptake in higher education seems to be limited. These games however can offer a great deal to a student's learning experience. Considering this value, this article proposed SherLOCKED, a new serious game created in the style of a 2D top-down detective adventure. SherLOCKED was designed to be used within an undergraduate cyber security course to complement lecture materials and content. A key motivation of the game was to overcome the challenges that students were facing with online-only learning because of the COVID-19 pandemic, including a lack of motivation and cognitive engagement with materials.

From our user study with a cohort of 112 university students, we found that the game was successful at providing a more enticing form of interaction which also assisted student's understanding and confidence with lecture content. We were also able to identify a number of key take away points for research in this domain more generally, including the importance of a strong narrative, the balance of informative and fun interfaces, game stories that are tailored to the subject context, and actionable and immediate feedback.

There are various avenues for future work, but there are two of particular interest. The first is to extend upon the game concept currently built. Currently the game only covers the initial lectures in the module, and therefore the others will need to be designed and implemented. Additionally, as mentioned above we would aim to explore ways to make the game more engaging and avoid issues of boredom (e.g. badges, interfaces and question styles). The second goal is to setup a long-term study to explore whether the expanded game results in better actual ongoing student engagement with content and actual student performance. This aims to tackle the current reliance on self-report data which can be biased. We believe that while the current version of SherLOCKED performed well, with improvements in the interface and via an extended user study, the game will be one that can be used within the undergraduate module for years to come.

References

1. Abt, C.C.: Serious games. University Press of America, New York (1987)
2. Aguilera-Hermida, A.P.: College students' use and acceptance of emergency online learning due to Covid-19. Int. J. Educ. Res. Open **1**, 100011 (2020)
3. Barata, G., Gama, S., Jorge, J., Gonçalves, D.: Engaging engineering students with gamification. In: 2013 5th International Conference on Games and Virtual Worlds for Serious Applications (VS-GAMES), pp. 1–8. IEEE (2013)
4. Chicone, R., Burton, T.M., Huston, J.A.: Using facebook's open source capture the flag platform as a hands-on learning and assessment tool for cybersecurity education. Int. J. Conceptual Struct. Smart Appl. (IJCSSA) **6**(1), 18–32 (2018)
5. Chothia, T., Novakovic, C.: An offline capture the flag-style virtual machine and an assessment of its value for cybersecurity education. In: 2015 USENIX Summit on Gaming, Games, and Gamification in Security Education (3GSE 2015). USENIX Association (2015). https://www.usenix.org/conference/3gse15/summit-program/presentation/chothia
6. Deeb, F.A., Hickey, T.J.: Teaching introductory cryptography using a 3d escape-the-room game. In: 2019 IEEE Frontiers in Education Conference (FIE), pp. 1–6. IEEE (2019)

7. Ford, V., Siraj, A., Haynes, A., Brown, E.: Capture the flag unplugged: an offline cyber competition. In: Proceedings of the 2017 ACM SIGCSE Technical Symposium on Computer Science Education, pp. 225–230 (2017)
8. Fortes Tondello, G., Premsukh, H., Nacke, L.: A theory of gamification principles through goal-setting theory. In: 51st Hawaii International Conference on System Sciences (2018)
9. González-Tablas, A.I., González Vasco, M.I., Cascos, I., Planet Palomino, Á.: Shuffle, cut, and learn: Crypto go, a card game for teaching cryptography. Mathematics **8**(11), 1993 (2020)
10. Hart, S., Margheri, A., Paci, F., Sassone, V.: Riskio: A serious game for cyber security awareness and education. Comput. Secur. **95**, 101827 (2020)
11. Heubl, B.: Retro-gaming boom during lockdown (2020). https://eandt.theiet.org/content/articles/2020/05/retro-gaming-boom-during-lockdown/ Accessed 16 Feb 2021
12. Jin, G., Tu, M., Kim, T.H., Heffron, J., White, J.: Evaluation of game-based learning in cybersecurity education for high school students. J. Educ. Learn. (EduLearn) **12**(1), 150–158 (2018)
13. Marczewski, A.: Periodic Table of Gamification Elements (2020). https://www.gamified.uk/user-types/gamification-mechanics-elements/ Accessed 16 Feb 2021
14. Mostafa, M., Faragallah, O.S.: Development of serious games for teaching information security courses. IEEE Access **7**, 169293–169305 (2019)
15. Nurse, J.R.C.: Cybercrime and you: How criminals attack and the human factors that they seek to exploit. In: The Oxford Handbook of Cyberpsychology. OUP (2019)
16. Roepke, R., Koehler, K., Drury, V., Schroeder, U., Wolf, M.R., Meyer, U.: A pond full of phishing games - analysis of learning games for anti-phishing education. In: Hatzivasilis, G., Ioannidis, S. (eds.) MSTEC 2020. LNCS, vol. 12512, pp. 41–60. Springer, Cham (2020). https://doi.org/10.1007/978-3-030-62433-0_3
17. Scholefield, S., Shepherd, L.A.: Gamification techniques for raising cyber security awareness. In: Moallem, A. (ed.) HCII 2019. LNCS, vol. 11594, pp. 191–203. Springer, Cham (2019). https://doi.org/10.1007/978-3-030-22351-9_13
18. Schreuders, Z.C., Butterfield, E.: Gamification for teaching and learning computer security in higher education. In: 2016 USENIX Workshop on Advances in Security Education (ASE 2016) (2016)
19. Sheng, S., et al.: Anti-phishing Phil: the design and evaluation of a game that teaches people not to fall for phish. In: Proceedings of the 3rd Symposium on Usable Privacy and Security, pp. 88–99 (2007)
20. Švábenský, V., Čeleda, P., Vykopal, J., Brišáková, S.: Cybersecurity knowledge and skills taught in capture the flag challenges. Comput. Secur. **102**, 102154 (2021)
21. Švábenský, V., Vykopal, J., Cermak, M., Laštovička, M.: Enhancing cybersecurity skills by creating serious games. In: Proceedings of the 23rd Annual ACM Conference on Innovation and Technology in Computer Science Education, pp. 194–199 (2018)
22. Welbers, K., Konijn, E.A., Burgers, C., de Vaate, A.B., Eden, A., Brugman, B.C.: Gamification as a tool for engaging student learning: a field experiment with a gamified app. E-Learn. Digit. Media **16**(2), 92–109 (2019)

A Reference Point for Designing a Cybersecurity Curriculum for Universities

Adéle da Veiga[✉] ⓘ, Elisha Ocholaⓘ, Mathias Mujingaⓘ, Keshnee Padayacheeⓘ,
Emilia Mwimⓘ, Elmarie Kritzingerⓘ, Marianne Loockⓘ, and Peeha Machakaⓘ

Security4U Research Group, School of Computing, College of Science, Engineering
and Technology, UNISA, Pretoria, South Africa

{dveiga,Ocholeo,mujinm,Padayk,mwimen,Kritze,Loockm,
machap}@unisa.ac.za

Abstract. The objective of this study is to propose a cybersecurity curriculum from a best practice perspective for universities and other higher educational institutions. Cybersecurity is a fast-growing part of the overall job market and cybersecurity skills shortage is a factor that needs attention worldwide. An updated approach is needed to build the cybersecurity labour force. A scoping literature review was applied on academic databases for proposed cybersecurity skills curricula. It was also applied on cybersecurity curricula offered by top universities as well as by studying cybersecurity curriculum frameworks and guidelines. The knowledge, skills, abilities and modules from the aforementioned were integrated to compile a holistic reference point for a cybersecurity curriculum. The study found that there is a global need for cybersecurity degrees and specifically for African countries like South African. More cybersecurity professionals need to be trained in the necessary technical abilities, combined by the necessary soft skills to be productive and fill the gaps in industry. This is possible by concentrating on this study's proposal namely a reference point for cybersecurity modules to be included in a cybersecurity curriculum.

Keywords: Cybersecurity · Curriculum · Skills · Education

1 Introduction

Cybersecurity skills challenges and a shortage of cybersecurity employees are experienced globally by organisations. It is estimated that there is a shortage of 3.12 million cybersecurity professionals across the globe [1]. The ISC found in their study that the cybersecurity skills workforce must be expanded by at least 89% to address the skills shortage, specifically in regions such as the Asia Pacific, followed by Latin America, North America and Europe [1]. In another study conducted by Check Point, 67% of the participating IT professionals across the world indicated that their staff lacked cybersecurity skills, with a continent-wide concern in Africa [2]. The African workforce will be expanding to represent 15% of the world's working population, with approximately 60% of Africa's population being under the age of 25 by 2030 [3]. With 87% of CEOs in Africa being concerned about the availability of key skills required on the continent [4], Africa has a unique challenge in this regard. While there is a gap in cybersecurity skills worldwide, studies also show that cybersecurity knowledge is one of the fastest growing skills required within public, private and government sectors [5]. Cybersecurity skills required range from technical skills, such as network and database skills, to non-technical skills, such as cybersecurity strategy, management, project management, training risk assessments and legal requirements [5]. One way to decrease the current cybersecurity skills shortage is through education. The need for cybersecurity education within the higher education sectors is growing rapidly [6]. It is therefore vital that universities and tertiary colleges adopt new curricula to address the cybersecurity skills shortage [2]. The responsibility to build the cybersecurity profession is partly that of the education system and education institutions [4]. In a study by Kaspersky, 62% of IT professionals indicated that education establishments have a key responsibility to train cybersecurity professionals, with only a third of the responsibility placed on industry [6].

While there is no universal curriculum for cybersecurity [7], there is a need for a holistic view to consider the content of guidelines such as CSEC2017 [8], but also the content that is currently offered by universities, and in addition also the work that is proposed by academic researchers for a cybersecurity curriculum, thereby providing an integrated point of reference. A consolidated view of cybersecurity skills as proposed in academic research and what is offered in practice by universities could be used by universities as a benchmark or point of reference to define their cybersecurity qualifications in order to aid in closing the cybersecurity skills gap. This research provides universities with a guideline for a cybersecurity curriculum from a best practice perspective, but also from an operational perspective as to what academic institutions are currently offering. It is of specific importance for countries like South Africa who also requires cybersecurity skills, but where there is a lack of cybersecurity degrees offered at tertiary institutions as found in this study.

2 Research Aims

In this research a scoping literature review [9] was applied to propose a reference point for a holistic academic cybersecurity curriculum for universities and other higher education institutions. The scoping review included:

- academic databases for proposed cybersecurity skills curricula;
- cybersecurity curricula offered by top universities; and
- cybersecurity curriculum frameworks and guidelines.

The results are consolidated to synthesise and propose a comprehensive point of reference for a cybersecurity curriculum for a tertiary educational context.

3 Background

Countries invest in acquiring modern technologies to secure their infrastructure within cyberspace. However, the success of these technologies depends on professionals with the appropriate cybersecurity related skills, knowledge and abilities for implementation. The cybersecurity skills shortage phenomenon, with few professionals having the skills and knowledge to protect networks, systems and data against malicious cyber attacks, arising from cyber warmongers, terrorists and cybercriminals. The cybersecurity skills gap has been recognised as a national vulnerability requiring a resolution in the UK government's cybersecurity strategy. The US government echoes the same sentiment, pointing out the need for qualified cybersecurity professionals [10]. Statistics show that the cybersecurity professionals shortage in the global labour market was at 2.93 million in 2018 [1], with a further 3.5 million global vacant positions for cybersecurity professionals estimated for 2021 [11]. (ISC)^2 [1] reports that 63% of their respondents confirmed a shortage of dedicated cybersecurity staff in their organisations; Capgemini [12] reports a widening digital gap for 55% of companies, with cybersecurity topping the demand list; Oltsik [13] observes that the shortage has impacted 70% of organisations over the past few years. With increased cybersecurity attacks and a shortage of cybersecurity skills, there is a great need for cybersecurity education.

Technologies and digital device adoption in South Africa (SA) has introduced diverse conveniences. However, this has also opened the doors for numerous cybercrime attacks on a global scale. High-profile data breaches have also been experienced in SA in recent years. A leakage of personal data affecting over 60 million users occurred in October 2017 [14]. The 2013 Protection of Personal Information (POPI) Act came to effect for the protection of personal information, including strengthening of security controls. However, its implementation has been slow, with only certain provisions currently implemented. In 2015, the government further responded by proposing the National Cybersecurity Policy Framework (NCPF) [15], which is yet to be implemented. The country is experiencing a lack of a skilled workforce, and cybersecurity professionals are among those in high demand. There is a need to strengthen the cyber talent pipeline, with a focus on a cybersecurity workforce. ICT technology advancements, regulations, cybersecurity incidents and increasing digitisation have shaped the cybersecurity labour market demand. The education and training of adequately skilled cybersecurity professionals is vital to fend off the global increase in sophisticated cyber attacks that have crippling effects on our way of life.

4 Research Methodology

4.1 Research Method

A scoping literature review [9] method was applied. The scoping review included three phases with a review of (a) cybersecurity curricula proposed in academic publications in the academic databases using the PRISMA (Preferred Reporting Items for Systematic reviews and Meta-Analyses) method, Sect. 4.2; (b) cybersecurity curricula of universities in South Africa and globally applying the Time Higher Education university ranking, Sect. 4.3; and (c) best practice and industry frameworks for cybersecurity curricula, Sect. 4.4.

4.2 Academic Publications Defining Cybersecurity Curricula

All academic studies that have considered a cybersecurity curriculum were eligible for the scoping review. The following search terms: [All: "cybersecurity curriculum"] OR [All: "cyber security curriculum"] AND [Publication Date: (01/01/2015 TO 12/31/2020)] were used. The databases selected for this review included ACM, IEEE and Scopus.

Table 1. Inclusion and exclusion criteria

Inclusion criteria	Exclusion criteria
IC1: Journal articles, conference proceedings, book chapters, reports	**EX1**: Posters, websites, keynote speeches
IC2: Empirical, theoretical or case study works on a cybersecurity curriculum design	**EX2**: Pedagogical methods (e.g. lab exercises), standalone modules (i.e. a discussion on the development of a standalone module), applications in other fields (e.g. engineering, healthcare), awareness campaigns, community involvement and training for professionals
IC3: Practices that have been implemented at tertiary level	**EX3**: Practices at school level
IC4: Articles written in 2015–2020	**EX4**: Articles prior to 2015

Using the PRISMA method, the process involved screening the papers by reviewing the title and the abstract's fitness for the study based on the criteria outlined in Table 1. The articles that remained were verified for suitability by reviewing the full-text version. The next step involved reviewing each article for their quality and relevance using five questions, Table 2, as adopted from Salleh et al. (2011). This checklist was appropriate, as the original study also considered pedagogical issues in higher education in computer science.

Table 2. Study quality checklist (adapted from Salleh et al. [16] and Kmet et al. [17])

Quality criteria	Reference
QC1: Was the article peer-reviewed?	[16]
QC2: Were the aims clearly stated?	[16]
QC3: Is the context clear? For example, the setting should be within a university	[17]
QC4: Is there a connection to a theoretical framework/wider body of knowledge?	[17]
QC5: Do the findings resonate with other research findings?	[16]

4.3 Results

The search and appraisal strategy applied generated a sample of **n = 8** studies from the respective databases, Table 3. The process involved three researchers who searched each database independently. If there was a dispute regarding a paper, the researchers collaborated and refined the exclusion criteria to focus on papers that provided a description or proposal of a curriculum in cybersecurity. Each researcher then considered the quality criteria and excluded further papers (excluded on QC3 and QC4). After consolidating the list of articles, it was found there was one duplicate, and this was eliminated, which generated a final sample of **n = 7**.

Table 3. PRISMA method

Database	#Records identified through database searching	#Records after duplicates removed	#Records screened	#Records excluded (exclusion/inclusion criteria)	#Full-text articles assessed for eligibility	#Full-text articles excluded, with reasons	#Articles included in the synthesis
IEEE	13	13	13	9	4	2^{QC3}	2
ACM	40	40	40	17	23	$20^{QC3\&4}$	3
SCOPUS	66	66	66	59	9	$6^{QC3\&4}$	3

Švábenský et al. [18] conducted a systematic review; however, while their search was wider, they only considered relevant conference papers (2010–2019). Their work provides a good basis toward this end and leveraged the CSEC2017 framework to identify the most common topics that were covered in cybersecurity curricula as summarised in Table 4. Bell and Oudshoorn [19] suggest that the methodology of developing a new programme should involve determining the focus areas and a consideration of exemplar programmes which could assist in that process. The Northwest Missouri State University offers a Bachelor of Science degree in cybersecurity [19] with a consideration of the eight knowledge areas of CSEC2017. The criteria proposed by the Accreditation Board for Engineering and Technology (ABET) [20] was also employed as well as input from industry stakeholders. Asghar and Luxton-Reilly [21] provide an overview of a Cybersecurity Master's Programme (University of Auckland) based on the ITiCSE framework as a case study. The six courses comprise four compulsory subjects (based on system security and security management) and ten electives (students choose two courses that focus on specialist strengths alongside the core knowledge). While the previous studies considered frameworks from a teaching and learning perspective, Jones et al. [22] embarked on a survey to identify the most relevant knowledge, skills, abilities (KSAs) that should be prioritised for a cybersecurity curriculum in order to prepare graduates for careers in cybersecurity using the NICE framework's KSAs as a basis. Buckley and Zalewski [23] highlight issues of teaching basic principles of cybersecurity at Florida Gulf Coast University. The curriculum is based on the CSEC2017 guidelines. They also compare CSEC2017 and $(ISC)^2$/CPHC [24] as guidelines for curriculum development and conclude that the former is more curriculum based while the latter is more technology based.

The authors developed two courses as part of an undergraduate Software Engineering programme: "Security Software" and "Introduction to Cybersecurity". Asghar, Swain and Biswal [25] report on the design and development of a cybersecurity concentration

Table 4. Academic cybersecurity curricula and related modules

Data-base	Description	Frameworks	Overview of modules
ACM	Predominately tertiary education in the USA [18]	CSEC 2017 Framework. A review of SIGCSE and ITiCSE conferences was also considered	The primary cybersecurity topics: Secure Programming and Software Development, Network Security and Monitoring, Human Aspects in Security, Cyber-Attacks, Malware, Hacking, Offensive Security and Exploitation, Cryptography, Authentication and Authorization
IEEE	Bachelor of Science degree in cybersecurity (Northwest Missouri State University) [19]	CSEC2017 Programme outcomes adopted from the ABET cybersecurity accreditation criteria	BSc programme structure: Introduction to Cybersecurity, Secure Programming, Incident Response, Cyber Risk Management, Digital Forensics and Ethical Hacking. Existing modules include: Professional Ethics, General Psychology, General Statistics, Discrete Mathematics, Computer Programming I and II, Data Structures, IT Hardware and Software, Network Fundamentals, Computer Organization, Database Systems, Operating Systems, Secure Systems Administration and Applied Cryptography
ACM	Cybersecurity master's programme (University of Auckland) [21]	ITiCSE 2018	Compulsory modules: Information Security, System Security, Network Security and Cryptographic Systems and ten electives: Smartphone Security, Human Computer Interaction, Advanced Analysis of Algorithms, Software Tools and Techniques, Data Communications, Information Systems Research, Telecommunications Management, Enterprise Systems, Research Methodology – Quantitative and Research Methodology – Qualitative. Students to select two of the ten electives

(continued)

Table 4. (*continued*)

Data-base	Description	Frameworks	Overview of modules
ACM	Proposed KSAs of cybersecurity curriculum [22]	NICE Framework	The KSAs that should be prioritised when developing cybersecurity course curricula relate to networks, vulnerabilities, programming and communication skills
Scopus	Part of an undergraduate software engineering programme (Florida Gulf Coast University) [23]	CSEC2017 (IEEE Computer Society, 2014) (Data Communication Networks: Open System Interconnection (OSI); Security Structure and Applications, 1991)	Software Security course with Cryptography, Network Security Protocols and Detection (Penetration Testing and Threat Modelling) Introduction to Cyber Security course with fundamental cybersecurity principles, practices and security controls and includes a cybersecurity laboratory (i.e. hands-on activities). The notion of protection mechanisms for implementing security services are covered from a software development cycle perspective
Scopus	Cybersecurity curriculum for computer science major students (South Carolina State University) [25]	ABET accredited computer science programme	The embedded programme courses include Introduction to Cybersecurity, Computer Forensics, Cryptography and Network Security, Application and Data Security with Privacy, Management of Information Security and a Cyber Security Capstone project
IEEE	Proposed graduate-level curriculum certificate [26]	Based on the Framing of Information Security Management: Prevention, Detection and Response	A graduate-level curriculum comprising the following areas: Prevention (e.g. penetration testing, ethical hacking); detection (e.g. intrusion detection systems) and response (e.g. digital forensics and incident response). Other areas proposed include cultural and global standardisation, legal issues, awareness, counter forensics and the theory of computer forensics

course for undergraduate students. The programme is based on the ABET accreditation at the South Carolina State University. In this case 15% of the coursework was devoted to cybersecurity. This programme was based on existing curricula and discussions with industry and scholars. While some curriculum models are based on established frameworks, other case studies provide approaches based on alternative perspectives. Santos,

Pereira and Mendes [26] propose a flexible curriculum based on the framing of prevention, detection and response for a graduate-level curriculum in cybersecurity. The core curriculum should consider prevention, detection and response.

The programmes listed in Table 4 highlight the wide scope of cybersecurity qualifications and various options of module selection of topics available to curriculum developers. Seven core modules crosscut these curricula, namely networks, cryptography, cybersecurity, forensics, programming human aspects and ethical hacking, with 34 unique modules across the seven curricula. It is worth pointing out that each of these curricula listed in Table 4 is based on a framework.

4.4 Cybersecurity Curricula of Universities

The Time Higher Education (THE) University rankings rank universities based on their academic research performance and their overall reputation and ratings by members of the academic community around the world [27]. Undergraduate programmes that are based solely on cybersecurity or incorporate an aspect of it were included in the scope. There were no undergraduate programmes in South African universities that focused solely on cybersecurity, but undergraduate programmes in the listed universities had modules that covered aspects of cybersecurity. Since a complete undergraduate course in cybersecurity was not found, it was concluded that South African universities do not have a formal undergraduate course in cybersecurity. Three websites were used to identify international universities for inclusion in the scope: www.educations.com; www.bachelorstudies.com; and www.barchelorportal.com. The researchers searched for 3- and 4-year bachelor's degrees in cybersecurity that are taught in English. educations.com returned 113 results, bachelorstudies.com returned 19 results and bachelorportals.com returned 64 results. The results were sorted by relevance and the THE university ranking. The cybersecurity programmes of the top 5 highly ranked universities according to THE [27] were then reviewed, with the results summarised in Table 5.

Cybersecurity or Security was the module that was most represented, with four of the university curricula including it. This was followed by the modules Forensics, Programming, Networks, Mathematics (including Discrete Mathematics) and Cyber Crime, which were each included in the curricula of three of the universities. There were 18 unique modules across the five universities.

4.5 Best Practice and Industry Frameworks for Cybersecurity Curricula

Organisations can use different international best practices to guide them in improving cybersecurity, education resources and curricula [33, 34]. According to Caruso [35], best practices have a wide scope. For this paper cybersecurity best practices are defined as documents that have structures, processes, practices and technologies that can aid in improving cybersecurity within an organisation. Security best practices can be seen as guidelines on security topics that are relevant and important within the industry sectors. It is therefore critical that educational curricula at higher education institutions be based on industry-required knowledge and skills. Best practices can be used as a basis to identify cybersecurity knowledge and transfer skills.

Table 5. Cybersecurity university degrees and related modules

University	Degree	University ranking	Overview of modules
Cardiff University	Computer Science with Security and Forensics [28]	191	Security, Forensics, Cryptography, Probability, Discrete Mathematics, Programming
Macquarie University	Bachelor of Commerce with a Major in Cyber Security Governance [29]	195	Cyber Security, Cybercrime, Information Systems and Business Processes, Blockchain for Business, Cyber Security and Privacy, Cyber Security Governance and Ethics, Information Systems Audit and Assurance
University of Winchester	BSc (Hons) Cyber Security [30]	201–300	Cyber Security and Networks, Artificial Intelligence, Network Security, Secure Systems Architectures, Risk Management and Cyber Security, Penetration Testing, Digital Forensic Investigation, Cyber Law and the Regulation of the Information Society, Globalised Crime, Organised Crime and Cyber Crime
Deakin University	Bachelor of Criminology/Bachelor of Cyber Security [31]	251–300	Crime and Criminology, Criminal Justice, Programming, Cyber Security, Discrete Mathematics, Secure Networking, Secure Coding, Computer Crime and Digital Forensics, Malware and Network Forensics, Ethical Hacking
Flinders University	Bachelor of Information Technology (Network & Cybersecurity Systems) [32]	251–300	Computing, Computer Programming, Electronics, Networks and Cybersecurity, Mathematics, Data Science, Software Engineering, Computer Networks, Cybersecurity, Enterprise Information Security

Two approaches can be used when designing a cybersecurity curriculum: 1) Using one existing best practice for the curriculum or 2) using a combination of frameworks and best practices to create a customised cybersecurity curriculum. There are numerous ways and methods to group and categorise cybersecurity topics relevant to educational curriculum development. In this research nationally accepted cybersecurity best practices were consulted to identify relevant cybersecurity topics and different options to group these topics. International documents consulted include Cybersecurity Curricular Guidelines (2017) [36]; CyBOK (2019); ISSP - Information Security Skills Framework (2010) [37]; NIST Cyber Security Framework (2014) [38] and Soc2 [39]. These documents were analysed to identify the different security related topics. The process of data saturation was used when identifying these topics. Data saturation is reached when results are repeating with low new contribution to the findings. Saturation was reached

Table 6. Security related topics

Access control	Improvements	Recovery planning
Adversarial behaviour	Incident management	Regulatory aspects
Anomalies & events	Information assurance methodologies	Research
Asset analysis & management	Information security strategy	Response planning
Attacks & defences	Infrastructure security	Risk assessment
Audit, assurance & review	Intrusion detection	Risk management
Awareness & training	Investigation	Secure development
Business continuity management	Law & regulation	Secure operations management
Business environment	Maintenance	Security architecture
Business improvements	Malware	Security incident handling
Communications	Management	Security innovation
Component & connection security	Management strategy	Security monitoring
Connection security	Mitigation	Security software life cycle
Cryptography	Network security	Security testing
Data security	Operational security management	Service delivery
Detection processes	Organisation security	Social security
Disaster recovery	Performance monitoring	Software security
Distributed systems security	Physical security	System security
Encryption	Policy & standards	Telecommunications
Firewalls	Privacy & online rights	Third party management
Forensics	Processing monitoring	Two factor authentication
Governance	Protection & procedures	Virtualisation
Hardware security	Protective technology	Vulnerability assessment
Human security	Quality assurance	Web & mobile security

after the five mentioned best practices [40]. Table 6 depicts the list of security topics derived from the collection documents. Some topics are not directly related to security such as communication or research, but is contextualised to security. For example, how to conduct research in cybersecurity or implementation of secure communications in networks or conducting awareness communication of the cybersecurity policy. Additional security topics can be added to this list. Within the design phase of a cybersecurity related curriculum, the topics (in Table 6) can be a baseline for the knowledge and skills based planning.

5 Reference Point for a Cybersecurity Curriculum

The modules derived from the 7 literature review papers as well as the modules derived from the 5 universities were consolidated to compute a unique list of 49 modules. The occurrence of each module across the 7 literature review papers (column A) and 5 university curricula (column B) were counted to determine the number of instances each module occurred across the curricula. The modules that occurred the most frequently were considered as the core or critical modules for inclusion in the cybersecurity curriculum. The framework topics from Table 6 were mapped to the list of 49 modules and a match was indicated by a "X" in column C. Only business continuity management, disaster recovery, security innovation, service delivery and third party management did not map to any of the modules and were thus added as possible additional modules, thereby increasing the module list to 53. The last column, "Total", portrays the modules that were represented in the literature review curricula and the university curricula and map to a topic in a framework. The modules are ranked according to the last total column in terms of the number or occurrence across the academic databases, best practice and existing curricula offered by universities covered in the scope of the study. This gives an indication of the most common modules that are currently included in proposed curricula, presenting an integrated view. Table 7 therefore outlines 53 modules in order of three tiers:

- Tier 1: Core modules for a cybersecurity curriculum
- Tier 2: Fundamental modules for a cybersecurity curriculum
- Tier 3: Elective modules for a cybersecurity curriculum

The research found that there is consensus that cybersecurity courses at undergraduate level will require a computing background and that cybersecurity courses have been embedded into existing Computer Science programmes. The modules in Table 7 range from specific cybersecurity topics like networks, ethical hacking and cyber attacks to more general topics like awareness, communication skills, electronics and general psychology. Therefore the development of any new cybersecurity curriculum will most likely have to include the core modules and a specific specialisation area as well as target a particular cohort of students using the fundamental and elective modules. A cybersecurity curriculum could be based on existing frameworks as mapped in Table 7, but it is proposed that these need to include industry stakeholders to review the relevance of topics proposed. From a pragmatic viewpoint as illustrated in the case study

Table 7. Reference point for a cybersecurity curriculum

	Modules	A	B	Total	Framework mapping to unique modules	C	Total
TIER 1	1. Networks	6	3	9	Network Security; Firewalls; Intrusion Detection; Component and Connection Security; Anomalies and Events; Adversarial Behaviour	X	10
	2. Cryptography	5	1	6	Cryptography; Encryption	X	7
	3. Cyber Security	3	4	7			7
	4. Forensics	3	3	6	Forensics; Investigation	X	7
	5. Programming	3	3	6			6
	6. Crime	1	3	4			4
	7. Mathematics	1	3	4			4
	8. Architecture	1	1	2	Security Architecture	X	3
	9. Ethical Hacking	2	1	3			3
	10. Human Aspects	2		2	Human Security; Social Security	X	3
	11. Law/legal	1	1	2	Law & Regulation; Regulatory Aspects	X	3
	12. Privacy	1	1	2	Privacy & Online Rights	X	3
	13. Risk Management	1	1	2	Risk Management; Risk Assessment; Mitigation	X	3
	14. Software Tools and Techniques, Engineering	1	1	2	Software Security	X	3
TIER 2	15. Audit and Assurance		1	1	Audit, Assurance & Review, Information Assurance Methodologies; Quality Assurance	X	2
	16. Authentication and Authorisation	1		1	Access Control; Two-Factor Authentication	X	2
	17. Awareness	1		1	Awareness & Training	X	2
	18. Business Processes		1	1	Business Environment	X	2
	19. Communication Skills	1		1	Communications	X	2
	20. Computing	1	1	2			2
	21. Cyber Attacks	1		1	Attacks & Defences	X	2
	22. Data Science	1	1	2			2

(*continued*)

Table 7. (*continued*)

Modules	A	B	Total	Framework mapping to unique modules	C	Total
23. Data Structures	1		1	Data Security	X	2
24. Enterprise Security		1	1	Organisation Security; Business Improvements; Asset Analysis and Management; Improvements; Infrastructure Security; Maintenance; Operational Security Management; Secure Operations Management	X	2
25. Ethics	1	1	2			2
26. Incident Response	1		1	Incident Management; Security Incident Handling; Detection Processes	X	2
27. IT Hardware and Software	1		1	Hardware Security; Physical Security; Protective Technology	X	2
28. Malware	1		1	Malware	X	2
29. Management of Information Security	1		1	Management; Management Strategy; Governance; Information Security Strategy; Policy & Standards; Protection and Procedures	X	2
30. Prevention, Detection	1		1	Response Planning; Recovery Planning	X	2
31. Research Methodology	1		1	Research	X	2
32. Smartphone Security	1		1	Web & Mobile Security	X	2
33. Software Engineering/Development	1		1	Secure Development; Security Software Life Cycle	X	2
34. System Security	1		1	System Security; Distributed Systems Security; Security Testing; Performance Monitoring; Processing Monitoring; Security Monitoring	X	2

(*continued*)

Table 7. (*continued*)

	Modules	A	B	Total	Framework mapping to unique modules	C	Total
	35. Telecommunications Management	1		1	Telecommunications	X	2
	36. Vulnerabilities	1		1	Vulnerability Assessment	X	2
TIER 3	37. Advanced Analysis of Algorithms	1		1			1
	38. Artificial Intelligence		1	1			1
	39. Block Chain		1	1			1
	40. Cultural and Global Standardisation	1		1			1
	41. Database Systems	1		1			1
	42. Electronics		1	1			1
	43. General Psychology	1		1			1
	44. General Statistics	1		1			1
	45. Information Security	1		1			1
	46. Operating Systems	1		1	Virtualisation		1
	47. Penetration testing		1	1			1
	48. Probability		1	1			1
	49. Secure Systems Administration	1		1			1
	50.				Business Continuity Management and Disaster Recovery	X	1
	51.				Security Innovation	X	1
	52.				Service Delivery	X	1
	53.				Third Party Management	X	1

of Buckley and Zalewski [23], the importance of leveraging existing strengths in the institution should be incorporated when designing the cybersecurity curriculum. This study identified that there is a lack of cybersecurity degrees in South African universities and the proposed modules in Table 7 for such a curriculum could serve as a reference point.

Alsmadi and Zarour [41] highlighted some issues with cybersecurity programs. First, the divide between theoretical knowledge and the practical skills. It is recommended that course material must consider knowledge, skills and ability (i.e. be able to innovate). Second the gap between industrial requirements and the knowledge base of students. The third problem is the lack of planning with respect to how to evolve with industry's needs. This study proposed a reference point that could be used towards the development of a cybersecurity curriculum that intends to be a strategy that addresses the first two challenges. In this demonstration, the reference point identified core modules such as Networks, Cryptography, Cybersecurity, Forensics and Programming, as obtained from current cybersecurity curricula and best practices. The development of the reference point involved a three-pronged approach using the PRISMA method for academic publications, best practice and industry frameworks as well as existing cybersecurity curricula of universities. It is envisaged that the proposed strategy can be used by academic institutions as a point of departure towards defining cybersecurity curricula, to map them for completeness and provide organisations with a point of reference for the cybersecurity skills they need. The literature review is useful in assisting further research and the aggregation and statistical support may be used by some when justifying and proposing new or enhanced cybersecurity curriculum. A limitation of this study is that only a literature review was conducted and with a lack of a cooperative approach with industry that could address the last challenge identified by Alsmadi and Zarour [41]. Future studies will extend the reference point to include qualitative and quantitative input that will assist in mapping the evolving needs of industry with theoretical knowledge and practice.

6 Conclusion

This study proposed a reference point for a cybersecurity curriculum that may be utilised within higher education institutions to graduate more cybersecurity professionals. A reference point is proposed for cybersecurity modules to be included in a cybersecurity curriculum that contributes to the cybersafety body of knowledge. The proposed curriculum focuses on core modules such as Networks, Cryptography, Cybersecurity, Forensics and Programming, as obtained from current cybersecurity curricula and best practices. The research included a three-phased approach using the PRISMA method for academic publications, best practice and industry frameworks as well as existing cybersecurity curricula of universities. It is envisaged that the proposed cybersecurity curriculum can be used by academic institutions to define their cybersecurity curricula, to map them for completeness and provide organisations with a point of reference for the cybersecurity skills they need.

References

1. (ISC)2: Cybersecurity Professionals Stand Up to a Pandemic. https://www.trendmicro.com/closethegap/wp-content/uploads/2018/11/2018-ISC2-Cybersecurity-Workforce-Study.pdf. Accessed 09 Mar 2021
2. Kagwiria, C.: Cybersecurity skills gap in Africa. https://www.afralti.org/cybersecurity-skills-gap-in-africa/. Accessed 09 Mar 2021
3. Shango, D.: Why the skills gap remains wider in Africa. https://www.weforum.org/agenda/2019/09/why-the-skills-gap-remains-wider-in-africa/. Accessed 09 Mar 2021
4. PricewaterhouseCoopers: CEOs' curbed confidence spells caution. https://www.pwc.com/gx/en/ceo-survey/2019/report/pwc-22nd-annual-global-ceo-survey.pdf. Accessed 09 Mar 2021
5. Furnell, S., Bishop, M.: Addressing cyber security skills: the spectrum, not the silo. Comput. Fraud Secur. **2020**, 6–11 (2020)

6. Kaspersky Lab: The Cybersecurity Skills Gap: a Ticking Time Bomb. https://media.kaspersky.com/uk/Kaspersky-Cyberskills-Report_UK.pdf. Accessed 09 Mar 2021
7. Bishop, M., Burley, D., Futcher, L.A.: Cybersecurity curricular guidelines. In: Ismini, V., Furnell, S. (eds.) Cybersecurity Education for Awareness and Compliance, pp. 158–180. IGI Global, Hershey (2019)
8. Joint Task Force on Cybersecurity Education: Curricula 2017 Cybersecurity Curriculum. http://www.csec2017.org/. Accessed 09 Mar 2021
9. Moher, D., Liberati, A., Tetzlaff, J., Altman, D.G., PRISMA Group: Preferred reporting items for systematic reviews and meta-analyses. Ann. Intern. Med. **89**, 264–270 (2009)
10. De Zan, T.: Mind the Gap: The Cyber Security Skills Shortage and Public Policy Interventions. https://ora.ox.ac.uk/objects/uuid:e9699fc6-279c-4595-b707-7fd0acc487b3/download_file?file_format=pdf&safe_filename=cyber-ebook-definitivo.pdf&type_of_work=Working+paper. Accessed 09 Mar 2021
11. Morgan, S.: 2018–2021 Cybersecurity Jobs Report. https://herjavecgroup.com/wp-content/uploads/2018/11/HG-and-CV-Cybersecurity-Jobs-Report-2018.pdf. Accessed 09 Mar 2021
12. Buvat, J., Turner, M., Slatter, M., Putter, R.K.: Cybersecurity Talent: The big gap in cyber protection. https://www.capgemini.com/wp-content/uploads/2018/02/the-cybersecurity-talent-gap-v8_web.pdf. Accessed 09 Mar 2021
13. Oltsik, J.: The Life and Times of Cybersecurity Professionals. https://www.esg-global.com/hubfs/issa/ESG-ISSA-Research-Report-Life-of-Cybersecurity-Professionals-Nov-2017.pdf?hsCtaTracking=a63e431c-d2ce-459d-8787-cc122a193baf%7Ce74f0327-0bbc-444a-b7a8-e2cd08d1999eCtaTracking=a63e431c-d. Accessed 09 Mar 2021
14. Veerasamy, N., Mashiane, T., Pillay, K.: Contextualising cybersecurity readiness in South Africa Namosha. In: van der Waag-Cowling, N., Leenen, L. (eds.) Proceedings of the 14th International Conference on Cyber Warfare and Securit. ACPI (2000)
15. Sutherland, E.: Governance of cybersecurity – the case of South Africa. Afr. J. Inf. Commun. **20**, 83–112 (2017)
16. Salleh, N., Mendes, E., Grundy, J.: Empirical studies of pair programming for CS/SE teaching in higher education: a systematic literature review. IEEE Trans. Softw. Eng. **37**, 509–525 (2011)
17. Kmet, L.M., Cook, L.S., Lee, R.C.: Standard quality assessment criteria for evaluating primary research papers from a variety of fields. Edmonton: Alberta Heritage Foundation for Medical Research (AHFMR). HTA Initiative #13 (2004)
18. Švábenský, V., Vykopal, J., Čeleda, P.: What are cybersecurity education papers about? A systematic literature review of sigcse and iticse conferences. In: Proceedings of the 51st ACM Technical Symposium on Computer Science Education, Portland, pp. 2–8 (2020)
19. Bell, S., Oudshoorn, M.: Meeting the demand: building a cybersecurity degree program with limited resources. In: Proceedings - Frontiers in Education Conference, FIE, pp. 1–7. IEEE (2019)
20. Criteria for Accrediting Computing Programs, 2018–2019 | ABET
21. Asghar, M.R., Luxton-Reilly, A.: A case study of a cybersecurity programme. In: Proceedings of the 51st ACM Technical Symposium on Computer Science Education, pp. 16–22. ACM, New York (2020)
22. Jones, K.S., Namin, A.S., Armstrong, M.E.: The core cyber-defense knowledge, skills, and abilities that cybersecurity students should learn in school: results from interviews with cybersecurity professionals. ACM Trans. Comput. Educ. **18**, 1–12 (2018)
23. Buckley, I.A., Zalewski, J.: Course development in the cybersecurity curriculum. In: Proceedings of the LACCEI International Multi-conference for Engineering, Education and Technology, pp. 24–26 (2019)

24. CPHC: Cybersecurity Principles and Learning Outcomes for Computer Science an IT-related Degrees: A Resource for Course Designers and Accreditors. (ISC)2 and The Council of Professors and Heads of Computing (2015)
25. Swain, N., Biswal, B.: Design and development of cybersecurity concentration courses and laboratory experiences for undergraduate students. ASEE Annual Conference and Exposition Conference Proceedings (2019)
26. Santos, H., Pereira, T., Mendes, I.: Challenges and reflections in designing Cyber security curriculum. In: 2017 IEEE World Engineering Education Conference (EDUNINE), pp. 47–51 (2017)
27. THE - Times Higher Education: World University Rankings (2020). https://www.tim eshighereducation.com/world-university-rankings/2020/world-ranking#!/page/0/length/25/ sort_by/rank/sort_order/asc/cols/stats. Accessed 09 Mar 2021
28. Cardiff University: Computer Science with Security and Forensics (BSc) - Study - Cardiff University. https://www.cardiff.ac.uk/study/undergraduate/courses/2021/computer-science-with-security-and-forensics-bsc. Accessed 09 Mar 2021
29. Macquarie University: Bachelor of Commerce with a Major in Cyber Security Governance | Macquarie University. https://courses.mq.edu.au/2020/domestic/undergraduate/bachelor-of-commerce-cyber-security-governance. Accessed 09 Mar 2021
30. University of Winchester: BSc (Hons) Cyber Security - University of Winchester. https://www.winchester.ac.uk/study/undergraduate/courses/bsc-hons-cyber-security/. Accessed 09 Mar 2021
31. Deakin University: Bachelor of Criminology/Bachelor of Cyber Security | Deakin. https://www.deakin.edu.au/course/bachelor-criminology-bachelor-cyber-security. Accessed 09 Mar 2021
32. Flinders University: Study the Bachelor of Information Technology (Network and Cyber-security Systems) - Flinders University. https://www.flinders.edu.au/study/courses/bachelor-information-technology-network-cybersecurity-systems?source=ecs-int-home. Accessed 09 Mar 2021
33. Ma, Q., Pearson, J.: ISO 17799: "Best practices" in information security management? In: Communications of the Association for Information Systems, pp. 577–591. Association for Information Systems (2005)
34. Coventry, L., Briggs, P., Blythe, J., Tran, M.: Using behavioural insights to improve the public's use of cyber security best practices, Northumbria (2015)
35. Osburn, J., Caruso, G., Wolfensberger, W.: The concept of "best practice": a brief overview of its meanings, scope, uses, and shortcomings. Int. J. Disabil. Dev. Educ. **58**, 213–222 (2011)
36. Joint Task Force on Cybersecurity Education: CyberSecurity Curricula. ACM, IEEE-CS, AIS SIGSEC, IFIP, New York (2017)
37. Professionals, Institute of Information Security: The IISP Skills Framework-Scoring levels for Skills Framework. https://apmg-international.com/sites/default/files/documents/products/iisp_skills_framework_v1_0.pdf. Accessed 09 Mar 2021
38. NIST: Framework for Improving Critical Infrastructure Cybersecurity. https://nvlpubs.nist.gov/nistpubs/CSWP/NIST.CSWP.04162018.pdf. Accessed 09 Mar 2021
39. AICPA: 2017 Trust Services Criteria for Security, Availability, Processing Integrity, Confidentiality, and Privacy. https://www.aicpa.org/content/dam/aicpa/interestareas/frc/assurance advisoryservices/downloadabledocu. Accessed 09 Mar 2021
40. Saunders, M., Lewis, P., Thornhill, A.: Research Methods for Business Students. Pearson Education Limited, London (2016)
41. Alsmadi, I., Zarour, M.: Cybersecurity programs in Saudi Arabia: issues and recommendations. In: 1st International Conference on Computer Applications & Information Security (ICCAIS), pp. 1–5. IEEE (2018)

A Conceptual Information Security Culture Framework for Higher Learning Institutions

Charles Mawutor Ocloo$^{(\boxtimes)}$ (ID), Adéle da Veiga(ID), and Jan Kroeze(ID)

School of Computing, College of Science, Engineering and Technology, UNISA, Pretoria, South Africa
{dveiga,kroezjh}@unisa.ac.za

Abstract. Education institutions within and outside Ghana continue to experience mass information leakages at an alarming rate even with the huge investment made in information technology infrastructure to secure their information assets. The lack of organisational commitment to enhance the non-technical aspects of information security — thus, information security culture (ISC) — largely accounts for the consistent rise of security breaches in institutions like the educational institutions. Securing information assets goes beyond technical controls and encompasses people, technology, policy, and operations. The aim of this paper is to identify a comprehensive list of the factors of ISC and construct a conceptual ISC framework (InfoSeCulF) that can be used to provide guidance for the cultivation of a strong ISC in higher learning institutions to secure information assets. A scoping literature review was conducted to determine what constitutes a comprehensive list of factors for cultivating ISC in higher learning institutions. The study proposes a comprehensive list of factors and provides a conceptual framework (InfoSeCulF) which serves as guide for cultivating a strong ISC in institutions.

Keywords: Information security culture · Dimensions · Factors · Framework · Organisation culture

1 Introduction

The increasing reliance of individuals and institutions on information and technologies has established the need for institutions to secure their information assets. The huge investments being made in technology to protect information assets are not yielding the desired result, and the lack of organisational commitment to enhance the non-technical aspects of information security (thus, information security culture) largely accounts for the consistent rise of security breaches in institutions [1]. Securing information assets "goes beyond technical controls and encompasses people, technology, policy, and operations" [2: 380]. Hence, focusing only on technical controls as the solution to the challenges of information security is not effective. Organisations must give equal attention to the human aspects of information security [2–5] to promote a strong information security culture (ISC) to achieve a holistic approach to tackling information security challenges.

© IFIP International Federation for Information Processing 2021
Published by Springer Nature Switzerland AG 2021
S. Furnell and N. Clarke (Eds.): HAISA 2021, IFIP AICT 613, pp. 63–80, 2021.
https://doi.org/10.1007/978-3-030-81111-2_6

For this study, the factors of ISC refer to components of information security culture such as information security policy and awareness that influence the creation of artefacts and shape assumptions, beliefs, values, attitudes and knowledge. Thus, factors influence ISC on the levels of Schein's definition of organisational culture which are assumptions and beliefs (for example, our members are our "human firewall"), espoused values, norms and knowledge (for example, members' security compliance increases the organisation's security) and artifacts (for example, an information security policy handbook). The shared information security values and beliefs of members of an organisation influence their behaviour. For the purpose of this study, organisational members of higher learning institutions refer to both staff and students of such institutions.

2   Research Aim and Question

This paper aims at identifying a comprehensive list of factors of ISC to construct a conceptual information security culture framework (InfoSeCulF) that can provide guidance to effectively cultivate a strong ISC in higher learning institutions to secure information assets. The study seeks to answer the research question:

- What constitutes a comprehensive list of factors for cultivating an information security culture in higher learning institutions?

Sections 1 and 2 provide the introduction and the aim of this study. The paper discusses what constitutes an ISC in Sect. 3, and the challenges of cultivating ISC in higher learning institutions in Sect. 4. Section 5 is a proposal of a list of factors required for cultivating a strong ISC in higher learning institutions. The InfoSeCulF is proposed in Sect. 6 and further discussed in Sect. 7. Limitations and future research work are discussed in Sect. 8, and Sect. 9 presents the conclusion.

3   Background

3.1   Understanding Information Security Culture

This study adopts a comprehensive definition of information security culture proposed by [6] to provide an understanding of what constitutes information security culture. Da Veiga, Astakhova, Botha and Herselman [6: 19] define information security culture as:

"Information security culture is contextualised to the behaviour of humans in an organisational context to protect information processed by the organisation through compliance with the information security policy and procedures and an understanding of how to implement requirements in a cautious and attentive manner as embedded through regular communication, awareness, training and education initiatives.

The behaviour over time becomes part of the way things are done, i.e., second nature, as a result of employee assumptions, values and beliefs, their knowledge and attitude towards and perception of the protection of information assets.

The information security culture is directed by the vision of senior management together with management support in line with the information security policy and influenced through internal and external factors, supported by an adequate ICT environment, visible in the artefacts of the organisation and behaviour exhibited by employees, thereby creating an environment of trust with stakeholders and establishing integrity."

The above definition was chosen because it is centred on [7] concepts of organisational culture adapted by [8] to the context of ISC and considers the impact of time on cultivating ISC. The definition provides a comprehensive view of ISC, focusing on six areas namely, knowledge, values and attitudes, behaviour, time, and assumptions, beliefs and perception.

The definition indicates that ISC refers to the security behaviour of members towards protecting the information assets of an organisation. The focus of ISC is on how human actions or inactions (behaviour) in relation to the management, access, sharing and communicating of information affects the security of organisational information assets. All human behaviour aspects are governed by norms [9]. This definition suggests that ISC is relative to an organisational setting, which informs the nature of ISC that ought to be promoted to secure the organisational information assets. The definition also lays emphasis on the essential role of senior management in establishing a strong ISC in organisations [10–12].

The definition indicates that the collective security behaviour of members (thus, ISC) evolves with time. Warrick [13] states that culture, whether purposely developed or left to chance, will certainly evolve with time. Therefore, strategies adopted in dealing with ISC challenges must be relevant to the challenges experienced at a particular period. Per this definition, ISC is greatly influenced by the underlying security assumptions, beliefs, knowledge and attitude promoted in an organisation, as affirmed by [14]. Hence, ISC seeks to address human behaviour so that information security becomes a second nature to employees [15] by defining constructs that create artefacts, shape assumptions, beliefs, values, attitudes and knowledge with respect to time. This implies that ISC in an organisation exists at the levels of security knowledge, assumptions, values, beliefs, attitudes, and artefacts of an organisation; the factors of ISC impact these levels of ISC.

3.2 Organisational Culture and Information Security Culture

A number of research studies [4, 8, 16, 17] have established the connection between organisational culture and ISC. Da Veiga and Martins [17: 72] indicate that "an information security culture (ISC) is a critical component of an organisation's information security programme. It must be embedded in the organisation, changed and influenced to direct employee, contractor and third-party behaviour, in order to reduce risk to the organisation's information assets". Making ISC part of the organisational culture [16] implies embedding ISC in an organisation to positively influence the information security behaviour of members. Organisational culture represents the dominant culture and ISC a subculture [17]. This is implying that ISC should not be functionally isolated from its operational environment (dominated by organisational culture) but must be cultivated within an organisational context.

Schlienger and Teufel [18: 405] indicate that "organizational culture is consequently expressed in the collective values, norms and knowledge of organizations" which impact the behaviour of members. Similarly, ISC is the collective information security knowledge, assumptions, values and artefacts within an organisation [8]. Hence, literature confirms there is a relationship between organisational culture and ISC [8, 17] with organisational culture as the superset and ISC as the subset, and both cultures having common cultural attributes and manifestations.

4   Cultivating Information Security Culture in Universities

The discussion on identifying the challenges of cultivating ISC in higher learning institutions was not limited to the Ghanaian context but considers the global situation due to the limited number of literature available on this subject at the time of this study. This offered an appreciation of the information security challenges confronting institutions of higher learning from a global perspective.

Higher learning institutions manage varied information technology resources which include people, IT systems, data or information, software and hardware [19] for the purpose of teaching, learning and research. The vast amount of student, staff, research and financial information owned by higher learning institutions makes them a breeding ground for cybercriminal activities. Kwaa-Aidoo and Agbeko [19] indicate that a successful attack launched on a university's information system will cause economic, operational, reputational, and legal damage.

Higher learning institutions continue to experience mass information leakages at an alarming rate even with the huge investment made in information technology infrastructure to secure their information assets, and the situation keeps worsening as ICT advances [20, 21]. As a result, the education sector has been tagged as a hotbed for data breaches [22].

There are several contributing factors to this trend, with the neglect of the human elements of information security as the ultimate factor [21]. "Unlike business enterprises that have substantial resources to invest into information security, educational institutions are more constrained" [19: 93], making it difficult for them to make adequate investments in establishing ISC.

Kwaa-Aidoo and Agbeko [19] state that the dynamic interactions that occur between students and IT resources in higher learning institutions in Ghana present the most demanding problems associated with establishing ISC. The promotion of Bring Your Own Device (BYOD) in higher learning institutions poses new security risks to institutional information on personal devices of staff [19].

Higher learning institutions in Ghana suffer security incidents such as online fraud, phishing, identity theft, password theft, unauthorized access, malware attacks and change of information on systems, with malware as the most common incident [19]. Hence, [19] states the need for regular information security training programmes for stakeholders of these institutions to mitigate such security risks.

The security investments made in higher learning institutions are highly focused on technical security controls, with little or no attention given to addressing the human elements of information security [21]. Hina, Panneer Selvam and Lowry [23: 1] indicate that "behavioural influence is still a challenge in the information security domain" which needs to be tackled. "An organization's investment in just technology does not eliminate the many security challenges" [1: 269]; equal investment in human factors is also required. The over-reliance on technical controls to secure information assets significantly contributes to the high number of data breaches recorded in higher learning institutions [20, 21, 23]. Hina and Dominic [21: 5] posit that "[t]echnological solutions and behavioral controls together bring a security culture within the organizations".

Moreover, the staff and students of higher learning institutions lack sufficient levels of information security awareness, leading to noncompliance of information security policies [20] which impacts ISC negatively. The lack of awareness in higher learning institutions has a significant correlation with security attacks like social engineering [24]. Therefore, higher educational institutions must invest in information security training for its workforce [20]. The lax attitude of staff, the culture of openness and availability of information, and the lack of a thorough security policy and plan in higher learning institutions make their IT systems vulnerable to data breaches [21, 25].

The IT security unit of higher learning institutions often develop and implement all information security strategies and procedures without involving end users and top management [21], though employees' and management's involvement is key to reducing employees' violations of security measures [26]. This causes a big communication gap which promotes noncompliance to information security policies and procedures [21]. Apart from the lack of complete and effective security policies and plan, an overwhelming majority of staff of higher learning institutions do not know and understand the content of the information security policies and procedures of their institution [21]. Another cause of the high rate of security breaches is the lack of effective monitoring measures [21].

Although higher learning institutions have invested hugely in implementing technical controls they still experience a consistent attitude of noncompliance with security policies which contributes to the mass leakage of information, reputational damage and possible lawsuits [20]. It is obvious that the information security challenges faced by higher learning institutions are mostly caused by the human elements, and, hence, can be well addressed by implementing a strong ISC. Glaspie and Karwowski [1: 270] state that "a positive information security culture can increase security policy compliance, strengthen the overall information security posture, and reduce financial loss caused by security breaches". It is eminent for higher education institutions to offer due attention to tackle the human issues of information security to implement a strong ISC to reduce the mass leakage of information.

5 Scoping Literature Review

This study adopted a scoping literature review and meta-analysis to identify the factors for cultivating and assessing ISC to propose an appropriate ISC framework that can be used for cultivating ISC in higher learning institutions in Ghana. While a scoping literature review is "an ideal tool to determine the scope or coverage of a body of literature on a given topic and give clear indication of the volume of literature and studies available as well as an overview (broad or detailed) of its focus" [27: 2], meta-analysis employs the use of statistical methods to summarise the results of the literature collected [28].

According to [27], one of the main purposes of conducting a scoping literature review is to identing key factors of a concept, making this method of review suitable for this study.

The scoping literature review was conducted by searching the content of five electronic databases namely ACM, AIS, Emerald, IEEE, Scopus, and Web of Science. The search for articles was conducted by combining keywords related to ISC into search phrases using Boolean operators. The keywords used to conduct the literature search are information security, culture, assessment, measurement, dimension, factors, framework, and maturity model. The terms dimension and factor are used interchangeably by different authors and are both included in frameworks and questionnaires. Hence, both terms were used as keywords to conduct the literature search to enable the researcher to identify a complete list of ISC factors.

The search was aimed at identifying English papers published from the year 2010 to 2019, where factors for cultivating or assessing ISC were identified. The list was limited to conceptual, and literature works that identified ISC factors or developed ISC framework or designed ISC questionnaire. However, conceptual and literature works with hypotheses that were only stated but not tested were excluded.

Existing frameworks and questionnaires were included because they are designed to comprise and measure factors. Therefore, frameworks and questionnaire were included in selecting the studies for this review as a comprehensive approach to identify all possible factors for assessing and cultivating ISC. This offers the advantage of capturing a holistic view of issues relating to ISC.

5.1 Results of Scoping Literature Review

Per the search conducted, 20 out of 177 initial works identified satisfied the eligibility criteria. Among these 20 works, 8 of them identified factors of ISC, 10 assessed ISC and 2 were works that did both. However, this review focuses on the factors of ISC. Hence, the researchers identified a total of 10 (thus, 8 + 2) papers that provide content on the factors of ISC.

5.2 Factors for Cultivating Information Security Culture

Table 1 provides an overview of related studies. It presents a summary of the ten studies identified during the literature search, indicating the factors proposed by each study and the research approaches by each.

The factors listed in Table 1 with similar description but captioned differently by different studies were recaptioned under the same name. For example, the factors captioned as information security policy, security policies, policy and procedures, and procedural countermeasures were all recaptioned as "Information Security Policy".

The total count of each factor used in the studies identified for this literature analysis were examined. The factors of studies 4 and 7 were counted as one since study 4 is an update of study 7. The result indicates that factors such as Top management support, Information security awareness, Information security policy and Information security training and education were consistently used, with Top management support as the most cited factor among the studies considered. Though Table 1 indicates the list of main factors proposed by the various studies considered, the subfactors of these main factors were further examined to establish some similarities that exist between these main factors to produce the final list of twenty-five main factors, namely Strategy, Technology, Organisation/Organisational Culture, People, Environment, Top management support, Information security awareness, Information security policy, Information security training and education, Information security risk and assessment, Information security compliance, Information security ownership, Deterrence and incentives, Technology protection and operations, Change management, National and ethical culture, Government initiatives, IT vendors, Information security knowledge, Budget, Information security knowledge sharing, Monitoring, Program Organisation, Trust, and Privacy.

These twenty-five factors of ISC identified are a synthesis of all the various aspects of ISC considered by the ten studies examined, to achieve a more comprehensive list of factors. This provides the foundation for developing a framework that provides a solution to a broad range of ISC issues to promote the cultivation of a strong ISC in organisations.

5.3 Literature Gaps Identified

The studies considered for this review as captured in Table 1 were either generic in context or conducted for a different context other than higher learning institutions. This indicate the need to conduct a study to develop a framework that fits the context of higher learning institutions since ISC must be contextualised.

Some of these studies [1, 29–32] only considered critical or few factors of ISC, indicating that the frameworks or list of ISC factors these studies proposed are not exhaustive and can be expanded to include other factors in different contexts. The results of the review conducted by [30] point out the fact that most of the frameworks considered are fragmented and present a limited view of ISC challenges which is still the case of this review as well. AlHogail and Mirza [30] emphasise the need to conduct more research that take a holistic view of ISC related issues to enable the development of comprehensive frameworks.

This brings to the fore the need to conduct further research that consolidates these fragmented frameworks or lists of ISC factors to present a holistic view of ISC challenges in specific contexts like the higher learning environment.

Although [29, 30], applied the STOPE view to develop an ISC framework, using the STOPE components as factors of this framework with no subfactors or underlining factors will make the implementation of this framework and the assessment of these factors difficult due to fact that the STOPE components capture a broad classification of the factors of ISC. There is a need to connect the STOPE components to factors of ISC for a better appreciation and implementation of the proposed framework.

Considering the impact of human behaviour on ISC and the technology aspects of information security on ISC, [1] notes the limited number of research studies on this subjects, hence advocates for more studies in these issues.

Per the literature analysis conducted, though management was listed as a factor for cultivating ISC by majority of the studies conducted, [1] again advocates the need to conduct research to assess the impact of role of management and other organisational members on ISC.

The literature analysis reveals the following gaps:

1. The need for more research that takes a holistic view (thus, a good appreciation) of ISC related issues to develop a comprehensive framework.
2. There are limited studies that discuss the impact of human behaviour on ISC and how the technology aspects of information security impact the human factors of ISC.
3. The need to conduct further studies for a good appreciation of the roles of management, employees, and other users in organisations and how that influence the cultivation of ISC.
4. The need to consider the tasks that originate due to the relationships between factors of ISC to develop an assessment instrument to assess the ISC level of organisations.
5. The frameworks proposed from the studies considered were either generic in context or focussed on different contexts other than higher learning institutions.

Table 1. Factors of information security culture

Study	Authour(s)	Factors	Approaches
1	Glaspie and Karwowski [1]	5 Factors: Information security policy; deterrence and incentives; attitudes and involvement; training and awareness; management support	Literature Review
2	Masrek, Harun and Zaini [33]	6 Factors: Management support; Policy and procedures; Compliance; Awareness; Budget; Technology	Literature Review
3	Nasir, Arshah, and Ab Hamid [34]	7 Factors: Procedural Countermeasures; Risk Management; Security Education, Training and Awareness (SETA; Policy enforcement Commitment (TMC); Monitoring (MON); Information Security Knowledge (ISK); Information Security Knowledge Sharing (ISKS)	Literature Review

(*continued*)

Table 1. (*continued*)

Study	Authour(s)	Factors	Approaches
4 & 7	AlHogail and Mirza [29, 30]	5 Factors: Strategy; Technology; Organisation; People; Environment	Literature Review Survey Validation
5	AlKalbani, Deng and Kam [31]	3 Factors: Management Commitment; Accountability; Information Security Awareness	Literature Review Quantitative Validation
6	Alnathee [35]	8 Factors: Top management support; Information security policy; Information awareness; Information security training and education; Information security risk and assessment; Information security compliance; Ethical conduct policies; Organisational culture	Literature Review
8	Alnatheer, Chan, and Nelson [32]	5 Factors: Security awareness; Information security ownership; Top management involvement; Policy enforcement; Security training	Literature Review Qualitative Quantitative Validation
9	Da Veiga and Eloff [14]	7 Factors: Leadership and governance; Security management and operations; Security policies; Security program management; User security management; Technology protection and operations; change	Literature Review Quantitative Validation
10	Dojkovski, Lichtenstein, and Warren [36]	8 Factors: National and ethical culture; Government initiatives; IT vendors; leadership/corporate governance; Organisational culture; Managerial; Individual and organisational learning; Organisational security awareness	Literature Review Qualitative Focus group discussion Validation

6 A Conceptual Information Security Culture Framework

The final list of factors obtained during the literature review has been used in this study to propose a comprehensive ISC framework (InfoSeCulF) for higher learning institutions grounded on the following:

1. STOPE view developed by [37]
2. Schein's concept of organisational culture [7]

The STOPE view used as the first or primary building block to provide the five development components of the InfoSeCulF. The theory of organisational culture which indicates the levels of culture was used as the second building block.

6.1 The STOPE View

The STOPE view, originally developed by [38], has been applied in conducting various research studies [29, 30, 37, 39–43]. This model has been used in various domains of information systems to support the development, integration, and evaluation of IT problems [30].

The STOPE development model is made up of five components namely, Strategy, Technology, Organisation, People and Environment. Security challenges are concerned with organisation, technology, people and environment which can be resolved by adopting appropriate strategies [38]. This presents a holistic view of ISC related issues. Per ISC's focus on context, these components of STOPE, though common to organisations, shows the uniqueness of each organisation, hence, the STOPE view focuses on context. These features make the STOPE view suitable for managing ISC-related issues, hence, it makes this model suitable for implementing ISC that fits within a context.

Each ISC factor (thus, underlining factor of ISC) of the InfoSeCulF, classified under a component of the STOPE view is influenced, developed, and implemented from the standpoint of the STOPE component that it is aligned with. The following paragraphs discuss the STOPE components.

The strategy component defines the development objectives and provides the directions (plan) for achieving these objectives within a time frame [40]. This component consists of ISC factors that serve as plans of action, policies, or best practices adopted to guide employees towards protecting information assets [29]. The strategy component of the InfoSeCulF consist of factors such as Top Management Support, Information Security Policy, Budget, Monitoring, Change and Program Organisation.

The technology component of the STOPE view caters for non-technical issues associated with the use of technology, such as vulnerability caused by how technology is designed, implemented or managed [38]. Although ISC focuses on the non-technical aspect of information security, technology impacts the nature of ISC cultivated in organisations, hence, ISC must consider the non-technical issues associated with technology-related measures that an institution adopts to help build the right values, assumptions and knowledge compatible with technological measures adopted, since technological components of information security affect how employees interact with information assets which translate into security culture [14, 30]. ISC factors such as Technology Protection and Operations, Information Security Risk and Assessment, and IT Vendors constitute the technology component of the InfoSeCulF.

The organisation component of the STOPE view is centred on the structure and culture of an organisation. This component is "the collection of information security related beliefs, values, assumptions, symbols, norms and knowledge that uniquely represent the organization" [29: 569]. Researchers [4, 16, 17] put it firmly that an ISC framework should be developed within an organisational context as it is strongly influenced by the culture and structure of an organisation. This component of the InfoSeCulF, made up of the organisational culture factor, aims at managing the security related cultural attributes to make ISC a part of the dominant organisational culture.

The people component of the STOPE view focuses on transforming the security behaviour of users with direct access to an organisation's information asset. Security behaviour originates from users' interactions with information assets, hence, ISC must manage human factors to improve the security behaviour of users [2, 30]. The factors that constitute the people component are Trust, Information Security Awareness, Information Security Training and Education, Information Security Compliance, Deterrence and Incentives, Information Security Ownership, Privacy, Information Security Knowledge, Information Security Knowledge Sharing and Monitoring.

The environment component of the STOPE model is "the identifiable external elements surrounding the organization that affect its structure and operations and in turn the security of the information assets and the information security culture" [30: 246]. For this reason, the effects of these external elements must be managed when implementing ISC. The factors that constitute the environment component of the InfoSeCulF are National and Ethical Culture and Government Initiatives.

6.2   The Relationship of STOPE Components

The InfoSeCulF adopts the relationship that exist between the STOPE components proposed by [30] in the context of ISC. This relationship which exists because of the interactions between the STOPE components signifies the existing interactions between the subfactors of the InfoSeCulF. This addresses the fourth literature gap stated under Sect. 5.3 for this study.

AlHogail and Mirza [30] argue that the environment component influences ISC, but not vice versa, hence, other components have no relationship to the environment component.

However, [30: 248] states that the relationship between the STOPE components "shows the relationship between factors through the information security culture (ISC)", and not between the factors and ISC. More so, the relationships between the STOPE components signify the underlying interactions between the subcomponents (factors) of the InfoSeCulF. Therefore, the researchers are of the view that there exist relationships between other components of the STOPE model and the environment component, making all the relationships bidirectional.

6.3 Schein's Concept of Organisational Culture

A good understanding of culture is to see it as existing at three different levels (artifacts, espoused values and basic assumptions) spanning from the level of very tangible manifestation that one can see and feel to those that are invincible (thus, deeply embedded), unconscious basic assumptions [7, 44]. Schein [44] posits that behaviour is the result of learned, shared, tacit assumptions that inform people's understanding of reality, resulting in the way people do things (culture).

Van Niekerk and Von Solms [8] argue that in the context of ISC, knowledge underpins and supports all three levels of organisation culture proposed by [44]. In the context of organisational culture, knowledge is ignored because it is assumed that the average employee has the requisite knowledge to perform core work functions. However, in the context of information security, it cannot be assumed that employees have the required security related knowledge to perform core work functions in accordance with security rules or standards, hence knowledge cannot be ignored [8]. For this reason, [8] introduces the fourth level (knowledge) of culture in the context of ISC.

Information security culture is made up of four levels. The artifact level refers to the visible products or phenomena that is observed when one encounters a group with an unfamiliar culture [7, 44]. Espoused values reflect consciously held beliefs that are carefully stated and practiced [7, 13]. Schein [7] refers to basic assumptions as the degree of agreement that originate from the repeated success of implementing certain beliefs and values, and the knowledge level refers to the information security related knowledge of employees [8]. Schein's concept of organisational culture [7] as adapted by [8] provides a good appreciation of what constitute an ISC and thus, provides a good premise for the development of the InfoSeCulF.

These four levels of ISC which collectively reflects the nature of ISC cultivated in an organisation are influenced by the factors of ISC, such as security awareness and security compliance. Hence, this research considers ISC existing at these four levels which collectively influence the security behaviour of members of an organisation.

7 The InfoSeCulF

The InfoSeCulF adopts the four components of the STOPE view as the ISC development component and the four levels of organisational culture (namely, knowledge, assumptions, beliefs and values, and artefacts). Figure 1 depicts the design of the InfoSeCulF developed for the cultivation of ISC. Each factor of the InfoSeCulF has been mapped to an ISC development component as a subcomponent. The STOPE components represent a holistic view of the categories of ISC issues that must be addressed by the factors of the InfoSeCulF to promote a strong ISC. Therefore, each factor of the InfoSeCulF must be developed and implemented to address the category of ISC that the issue is mapped to. The twenty-one factors of the InfoSeCulF influence the cultivation of ISC which reflects at the levels of ISC which are knowledge, assumptions, espoused values, and artifacts.

These factors of the InfoSeCulF can address the ISC challenges of higher learning institutions. For example, the top management commitment factor is key to addressing the challenge of establishing a strong ISC in higher learning institutions due to the lack of management commitment. Again, the information security policy factor − if comprehensively developed with the involvement of all stakeholders – will significantly promote security ownership and impact the security behaviour of members. This implies that this list of factors fits the context of higher learning institutions, hence, it answers the research question for this study. The design of the InfoSeCulF at this stage is a generic framework which is not specific to the context of Ghana and can be applied in institutions within or outside the educational sector, hence, further research is needed to validate the InfoSeCulF to tailor it to the context of Ghana.

The following bullet points provide information on the factors of the InfoSeCulF.

- Organisational Culture: This factor refers to the collective security related assumptions, values, beliefs, and knowledge of an organisation. Its aim is to ensure that these security related attributes of higher learning institutions are in sync with information security measures to motivate organisational members to comply with security guidance to promote ISC.
- Top Management Commitment: This refers to senior management's appreciation of security functions and involvement in activities to protect the information assets of its organisation. This factor is key to implementing ISC [35].
- Information Security Policy: This consists of required guidelines or rules established by an organisation (higher learning institution) to guide all information security matters to influence a positive security behaviour to protect information assets [1, 35].
- Information Security Training and Education: This factor refers to the provision of training and education to enable organisational members to acquire the requisite knowledge and skill of dealing with matters of information security.
- Information Security Risk and Assessment: This factor identifies and analyses the information security risk an institution is exposed to and assesses possible threats and their effects on the institution, and actions required to avoid or mitigate the risk [45].
- Deterrence and Incentives: This factor refers to the mechanism for holding members of an organisation accountable to adhering to its information security policy and procedures via the use of punitive measures and rewards. This is very important as it provides a strategy to compel and motivate organisational members to adhere to security policies.
- Technology Protection and Operations: This factor addresses soft issues that arise due to the management of assets and security incidents, development of technical systems, business continuity and management, and other security-related technical operations to protect organisational information assets [14].
- Change Management: This factor manages the security changes that occur in the way of doing things as a result of the implementation of new information security reforms to ensure a more reliable and stable working environment [29].
- National and Ethical Culture: This factor manages the impact of national culture on cultivating ISC [46] and ethical values and beliefs which define what is right or wrong in the context of information security.

- Government Initiatives: This factor manages information security interventions made by governments (such as national information security regulations, policies, guidelines, information security benchmarking and security awareness promotion programmes), all in a bid to promote information security to protect the national digital space and information assets.
- IT Vendors: This factor defines and manages security-related processes and procedures in relation to pre- and post-validation of IT systems supplied by vendors to an organisation to avoid or reduce the risk of compromising their information assets.
- Budget: This refers to information security budget practice (ISC activities) and investment (ISC action taken to gain benefits for attaining ISC goals) made by institutions to attain a reliable and an effective information security culture [33].
- Program Organisation: This factor addresses the programming or systemising of series of ISC activities in order to achieve the collective goals of protecting information assets for the implementation of a successful ISC programme.
- Information Security Knowledge Sharing: This factor ensures the availability of security knowledge in the organisation by having members externalise the information security knowledge they have acquired by sharing and [internalise] [by] learning security practices from each other [34].
- Monitoring: Monitoring refers to hidden activities employed to check and ensure the security compliance and behaviour of organisational members and, to some extent, assess the belief and trust of members of an organisation [34].
- Trust: This factor deals with building mutual trust between all parties to promote the joint or team operation in the performance of information security tasks in an organisation [47].
- Privacy: This factor manages the appropriate collection and use of personal information stored on a computing system to avoid compromising information assets.
- Information Security Awareness: Rahman, Lubis and Ridho define information security awareness as "a state of consciousness where [a] user [is] ideally committed to the rules, recognize the potentiality, understand the importance of responsibilities and act accordingly" [48: 361].
- Information Security Compliance: This factor refers to "human information system behaviors with regard to information security policies" [49: 1], indicating the extent at which the information security behaviour of organisational members is in adherence with the information security policy of an organisation.
- Information Security Knowledge: This factor deals with providing the requisite information security related knowledge to organisational members to influence the cultivation of a stable information security culture at the other three levels of culture, thus, assumptions, values and artefacts [8].
- Information Security Ownership: This deals with instilling a sense of ownership in organisational members that impact their information security behaviour by ensuring that members have a good appreciation of their roles and responsibilities in championing the ISC course of their organisation.

This framework makes a contribution to research by consolidating the different factors of ISC proposed by other researchers to provide a more comprehensive ISC framework that covers a broader scope of issues associated with cultivating ISC. The

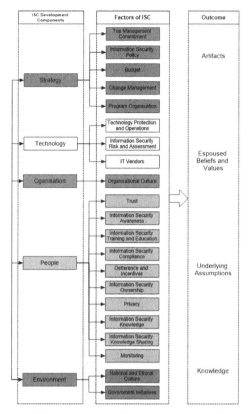

Fig. 1. Proposed information security culture framework (InfoSeCulF)

InfoSeCulF also provides the knowledge on how the underlining factors of ISC such as information security policy, information security awareness and compliance are classified under the main (broader) categories of issues associated with ISC (thus, the STOPE components). This indicates the role played or security related issues tackled by each factor of ISC, providing an effective way to assess and implement an ISC programme.

8   Limitations and Future Research

This study is limited in the sense that the proposed InfoSeCulF is a conceptual framework, though its factors provide a solution to the challenges associated with cultivating ISC in higher learning institutions, hence, in future work, the researchers intend to conduct a study to evaluate the InfoSeCulF using expert reviewers (information security professionals in higher learning institutions) to validate its comprehensiveness and usefulness and to customise it further to the context of higher learning institutions in Ghana.

9   Conclusion

A scoping literature review was conducted to determine what constitutes a comprehensive list of factors for cultivating ISC in higher learning institutions. The factors identified through the scoping review exercise were explored to propose the InfoSeCulF. The proposed framework (InfoSeCulF) is an integration of the STOPE model with the factors of ISC, where the five components of the STOPE model developed by [38] have been applied in the context of ISC as key components of implementing a successful information security culture. Hence, the InfoSeCulF can be regarded as an extended STOPE model, which can be used for establishing a strong ISC in institutions, especially higher learning institutions.

The InfoSeCulF is a holistic and theoretically sound framework that can assist management and information security professionals in cultivating an effective ISC in higher learning institutions. The development of this framework is motivated by available ISC frameworks, the STOPE view developed by [38] and the theory of organisational culture [7, 8].

References

1. Glaspie, H.W., Karwowski, W.: Human factors in information security culture: a literature review. In: Nicholson, D. (ed.) AHFE 2017. AISC, vol. 593, pp. 269–280. Springer, Cham (2018). https://doi.org/10.1007/978-3-319-60585-2_25
2. Caballero, A.: Information Security Essentials for IT Managers: Protecting Mission-Critical Systems. Morgan Kaufman Publishers, Waltham, MA (2013)
3. Singh, A.N., Gupta, M.P., Ojha, A.: Identifying factors of 'organizational information security management.' J. Enterp. Inf. Manag. 27(5), 644–667 (2014)
4. Tang, M., Li, M., Zhang, T.: The impacts of organizational culture on information security culture : a case study. Inf. Technol. Manag. 17(2), 179–186 (2016)
5. Alhogail, A., Mirza, A., Bakry, S.H.: A comprehensive human factor framework for information security in organizations. J. Theor. Appl. Inf. Technol. 78(2), 201–211 (2015)
6. Da Veiga, A., Astakhova, L.V., Botha, A., Herselman, M.: Defining organisational information security culture – Perspectives from academia and industry. Comput. Secur. 92, 1–52 (2020)
7. Schein, E.H.: Organizational Culture and Leadership. Jossey-Bass, Third. San Francisco (2004)
8. Van Niekerk, J.F., Von Solms, R.: Information security culture: a management perspective. Comput. Secur. 29(4), 476–486 (2010)
9. Anderson, J.E., Dunning, D.: Behavioral norms: variants and their identification. Soc. Personal. Psychol. Compass 8(12), 721–738 (2014)
10. Mokwetli, M., Zuva, T.: Adoption of the ICT security culture in SMME's in the Gauteng Province, South Africa. In: 2018 International Conference on Advances in Big Data, Computing and Data Communication Systems (icABCD) (2018)
11. Merhi, M.I., Ahluwalia, P.: Top management can lower resistance toward information security compliance. 2015 International Conference on Information Systems. Exploring the Information Frontier ICIS 2015, pp. 1–11 (2015)
12. Glaspie, H.: Assessment of Information Security Culture in Higher Education, p. 155 (2018)
13. Warrick, D.D.: What leaders need to know about organizational culture. Bus. Horiz. 60(3), 395–404 (2017)

14. Da Veiga, A., Eloff, J.H.P.: A framework and assessment instrument for information security culture. Comput. Secur. **29**(2), 196–207 (2010)
15. Okere, I., Van Niekerk, J., Carroll, M.: Assessing information security culture: a critical analysis of current approaches. In: The Proceedings of IEEE Conference on Information Security for South Africa, pp. 136–143 (2012)
16. AlHogail, A., Mirza, A.: Information security culture: a definition and a literature review. In: 2014 World Congress on Computer Applications and Information Systems (WCCAIS) (2014)
17. Da Veiga, A., Martins, N.: Defining and identifying dominant information security cultures and subcultures. Comput. Secur. **70**, 72–94 (2017)
18. Schlienger, T., Teufel, S.: Analyzing information security culture : increased trust by an appropriate information security culture iimt (international institute of management in telecommunications). In: Proceedings of 14th International Workshop on Database and Expert Systems Applications, pp. 405–409 (2003)
19. Kwaa-Aidoo, E.K., Agbeko, M.: An analysis of information system security of a Ghanaian university. Int. J. Inf. Secur. Sci. **7**(2), 90–99 (2016)
20. Rajab, M., Eydgahi, A.: Evaluating the explanatory power of theoretical frameworks on intention to comply with information security policies in higher education. Comput. Secur. **80**, 211–223 (2019)
21. Hina, S., Dominic, D.D.: Compliance: a perspective in higher education institutions. In: Proceedings of 5th International Conference on Research Innovation Information Systems, pp. 1–6 (2017)
22. Dignan, L.: Ransomware incidents surge, education a hotbed for data breaches, according to Verizon (2017). http://www.zdnet.com/article/ransomware-incidents-surge-education-a-hotbed-for-data-breaches-according-to-verizon/. Accessed 18 Aug 2017
23. Hina, S., Panneer Selvam, D.D.D., Lowry, P.B.: Institutional governance and protection motivation: theoretical insights into shaping employees' security compliance behavior in higher education institutions in the developing world. Comput. Secur. **87**, 1–15 (2019)
24. Metalidou, E.: Human Factor and Information Security in Higher Education (2014)
25. Saltzman, J.: Designing Information Systems Security Policy in Higher Education in Higher Education (2004)
26. Alshare, K.A., Lane, P.L., Lane, M.R.: Information security policy compliance: a higher education case study. Inf. Comput. Secur. **26**(1), 91–108 (2018)
27. Munn, Z., Peters, M.D.J., Stern, C., Tufanaru, C., McArthur, A., Aromataris, E.: Systematic review or scoping review? Guidance for authors when choosing between a systematic or scoping review approach. BMC Med. Res. Methodol. **18**(1), 1–7 (2018)
28. O'Kelly, F., DeCotiis, K., Aditya, I., Braga, L.H., Koyle, M.A.: Assessing the methodological and reporting quality of clinical systematic reviews and meta-analyses in paediatric urology: can practices on contemporary highest levels of evidence be built? J. Pediatr. Urol. **16**(2), 207–217 (2020)
29. AlHogail, A.: Design and validation of information security culture framework. Comput. Human Behav. **49**, 567–575 (2015)
30. AlHogail, A. Mirza, A.: A proposal of an organizational information security culture framework. In: Proceedings of 2014 International Conference on Information, Communication Technology and System, ICTS 2014, pp. 243–249 (2014)
31. AlKalbani, A., Deng, H., Kam, B.: Organisational security culture and information security compliance for e-government development: the moderating effect of social pressure. In: 19th Pacific Asia Conference of Information Systems PACIS 2015 Proceedings, p. 65, January 2015
32. Alnatheer, M., Chan, T., Nelson, K.: Understanding and measuring information security culture. In: PACIS 2012 Proceedings (2012)

33. Masrek, M.N., Harun, Q.N., Zaini, M.K.: Information security culture for Malaysian public organization: a conceptual framework. In: 4th International Conference on Education and Social Sciences 6–8 (INTCESS 2017), pp. 156–166 (2017)
34. Nasir, A., Arshah, R.A., Ab Hamid, M.R.: Information security policy compliance behavior based on comprehensive dimensions of information security culture: a conceptual framework. In: ACM International Conference Proceeding Series, vol. Part F1282, pp. 56–60 (2017)
35. Alnatheer, M.A.: Information security culture critical success factors. In: Proceedings - 12th International Conference on Information Technology: New Generations, ITNG 2015, pp. 731–735 (2015)
36. Dojkovski, S., Lichtenstein, S., Warren, M.: Enabling information security culture: influences and challenges for Australian SMEs. In: ACIS 2010 Proceedings (2010)
37. Bakry, S.H.: Development of e-government: a STOPE view. Int. J. Netw. Manag. **14**(5), 339–350 (2004)
38. Bakry, S.H.: Development of security policies for private networks. Int. J. Netw. Manag. **13**(3), 203–210 (2003)
39. Adhiarna, N., Hwang, Y.M., Park, M.J., Rho, J.J.: An integrated framework for RFID adoption and diffusion with a stage-scale-scope cubicle model: a case of Indonesia. Int. J. Inf. Manage. **33**(2), 378–389 (2013)
40. Bakry, S.H., Bakry, F.H.: A strategic view for the development of e-business. Int. J. Netw. Manag. **11**(2), 103–112 (2001)
41. Bin-Abbas, H., Bakry, S.H.: Assessment of IT governance in organizations: a simple integrated approach. Comput. Human Behav. **32**, 261–267 (2014)
42. Saleh, M.S., Alfantookh, A.: A new comprehensive framework for enterprise information security risk management. Appl. Comput. Inform. **9**(2), 107–118 (2011)
43. Esteves, J., Joseph, R.C.: A comprehensive framework for the assessment of e-government projects. Gov. Inf. Q. **25**(1), 118–132 (2008)
44. Schein, E.H.: The Corporate Culture Survival Guide, vol. 17, no. 4.CA: Jossey-Bass, San Francisco (2009)
45. Naseer, H., Shanks, G., Ahmad, A., Maynard, S.: Towards an analytics-driven information security risk management: a contingent resource based perspective. In: Proceedings of the 25th European Conference on Information Systems, ECIS, 2017, pp. 2645–2655 (2017)
46. Govender, S., Kritzinger, E., Loock, M.: The influence of national culture on information security culture. In: 2016 IST-Africa Week Conference, pp. 1–9 (2016)
47. Da Veiga, A., Astakhova, L.V., Botha, A., Herselman, M.: Defining organisational information security culture – perspectives from academia and industry. Comput. Secur., 101713 (2020)
48. Rahman, A., Lubis, M., Ridho, A.: Information security awareness at the knowledge-based institution: its antecedents and measures. Procedia - Procedia Comput. Sci. **72**, 361–373 (2015)
49. Lembcke, T.B., Trang, S., Plics, P., Masuch, K., Hengstler, S., Pamuk, M.: Fostering information security compliance: comparing the predictive power of social learning theory and deterrence theory. In: 25th Americans Conference on Information Systems AMCIS 2019, no. Bandura 1977, pp. 1–10 (2019)

What Can We Learn from the Analysis of Information Security Policies? The Case of UK's Schools

Martin Sparrius⬤, Moufida Sadok(✉)⬤, and Peter Bednar⬤

University of Portsmouth, Portsmouth, UK
{martin.sparrius,moufida.sadok,peter.bednar}@port.ac.uk

Abstract. Security standards consider that developing a security policy is a cornerstone in information security management. In practice, the development of a security policy is contextually dependent and there is no agreement on what organisations should include in their security policies. This paper argues that analysing information security policy documents could potentially provide new insights into existing issues with security practices. The paper explores and analyses the content and form of 100 UK schools' information security policies to assess their scope and accessibility. The key findings show that the content varied widely between schools but tended to have a technical focus, many security policies had not been updated to address changes to work practices due to the Covid-19 situation and many policies have poor readability scores preventing readers from engaging with them.

Keywords: Information security · UK schools · Information security policy · Readability score · Covid-19 · ISO 27002

1 Introduction

Based on risk analysis, an information security policy (ISP) determines the critical assets that need to be protected, and includes procedures and control measures to prevent and respond to security incidents and breaches. ISO/IEC 27002 [1] stipulates that the objective of security policy is to provide management direction and support for information security in agreement with business requirements and relevant laws and regulations. The security standard also recommends that the statement of ISP objectives and scope should be fully documented. The document should provide information and instructions about how to implement the ISP and should include for example, authentication procedures, roles and responsibilities definition, awareness and training programs planning, business recovery measures and sanctions associated with policy violations. Specific parts of the security policy documents should be communicated to all users and relevant external partners.

Previous research [2] has highlighted the importance of using metrics to assess the quality of an ISP. In this paper, we argue that the analysis and review of security policy

© IFIP International Federation for Information Processing 2021
Published by Springer Nature Switzerland AG 2021
S. Furnell and N. Clarke (Eds.): HAISA 2021, IFIP AICT 613, pp. 81–90, 2021.
https://doi.org/10.1007/978-3-030-81111-2_7

documents have the potential to provide useful information about the main features of an organisation's vision on information security management.

Schools within the United Kingdom (UK) collect and store large amounts of data on their students, parents, and staff. This makes them an attractive target for cyber-attacks, and it has been noted by previous studies that data breaches and cyber-attacks targeting educational organisations have been on the rise [3, 4]. In their Data Breaches Investigation from 2021, Verizon found that 96% of the cyber-attacks involving educational organisations were financially motivated and that they specifically targeted personal data held by these organisations, with Social Engineering being the most common method of attack (47%) [5]. Subsequent to the implementation of the GDPR, it was found that the UK education sector was more likely than other UK sectors to have an ISP in place (75%) [6]. There appears to however been no independent academic research into the nature and quality of the content of UK school ISPs or how staff interact with them.

This paper reports the results of content analysis of 100 UK schools to assess their scope, the relevance of their components and the accessibility of their contents. It is organized as follows: the next section provides some theoretical background to this research. The third section details how ISPs were selected and analysed. The last section discusses the key findings and includes concluding remarks.

2   Background

While there is a wide recognition that an ISP is a key component of an effective information security governance, research in information security suggests that there are different views of what the content of an ISP is supposed to cover [7] and the form these policies take [2]. Some argue that ISP directives need to be detailed in a well-elaborated document [8–10]. Others suggest that only particular aspects of information use need to be covered such as remote working and security incident reporting. The content of an ISP can also address human behaviour and target different groups of users [11]. In this context, ISP document specifies guidelines and procedures that employees must adhere to in their daily interactions with the IT system [12]. The identification of the rights and responsibilities of the organisation members is particularly useful to assist with future decisions when handling information [13].

An ISP document may also outline the specific actions to prevent, respond to and mitigate security incidents. This could include detailed description of monitoring, mitigation and investigation activities that should be assigned to an incident response team (IRT). Monitoring is particularly important since security attacks are growing in frequency, severity and impact and the role of an IRT is crucial in gathering, analysing and archiving digital evidences. When it comes to guides for ISP content, organisations can choose from many different frameworks and could for example refer to security standards such as ISO27002 and/or EU directives for processing personal information. It is, however, challenging in practice to craft a fit-for-purpose ISP as this requires a thorough contextual analysis of an organisation's strategy, structure and culture. Karyda et al. [14] suggest that contextual factors such as organisational structure, organisational culture, management support, users' participation in the formulation process, training and education influence the formulation and implementation of ISPs. Karlsson et al. [15]

found that employees experienced difficulties in following policies due to inadequate explanation and use of terms, inconsistent explanations of the controls, and unexplained policy architecture. A critical analysis of a sample of security policies from the UK's National Healthcare Service by Stahl et al. [16] concluded that security policies can privilege certain groups of stakeholders such as managers and information technology (IT) professionals and do not sufficiently integrate the views and concerns of doctors and nurses about medical matters. Inadequate involvement of staff makes it even less likely that the existence of security policies will lead to effective implementation or relevance from users' perspective [17]. Although an ISP document could include rich and useful information about an organisation's vision of information security, it has been noted that how the policy is constructed can also have a dramatic effect on its effectiveness [2]. In addition, collecting ISPs documents for analysis is very challenging [18], with many organizations regarding the analysis of this documentation as very intrusive [3] and there is still a substantial gap in understanding what organisations include in their ISPs.

In the 2021 UK government survey of schools and colleges it was found that approximately 75% of schools had developed an ISP [6]. However, 47% of the surveyed schools reported multiple security breaches, with phishing (85%), malware (12%) and DDoS (12%) attacks forming the bulk of successful attacks [19]. This discrepancy between having an ISP and still suffering high levels of successful attacks has been highlighted in previous research [3]. This is a cause for concern and it is possible that UK schools ISPs have the same inherent problems over content and form that have been highlighted in other sectors. This paper argues that the analysis of both the content and form of ISPs from UK primary and secondary schools will provide insights into existing issues with security practices within schools.

3 Data Collection and Analysis

UK schools generally publish their policies for parental review and therefore are accessible in the public domain. The ISPs for the study were obtained using two different search engines (Google and Duck Duck Go), allowing the use of different searching algorithms to produce different search results. The keywords used in this search were "Information Security", "Policy" and "UK School", with other variations and additions as the search progressed. To ensure the policies were up to date each policy was double-checked on the school's website by either checking each relevant policy webpage or performing a search using the website's search tool. E-Safety and Safe Internet use policies were disregarded as having a primary focus on students, rather than on staff. Additionally, policies which were too specific in nature (BYOD, GDPR, Use of Mobile Phones) were also disregarded because, as Weidman and Grossklags noted, while smaller, issue-specific policies are useful for an organisation, it is important to have a consolidated high-level policy to provide a foundation for an organisation's ISP [3]. The final sample comprised a total of 100 policies from 73 primary schools and 27 secondary schools which is broadly in line with the expected ratio of UK primary and secondary schools [19]. Next, the UK Government school database [19] was used to collect data on each school, such as school capacity and organisation type. The policies where then loaded into an NVivo database and relevant data for each school added as attributes prior to the initial coding. Initial coding used two categories: Security Management (Organisational Philosophy, Information Security Structure) and Computer Security (Technical Controls, Specific User Responsibilities). These categories were based on Weidman and Grossklags' analysis of university ISPs [3], then the coding was refined using an iterative analysis of a sample of 10 policies. Coding was assigned to content that met the required criteria, irrespective of the potential quality or accuracy of the content. Each policy was then entered into a website readability calculator, Readable, to obtain the word count, Flesch Reading Ease and Simple Measure of Gobbledygook (SMOG) scores. These results were then added to the attribute date for each policy.

3.1 Content of ISPs

As previously stated, coding only notes the presence of content that corresponds to the relevant code. All 100 policies had some relevant text; however, no single policy had all the desired content. For each age focus (primary and secondary schools), the sum of policies which contained the specific content code was divided into the total number of policies for that age focus. The results are presented in Tables 1 and 2.

Table 1. Percentage of schools ISPs containing Security Management content

Content code	Primary schools	Secondary schools
Clearly states who issued policy	59%	**88%**
Has a next review date	57%	68%
Has an effective from date	78%	92%
Explicitly provides motivation or justification for policy	**93%**	88%
Clearly states who is affected by the policy	**93%**	88%
Defines responsibilities for standard roles	42%	32%
Defines responsibilities for specific roles	70%	52%
Mentions methods of enforcement	54%	68%
Mentions nature of sanctions	70%	72%
Has detailed technical items	55%	48%
Has Information Security definitions	**16%**	**28%**
References Computer Misuse Act	35%	48%
References GDPR or Data Protection	82%	80%
Refers to other school policy documents	86%	88%

3.2 Accessibility

Accessibility is generally recognised as how easy it is for a person to read and understand a piece of text [20]. To extend upon the work done by Weidman and Grossklag [3]

Table 2. Percentage of schools ISPs containing Computer Security content

Use of:	Primary schools	Secondary schools
Account control	54%	48%
Anti-virus or malware	64%	56%
Awareness campaign	42%	28%
Backups	53%	44%
BYOD conditions	64%	60%
Encryption	69%	76%
Firewalls	42%	44%
Locking stations	62%	72%
Multi-Factor Authentication	**4%**	**8%**
Passwords	**85%**	**88%**
Patching schedule	24%	40%
Physical security procedures	73%	80%
Public Wi-Fi usage restrictions	14%	8%
Definitions for security breaches	22%	44%
IS incident response guidelines	**80%**	**88%**
Software licensing and software restrictions	66%	60%
Spam or Phishing emails guidance	22%	32%

the same measures of accessibility (readability and word count) were investigated. To calculate the readability score, Flesch Reading Ease was used due to its popularity in research [21], and Simple Measure of Gobbledygook (SMOG) due to its recommended use by the UK's National Health Service [20]. Flesch Reading Ease bases its results on word/sentence length ratios and syllables/word ratios. The scoring ranges from 0–100, and Flesch has a recommended target of 30–50 [3]. SMOG examines the number of polysyllabic words, perceived as being difficult words, compared to the number of sentences in the text. SMOG ranges from 1 to 20, with a higher score being harder to read, and a recommended target of 12–13. The NHS suggests that a score of 14 or higher would result in most adults battling to read the text [20]. The accessibility results are presented in Table 3.

Table 3. Accessibility analysis of ISPs

	Mean	Standard deviation	Minimum	Maximum
Flesch Reading Ease	42.7	7.9	18.1	65.2
SMOG	12.9	1.43	10.1	15.5
Word count	3962	3327	424	20352

The mean Flesch Reading Ease (42.7) and SMOG scores (12.9) both fall within the recommended targets, but have a high standard deviation with outlier policies tending to occur in the regions of lower readability. The average ISP consisted of approximately 10 pages of content, but the standard deviation for this was very high and there were a number of policies sitting at the extreme ends of the range. Based on the results from Weidman and Grossklags' study [3], further analysis was conducted to see if there was a correlation between readability and either wordcount or technical content [3]. Bivariate analysis of the word count and reading difficulty revealed that there was a significant positive correlation between the word count of the policies and improved readability (Table 4). This confirmed Weidman and Grossklags' findings that an increased word count resulted in improved readability [3].

Table 4. Bivariate analysis of word count against readability scores (Note *p < 0.01; **p < 0.001)

	Flesch Reading Ease	SMOG score
Word count of ISP	.386**	−.202*

Bivariate analysis of the coded content and the readability scores was also conducted to see if the presence of technical content significantly decreased accessibility. Selected results with significant correlations are reported in Table 5 and confirm, particularly for the Flesch Reading Ease score, that the presence of a coded technical control increased with readability. While there are only a few contrary correlations in the SMOG results, this analysis still appears to indicate that the presence of the content does not in itself make the text harder to access. This result contrasts with Weidman and Grossklags' result and suggests that other factors are decreasing the readability [3].

Table 5. Bivariate analysis of the presence of technical content against readability scores (Note *p < 0.01; **p < 0.001)

	Flesch Reading Ease score	SMOG score
Has detailed technical items	.294**	.211*
Mentions account control		.293**
Mentions anti-virus or malware	.296**	
Mentions BYOD conditions	.280**	.243*
Mentions locking stations	.249*	
Mentions passwords	.553**	
Mentions physical security	.274**	
Mentions security breaches or incidents	.244*	

3.3 Updating of ISPs

The outbreak of Covid-19 has created new challenges and working conditions within UK schools. These schools have had to shift to working from home during the Covid-19 outbreak and staff and schools have had to make use of programs, such as Microsoft Team and Google Meet, with which they have potentially had relatively little or no training. To examine if this work shift was mirrored within the school's ISPs, all 100 ISPs were revisited one year after the initial collection. Each original policy was examined to see if it had been due an update, either as stipulated by a published review date or if two years had passed since the last published change. Policies with no included dates were placed in a separate category. Each policy was examined to see if there had been changes in any of the following: dates and names, structure/writing style, content, changed into a new type of policy. The final analysis placed each policy into one of three groups: due, an update, not due an update and no date mentioned. Each of these categories was sub-divided into five categories: No Change − policy was identical to original policy; Superficial change − a date or person's name was changed; Meaningful − Substantial content change was present (both positive and negative); Different policy − such as becoming an Acceptable Use or GDPR policy; No longer present − policy has been removed and can no longer be found on the website or via Google search.

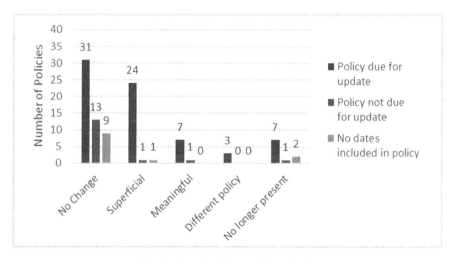

Fig. 1. Results of the update analysis

Figure 1 shows that 72 of the 100 policies were due to be updated, with 41 of those policies having received some form of revision. Of the remaining 28 policies that either lacked any date information or were not due to be revised only three had been revised.

4 Discussion and Conclusions

The results from the content analysis revealed a wide variation between ISPs in terms of both organisational and technical content. Analysis of the technical controls found that controls regarding passwords, physical security, encryption, locking workstations and information security incident response guidelines are the most encountered items within the policies. This is in line with the requirements for GDPR compliance and is a legal obligation for UK schools to avoid financial penalties in the event of a data breach [22]. Additional technical items referring to account control, anti-virus, backups, patching and firewalls occur inconsistently, with several policies implying their presence but not providing any detail. The least common items deal with security issues that involve staff interactions with the broader IT world such as spam/phishing attacks, public Wi-Fi usage and awareness of IS threats. There is little indication within the policies of why these are under-represented but considering that Multi-Factor Authentication is effectively non-existent in the surveyed policies, it is possible that the policies are focusing on aspects which are deemed to be of a higher priority or are more easily managed. This skewed focus in the studied policies is concerning, particularly in regards to raising awareness (35% across all schools) and defining what exactly a security breach is (33% across all schools), as it leaves the staff unprepared for the Social Engineering attacks that UK government has identified as the most likely to affect UK schools [4].

ISP content differed between Primary and Secondary schools. Primary schools focused more on justifying content (93% vs 88%) and explaining roles (70% versus 52%) while Secondary schools tended focus more on policy administration, such as dates (78% vs 92%) and technical controls, such as monitoring staff accounts (54% vs 68%). Primary schools tend to be substantially smaller than secondary schools and this is likely to have a knock-on effect in terms of their financial resources and staffing resources. This difference in resources will lead to a split in how primary and secondary schools approach their information security management, with secondary schools more likely to have the resources to develop a dedicated IT team and assign a senior manager to deal with information security.

Accessibility analysis of the school ISPs found that there was substantial variation in the readability of the policies, representing a wide range of writing styles. With a mean Flesch Reading Ease of 42.7 and a SMOG score of 12.9, the policies can be considered to have an average or higher readability difficulty. For these scores, the average policy would require 11 years of education to reliably access the content and would exclude approximately 50% of the UK population [19]. During the analysis, it was also noted that there was a large variation in word count for the policies. In their analysis of policy accessibility, McDonald and Cranor used a value of 250 words per minute to find the time spent reading a policy [23]. Using that same value, it was calculated that an ISP with the mean word count of just under 4000 words would take 16 min to read. Though most of the policies cluster on the short side, there are six policies that would take an hour or more to read.

In conclusion, there are some good examples within the sample of ISPs that have high accessibility, cover attacks targeting the human factors and have evolved to keep track of current threats. Most of the ISPs however are static and focus primarily on routine technical content. This is to some extent alarming as human factors are equally important in ensuring effective security practices. According to Cyber Security Breaches Survey 2021 [6], the largest number of breaches involve staff interaction with the broader IT environment (redirects, phishing, malware), which correspond to the least common items in the school ISP (spam/phishing attacks, public Wi-Fi usage and awareness of security threats). This implies that the current ISPs have a substantial weakness involving human-IT interactions. This result is consistent with previous research highlighting that actual work practices and routines of most employees were often ignored in the development and operation of security management efforts [24]. Further, the accessibility analysis of the analysed ISPs found that they are on average difficult to access and require a substantial time commitment due to policy length. This raises concerns around the effective implementation of the ISP as the staff are unlikely to engage with the content. Future research could explore the interaction of teachers with ISPs, their perception about their usefulness, and to what extent they reflect and address teachers' work practices in their everyday situation. In addition, further research needs to be conducted into how UK schools can develop their ISPs in order to meet the challenges of managing information security and engaging staff successfully.

References

1. Standard, I.: ISO/IEC 27002 - Code of practice for information security management (2005)
2. Goel, S., Chengalur-Smith, I.N.: Metrics for characterizing the form of security policies. J. Strateg. Inf. Syst. **19**, 281–295 (2010). https://doi.org/10.1016/j.jsis.2010.10.002
3. Weidman, J., Grossklags, J.: What's in your policy? An analysis of the current state of information security policies in academic institutions. In: 26th European Conference on Information Systems: Beyond Digitization – Facets of Socio-Technical Change, ECIS 2018, pp. 1–16 (2018)
4. Laszka, A., Farhang, S., Grossklags, J., On the Economics of Ransomware. Lecture Notes in Computer Science (including Subseries Lecture Notes in Artificial Intelligence and Lecture Notes in Bioinformatics). 10575 LNCS, pp. 397–417 (2017). https://doi.org/10.1007/978-3-319-68711-7_21
5. Verizon: 2021 data breach investigations report. Verizon Bus. J. (2021). https://doi.org/10.1057/s41280-018-0097-z
6. Department for Digitial, Culture, M & S.: Cyber security breaches survey 2021 - Education institutions findings annex (2021). https://doi.org/10.1016/s1361-3723(20)30037-3
7. Paananen, H., Lapke, M., Siponen, M.: State of the art in information security policy development. Comput. Secur. **88**, 101608 (2020). https://doi.org/10.1016/j.cose.2019.101608
8. David, J.: Policy enforcement in the workplace. Comput. Secur. **21**, 506–513 (2002). https://doi.org/10.1016/S0167-4048(02)01006-4
9. Klaić, A.: Overview of the state and trends in the contemporary information security policy and information security management methodologies. In: MIPRO 2010 - 33rd International Convention on Information, Communication and Technology Electron Microelectron Proceedings, pp. 1203–1208 (2010)
10. Pathari, V., Sonar, R.: Identifying linkages between statements in information security policy, procedures and controls. Inf. Manag. Comput. Secur. **20**, 264–280 (2012). https://doi.org/10.1108/09685221211267648
11. Doherty, N.F., Anastasakis, L., Fulford, H.: The information security policy unpacked: a critical study of the content of university policies. Int. J. Inf. Manage. **29**, 449–457 (2009). https://doi.org/10.1016/j.ijinfomgt.2009.05.003
12. Cram, W.A., Proudfoot, J.G., D'Arcy, J.: Organizational information security policies: a review and research framework. Eur. J. Inf. Syst. **26**, 605–641 (2017). https://doi.org/10.1057/s41303-017-0059-9

13. Baskerville, R., Siponen, M.: An information security meta-policy for emergent organizations. Logist. Inf. Manag. **15**, 337–346 (2002). https://doi.org/10.1108/09576050210447019

14. Karyda, M., Kiountouzis, E., Kokolakis, S.: Information systems security policies: a contextual perspective. Comput. Secur. **24**, 246–260 (2005). https://doi.org/10.1016/j.cose.2004.08.011

15. Karlsson, F., Hedström, K., Goldkuhl, G.: Practice-based discourse analysis of information security policies. Comput. Secur. **67**, 267–279 (2017). https://doi.org/10.1016/j.cose.2016.12.012

16. Stahl, B.C., Doherty, N.F., Shaw, M.: Information security policies in the UK healthcare sector: a critical evaluation. Inf. Syst. J. **22**, 77–94 (2012). https://doi.org/10.1111/j.1365-2575.2011.00378.x

17. Dhillon, G., Torkzadeh, G.: Value-focused assessment of information system security in organizations. Inf. Syst. J. **16**, 293–314 (2006). https://doi.org/10.1111/j.1365-2575.2006.00219.x

18. Kotulic, A.G., Clark, J.G.: Why there aren't more information security research studies. Inf. Manage. **41**(5), 597–607 (2004)

19. Department for Education: Schools, pupils and their characteristics (2019). https://www.gov.uk/government/statistics/schools-pupils-and-their-characteristics-january-2019

20. NHS: Use a readability tool to prioritise content - NHS digital service manual. https://service-manual.nhs.uk/content/health-literacy/use-a-readability-tool-to-prioritise-content

21. Feng, L., Jansche, M., Huenerfauth, M., Elhadad, N.: A comparison of features for automatic readability assessment. Coling 2010 – Proceedings of the 23rd International Conference on Computational Linguistics, vol. 2, pp. 276–284 (2010)

22. Department for Education: Statutory policies for schools and academy trusts - GOV.UK. https://www.gov.uk/government/publications/statutory-policies-for-schools-and-academy-trusts/statutory-policies-for-schools-and-academy-trusts

23. McDonald, A., Cranor, L.: The cost of reading privacy policies. Isjlp. **4**, 543–568 (2008). https://doi.org/10.1136/bmj.c2665

24. Sadok, M., Alter, S., Bednar, P.: It is not my job: exploring the disconnect between corporate security policies and actual security policies in SMEs. Inf. Comput. Secur. **28**(3), 467–483 (2020)

A Wolf, Hyena, and Fox Game to Raise Cybersecurity Awareness Among Pre-school Children

Dirk P. Snyman$^{(\boxtimes)}$ [iD], Gunther R. Drevin [iD], Hennie A. Kruger [iD],
Lynette Drevin [iD], and Johann Allers [iD]

School of Computer Science and Information Systems, North-West University,
Potchefstroom, South Africa
`dirk.snyman@nwu.ac.za`

Abstract. Currently, children have a greater exposure to cyberspace and cyber threats than any previous generation. Digital technologies are evolving continuously with the result that cell phones, tablets and similar devices are more accessible to both young and old. Technological advancements create many opportunities, however it also exposes its users to many threats. Pre-school children are especially vulnerable to these threats, as they are rarely made aware of, or empowered to defend themselves against these threats. An approach to solving this problem is to create a mobile serious game that promotes cybersecurity awareness among pre-school children. The focus of this paper is the part of the game that promotes the use of strong passwords and not sharing these passwords with one's friends.

Keywords: Serious mobile games · Strong passwords · Raising awareness with storytelling · Online safety for pre-school children

1 Introduction

Most of the technological advancement taking place in Africa and especially in South Africa, is in the mobile sphere [13]. This is mainly due to the fact that currently young people are the main clients of the digital uptake in developing countries and that mobile devices are easier and cheaper to acquire than other digital devices [5]. The result is that the younger generation has more exposure to technology than previous generations. This provides a big driving force for technological advances in developing countries.

The advancement in technology has many advantages to developing countries and it presents the younger generations with many new opportunities. The downside of these advantages and opportunities is that they are often accompanied with danger. This increases the likelihood that young people will be exposed to negative online experiences and cyber threats. The threat to young people is

Published by Springer Nature Switzerland AG 2021
S. Furnell and N. Clarke (Eds.): HAISA 2021, IFIP AICT 613, pp. 91–101, 2021.
https://doi.org/10.1007/978-3-030-81111-2_8

greater than it is to other groups due to the fact that they have insufficient know-how of how to be digitally safe [5]. Being digitally safe involves the ability to distinguish between opportunities and threats or dangers as well as to act responsibly when online [13].

In the case of pre-school children, their risk to the threats and dangers of cyberspace is much higher as they are exposed to these threats from a very young age without being equipped with the knowledge and ability to protect themselves against these threats [13]. A large amount of cybersecurity educational material and awareness strategies exist, however very few of these resources are aimed at pre-school children. The problem is that pre-school children have different and specific requirements when it comes to learning. As most pre-school children are not able to read or write, it is necessary to use different ways to present information and include different methods of learning. Content also needs to be presented in a way that is fun and easy to understand thereby ensuring the children's interest and motivation to participate.

The use of mobile devices, by pre-school children, to access cyberspace poses a security risk for the children. However, the opportunity is also presented to use these devices as a tool to educate them about the dangers and threats of cyberspace. Children learn through playing games [14], therefore using a serious game on a mobile device can be a viable approach to introducing them to cybersecurity concepts.

A serious game is an approach whereby serious aspects, with the intention to instruct, are presented in the guise of a video game [3]. It could be possible to educate pre-school children about the dangers of cyberspace by using a serious game that is appealing to them and to deploy it on the mobile devices that they are familiar with. In this way it could be possible to enable them to act and protect themselves against these dangers.

The purpose of this paper is to present a proof of concept of a serious game that can be used to promote awareness of cybersecurity among pre-school children in the context of developing countries, specifically South-Africa. This paper is based on a Master's dissertation [2][1].

The remainder of the paper is structured as follows: In Sect. 2, a cursory discussion on cybersecurity is presented, followed by cybersecurity awareness for children in Sect. 3. Section 4 is dedicated to existing serious game implementations for cybersecurity awareness for pre-school children. The implementation of the game in this research is discussed in Sect. 5. A reflection on the implementation of the game is provided in Sect. 6 and Sect. 7 ends with a conclusion and future work.

2   Cybersecurity

Cyberspace has become a vital and irreplaceable part of modern society. Not only do billions of users visit it daily, but it also contains data and information of,

---

[1] This study was conducted with ethical approval of the Faculty of Natural and Agricultural Sciences Ethics Committee of the North-West University, ethics number NWU-01159-20-A9.

and on, people, companies, and governments. This information includes sensitive data such as, protected health information, personal information, intellectual property and governmental and industrial information systems.

As threats in cyberspace can affect personal and private information, a form of digital security must be implemented by users of cyberspace to ensure that a safe cyber environment is maintained.

A common approach to protect assets from unauthorised access in cyberspace is the use of some form of authentication and verification to prove that the user, who is attempting to gain access, does indeed have the right to do so. The most common implementation of this method is the use of passwords. Creating strong passwords is a very simple, yet crucial step in protecting assets in cyberspace. Criteria that are commonly used to evaluate strong passwords are length, complexity and randomness [9].

3   Cybersecurity Awareness for Pre-school Children

The purpose of creating awareness of cybersecurity is to focus an individual's attention on issues regarding cybersecurity. These awareness activities are aimed at enabling individuals to recognise cybersecurity threats and to respond to them in an appropriate way [11]. Cybersecurity awareness is aimed at users of cybertechnology and therefore the human element of cybersecurity is addressed.

There are a number of elements that need to be considered when developing a cybersecurity awareness campaign. One of these elements is simplicity. For an awareness campaign to be successful, it is important that the user feels in control of the situation and can follow specific behaviours [1]. By keeping the rules simple and consistent, the user's perception of control will make it easier to accept the new behaviour [4]. Another element is the use of engaging material that is appropriate for the target group [4]. This presents a challenge when the awareness campaign is aimed at a very specific audience, such as pre-school children. Some examples of awareness campaigns for children are presented in the following sub-section.

3.1   Example Resources from Literature

Cyberspace can be dangerous and therefore children, and more specifically pre-school children, need to be made aware of the dangers from a young age, but relatively few resources are available for use with this target demographic. Three examples from literature to increase awareness of cybersecurity issues among children (some without the specific focus on pre-school children) are given in Table 1.

Table 1. Cybersecurity resources for children [2]

Title	Content
Digital wellnests: Let us play in safe nests [8]	A book that consists of concepts, poems and messages set in the animal kingdom. It also inludes a number of digital wellness and cybersecurity morals
Be Internet awesome[a]	Resources that explore four different in-game worlds that teaches the user cybersafety lessons on issues such as responsible communication, recognising potential scams, using strong passwords, and taking action against inappropriate behaviour. It also includes a curriculum for educators
Savvy Cyber Kids[b]	A book series aimed specifically at children, in which the following digital wellness and cybersecurity elements are identified, *viz.* online anonymity; online bullying; and limiting screen time

a https://www.google.ch/goodtoknow/web/curriculum/
b https://savvycyberkids.org/families/kids/

When comparing the above mentioned resources, the work of Fischer and Von Solms [8] has the best alignment with the aim of this study. Their book identifies relevant cybersecurity topics and is specifically aimed at pre-school children, while in comparison, *Internet awesome* and *Savvy cyber kids* identify a smaller number of core issues. In *"Digital wellnests: Let us play in safe nests"* simple explanations are used and the main characters are depicted using animals that children are familiar with and can relate to. There are four main sections in the book. The first section has a foreword and introduction aimed primarily at the parent, guardian or teacher. A few technology-related concepts are discussed and illustrated, using drawn representations, in the second section. The third section contains a number of poems which form the main content of the book. These poems feature animals that are busy interacting with technology and each poem ends with a moral lesson. The following is an example of a typical cybersecurity scenario (in this case, the use of strong passwords) that is addressed by the poems in the book:

Three friends, Wolf, Hyena and Fox, discuss how to create strong passwords. Wolf recommends that they share each other's passwords and Hyena agrees, until Fox warns them to never share their passwords with others.
— The moral of the story is to create strong passwords and to keep these passwords a secret from others. Good password practices are a big part of cybersecurity and it is essential to improve one's online security.

Finally, the fourth section of the book consists of 14 short, easy to remember, messages that serve as important cybersecurity-related lessons. The messages loosely match the lessons presented by the poems. The following example is the message that closely matches the lesson given by Wolf, Hyena and Fox:

"Remember, remember to never forget. A strong password is not the name of your pet. It's letters and numbers all mixed together. Hard to guess, but easy to remember." [8, p. 38].

To better understand how to raise awareness of cybersecurity among pre-school children it is necessary to identify how pre-schoolers learn and develop important skills. This is addressed in the following sub-section.

3.2 Play as a Mode of Awareness and Knowledge Acquisition

Children, especially pre-school children, use the following five ways to become aware of, and learn to interact with their environment [12]:

- Observation - Learning visually using observation and imitation;
- Listening - Auditory learning;
- Exploring - Investigative learning;
- Experimenting - Learning by trial and error; and
- Asking questions - Inquisitive learning.

However, not all children learn in the same way. While some children respond better to teaching modes that involve observing and listening, others receive more stimulation from practical experimentation and asking questions. At their age, pre-school children learn through play [14] as it is a fun way to learn and presents the opportunity to observe, listen, explore, experiment and ask questions to solve problems, irrespective of a child's preferred learning mode. All forms of learning can therefore be stimulated using a single learning medium.

As a child's parent, teacher or guardian knows how the child learns best, their involvement is important to guide the child to optimize learning.

From the discussion above, it is clear that play can encompass many modes of learning at once. In the next section, the use of serious games, as a form of play with the intention of teaching and learning, is discussed.

4 Serious Games for Pre-school Children

Pre-school children learn through play [14], therefore educators and parents are given the opportunity to use games to assist in teaching children new skills and knowledge. As children are already exposed to digital technology [6], the use of games for teaching and spreading awareness appears to be a viable approach. This is evident by the number of serious games aimed at young children.

A non-exhaustive list of serious games targeted at young children with the goal of teaching or spreading awareness of cybersecurity is given in Table 2. The games listed here serve as a reference when creating a serious game on cybersecurity for children in general. A gap exists in the current literature as are no games with a focus on pre-school children [10] and, therefore, the novelty of this research is the creation of such a game to contribute to filling this gap.

Table 2. Serious games for children [2, 10]

Game name	Cybersecurity topics
Interland[a] (Serious game implementation of the "Internet awesome" resources from Table 1)	- Communicate responsibly; - Know the signs of a potential scam; - Create a strong password; and - Set an example and take action against inappropriate behaviour
Carnegie Cadets[b]	- Staying safe online - Protection against viruses and malware - Using social networks responsibly
CyberKids[c]	- Strong passwords - Vulnerability identification
PBS Cybersecurity Lab[d]	- Staying safe online - Spotting scams - Defending against cyber attacks

[a] https://beinternetawesome.withgoogle.com/en_us/interland
[b] http://www.carnegiecyberacademy.com/
[c] https://doi.org/10.1109/SCCC51225.2020.9281253
[d] https://www.pbs.org/wgbh/nova/labs/lab/cyber/

In an attempt to create a framework for games aimed specifically at pre-school children, Callaghan and Reich [6] identified the following educational design elements based on how they learn:

Clear and Simple Goals – Children learn best with clear instructions and modelling which allows them to draw connections to their existing beliefs and frames of reference [7];

Quality of Feedback and Rewards – Using feedback is important tool to encourage children and notifies them if they are doing something wrong. Visual and auditory feedback can be combined to make it easy for the child to understand and should therefore rather be used as most pre-school children are unable to read;

Structure of Challenge – The structure of a challenge should match the level of performance of the target audience. The level of a challenge can be increased gradually as the child understands more of the material. Furthermore, its difficulty should be decreased when the child appears to struggle; and

Motion based Interactions – Motion-based interactions can serve as an alternative to complex touch screen activities that might be too difficult for many children. Game interaction should be aligned with the physical capabilities of pre-school children. Touchable object sizes, simplified touchscreen motions, etc. will improve the total experience of the child.

All these elements are necessary for a game to be appropriate for pre-school children and should therefore be implemented in the mobile serious game that is to be created for this study.

5   Serious Game Implementation

In this section, an overview of the serious game that was developed in this study is given by discussing the layout and function of each scene and its components.

The game starts with the main menu which serves as a selection screen for choosing a story scene which includes a poem and related quiz and game to be played. A screenshot of the main menu scene is given in Fig. 1. The two green arrows pointing left and right are used to navigate through the poems. The story currently shown is that of Wolf, Hyena and Fox as shown in the center of Fig. 1, and is an animation that can selected. When this part of the screen is tapped, focus will be switched to the chosen story.

Fig. 1. Application main menu

Once a story is selected in the main menu scene, the related poem's first scene will be displayed and read out loud to the child. This specific poem forms the basis for the related cybersecurity theory on password complexity [9], presented at the appropriate level [13]. The poem progresses by tapping anywhere on the screen to move to its next screen. The purpose of this scene is to make the child aware of the dangers of cyberspace in an enjoyable way.

Once the moral and reflection questions in the poem scene (Fig. 2) is completed, the quiz scene (Fig. 3) is entered. In this scene it is determined whether or not the child understands the issue that was described in the poem by motivating him/her to answer four questions, about the topic, that are chosen randomly from a question pool. The random selection of questions is done to provide a form of replayability and thereby to ensure that no pattern is memorised when answering the questions. Progress is not blocked if the questions are answered incorrectly. The first reason for not blocking progress, is the objective of the game is not a formal assessment of the child's understanding of the dangers, but rather the raising of awareness on the matter. Secondly, the quiz is only a tool for the parents, teachers and guardians to be used to encourage the child and also to keep track of their effort and progress.

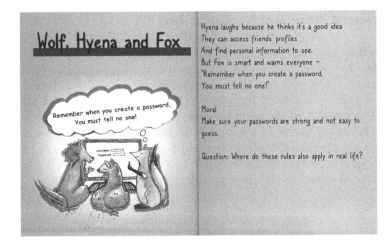

Fig. 2. Poem scene (page two of two)

Fig. 3. Quiz question screen showing one of five possible cybersecurity questions based on the poem topic

The final scene allows the child to play a mini-game which is based on the poem that was selected. The game serves as a fun reward for completing the poem and quiz scenes. Before the game starts, the instructions and goal of the game are displayed on the screen and it is read out loud (Fig. 4). A slider is used to set the difficulty level of the game.

In the Wolf, Hyena and Fox game (Fig. 4) the child has to flip over tiles to reveal the images underneath. If two tiles with non-matching images are flipped, they are flipped back. If the images match, the tiles are left facing upwards permanently. The images are spread randomly between the tiles and each tile has exactly one match. The goal of this game is to match each tile with an identical tile. There is no scoring in the game and, therefore, it cannot be lost. The game is an exercise in memory and the theme of the message of the game is to remember the passwords that one creates. The number of tiles increase if a higher difficulty level is selected.

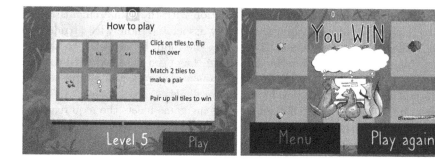

Fig. 4. Wolf, Hyena and Fox game

After completing the game, a message is displayed to indicate success or failure. This message is accompanied by an animation that relates to the poem. An option is presented to play again or return to the main menu. If the user decides to play again, the user is redirected to the level selection screen. The following section is dedicated to a reflection on the game.

6 Reflection

The aforementioned game design elements that were identified from the framework of Callaghan and Reich [6] are revisited in this section and used to reflect on the success of the implementation of the game:

Clear and Simple Goals – The aim of the game is to introduce the pre-school player to cybersecurity concepts at an appropriate level. Some specific activities that are used to meet this aim include listening (poem scene), reflecting (quiz scene), and playing (game scene). The goals for each of these activities are restricted to one outcome each, simple to understand, and the associated completion time of the activities are kept short to match the attention span of pre-school children.

Quality of Feedback and Rewards – During the reflection activity, real-time feedback is provided on the answers on the quiz with large recognisable symbols (ticks and crosses), accompanied by auditory feedback in the form of easily recognisable chimes. The game further rewards the player with an array of icons, once more featuring the characters from the poem, that indicate the level of performance in the reflection activity. Depending on the outcome of the playing activity, a completion screen reaffirms the positive or negative result upon completing the game.

Structure of Challenge – The challenge level of the final activity can be adjusted to match the relative ability of the player to play the game. As a player becomes more familiar and skilled, the difficulty can be increased accordingly to provide an ongoing challenge.

Motion Based Interactions – Motion interaction with the game remains a challenge to implement. Motion input is typically associated more with arcade style games, rather than serious games. Therefore, the input is restricted to tapping and touching gestures. The interface, however, has been designed with the preschooler in mind and incorporates bigger touch elements and simple actions appropriate to a player with developing motor skills.

Apart from this cursory reflection on how the game meets the required game design elements, further evaluation was performed in the form of an expert review of the game in its entirety and not only on the implementation of the poem aimed at strong passwords. This review was done by six experts in the field of pre-school education in the form of a questionnaire with a predetermined scoring system for evaluating the game, followed up by a telephonic interview for qualitative feedback. The reviewers believed the game to be an overall success and scored the game highly (average score of 4.5/5) on factors such as fun, suitability for pre-school children, and the effectiveness of conveying cybersecurity awareness. Due to space considerations, the full review is not shown here and the reader is referred to related work that describes this in detail [2].

This study is concluded in the following section.

7   Conclusion and Future Work

The aim of this paper was to present a mobile serious game that is appropriate to promote awareness of cybersecurity issues among pre-school children. An overview of cybersecurity awareness for children and related resources were provided, followed by a brief discussion on the relevant learning modes that relate to children. Existing serious games for the promotion of good cybersecurity practices among children were discussed. Subsequently, the implementation of a serious game, specifically for pre-school children was described. The specific example regarding the use of passwords was used as an example of one of the topics that is covered in the game and the book that it is based on. The paper is concluded by contributing a reflection on the success of the implementation, based on a framework of educational design elements from literature and a short summary of an expert evaluation of the game.

Future work include the expansion of the game to include more information security scenarios, characters, and games.

References

1. Ajzen, I.: Perceived behavioral control, self-efficacy, locus of control, and the theory of planned behavior. J. Appl. Soc. Psychol. **32**(4), 665–683 (2002). https://doi.org/10.1111/j.1559-1816.2002.tb00236.x
2. Allers, J.: A mobile serious game to promote digital wellness among pre-school children. Master's thesis, North-West University, South Africa (2021)
3. Alvarez, J., Djaouti, D., et al.: An introduction to serious game - definitions and concepts. Serious Games Simul. Risks Manage. **11**(1), 11–15 (2011)

4. Bada, M., Nurse, J.R.: The social and psychological impact of cyberattacks. In: Benson, V., Mcalaney, J. (eds.) Emerging Cyber Threats and Cognitive Vulnerabilities, pp. 73–92. Academic Press (2020). https://doi.org/10.1016/B978-0-12-816203-3.00004-6

5. Burton, P., Leoschut, L., Phyfer, J.: South African Kids Online : A glimpse into children's internet use and online activities. Technical Report, UNICEF (2016). http://www.cjcp.org.za/uploads/2/7/8/4/27845461/south_african_kids_online_brochure.pdf

6. Callaghan, M.N., Reich, S.M.: Are educational preschool apps designed to teach? an analysis of the app market. Learn. Media Technol. **43**(3), 280–293 (2018). https://doi.org/10.1080/17439884.2018.1498355

7. Cowley, B., Charles, D., Black, M., Hickey, R.: Toward an understanding of flow in video games. Comput. Entertainment **6**(2), 1–27 (2008). https://doi.org/10.1145/1371216.1371223

8. Fischer, R., Von Solms, S.: Digital wellnests. African Centre of Excellence for Information Ethics (2016)

9. Furnell, S.: Password meters: inaccurate advice offered inconsistently? Comput. Fraud Secur. **2019**(11), 6–14 (2019). https://doi.org/10.1016/S1361-3723(19)30116-2

10. Hill, W.A. Jr., Fanuel, M., Yuan, X., Zhang, J., Sajad, S.: A survey of serious games for cybersecurity education and training. In: KSU Proceedings on Cybersecurity Education, Research And Practice, pp. 1–15 (2020)

11. Kissel, R.: Glossary of key information security terms. Technical Report, Revision 2, National Institute of Standards and Technology, Gaithersburg, MD (2013). https://doi.org/10.6028/NIST.IR.7298r2

12. Matthews, D., Lieven, E., Tomasello, M.: How toddlers and preschoolers learn to uniquely identify referents for others: a training study. Child Dev. **78**(6), 1744–1759 (2007). https://doi.org/10.1111/j.1467-8624.2007.01098.x

13. Von Solms, S., Fischer, R.: Digital wellness : Concepts of cybersecurity presented visually for children. In: Furnell, S., Clarke, N.L. (eds.) Eleventh International Symposium on Human Aspects of Information Security & Assurance (HAISA 2017), vol. 11, pp. 156–166 (2017)

14. Yogman, M., Garner, A., Hutchinson, J., Hirsh-Pasek, K., Golinkoff, R.M.: The power of play: a pediatric role in enhancing development in young children. Pediatrics **142**(3), (2018). https://doi.org/10.1542/peds.2018-2058

Evaluation Strategies for Cybersecurity Training Methods: A Literature Review

Joakim Kävrestad[(✉)] and Marcus Nohlberg

University of Skövde, Skövde, Sweden
{joakim.kavrestad,marcus.nohlberg}@his.se

Abstract. The human aspect of cybersecurity continues to present challenges to researchers and practitioners worldwide. While measures are being taken to improve the situation, a vast majority of security incidents can be attributed to user behavior. Security and Awareness Training (SAT) has been available for several decades and is commonly given as a suggestion for improving the cybersecurity behavior of end-users. However, attackers continue to exploit the human factor suggesting that current SAT methods are not enough. Researchers argue that providing knowledge alone is not enough, and some researchers suggest that many currently used SAT methods are, in fact, not empirically evaluated. This paper aims to examine how SAT has been evaluated in recent research using a structured literature review. The result is an overview of evaluation methods which describes what results that can be obtained using them. The study further suggests that SAT methods should be evaluated using a variety of methods since different methods will inevitably provide different results. The presented results can be used as a guide for future research projects seeking to develop or evaluate methods for SAT.

Keywords: Security · Evaluation · Methods · Awareness · Training · User

1 Introduction

It is well-established that insecure user behavior is one of the major challenges in cybersecurity [36]. Targeting users rather than technology is common practice for many attackers, and the need to make users more resilient to social engineering is apparent. As such, there is an obvious need to improve user behavior in regards to cybersecurity [6]. To this end, users must be helped to understand the consequences of their actions and learn how to act more securely [13]. For that purpose, user training is the go-to solution suggested in scientific research and offered by practitioners [23,32].

Security and Awareness Training (SAT) has been discussed in the scientific literature for at least two decades [38]. However, recurring reports of attacks suggest that the problem of insecure user behavior is nowhere near being solved.

© IFIP International Federation for Information Processing 2021
Published by Springer Nature Switzerland AG 2021
S. Furnell and N. Clarke (Eds.): HAISA 2021, IFIP AICT 613, pp. 102–112, 2021.
https://doi.org/10.1007/978-3-030-81111-2_9

On the contrary, industry reports describe that human-related attacks are the most common attacks, suggesting that up to 95% of attacks include the human element [12,15,39]. Some researchers even suggest that organizations' training programs are often not grounded in empirical evidence of their effectiveness [1,2]. Seeing how the problem of insecure user behavior is certainly not resolved, the need for further research into this area is apparent.

The goal of any SAT effort is to convey knowledge to the user so that she knows what to do, understands why to do it and how to do it [38]. As such, the ultimate goal is to improve the user behavior regarding security by providing the user with knowledge and understanding. Recent research suggests that providing knowledge is not enough as knowing what to do does not necessarily translate to correct behavior [4,31]. It is easy to argue that the proper way to evaluate SAT efforts would be to evaluate the actual outcome, the effect on cybersecurity behavior. However, such studies bring practical as well as ethical concerns. Studies on human behavior must adhere to rigorous ethical principles that impact what can be done and how, as exemplified by [35]. Practically, experimental evaluations are hard to perform, leaving room for the use of other evaluation methods [46].

This paper aims to explore recently published work in the domain of end-user cybersecurity training to identify how such training methods are evaluated and outline considerations related to the identified evaluation methods. This was done through a structured literature review where included papers were analyzed using thematic coding. The results provide insight into what evaluation methods that are used for the evaluation of SAT and what results that can be expected from them. As such, it can be used to guide future research into SAT development by providing a reference for making informed methodological decisions and respond to the need for empirically evaluated SAT methods. The results also identify what SAT methods that have been evaluated in recent research.

2   Methodology

The study was performed as a structured literature review (SLR) which followed the process outlined by [30]:

1. Formulate a research question or aim.
2. Perform literature searches.
3. Apply inclusion and exclusion criteria.
4. Perform quality assessment.
5. Extract data.
6. Analyze data.

As described by [22,27], selecting search terms and databases are essential tasks in an SLR. The search term used in this study was designed to be inclusive and capture all papers discussing end-user cybersecurity training. While a more restrictive query could have been designed, we argue that a broad search is more likely to capture all relevant studies, even if it results in a higher manual workload regarding the application of selection criteria. The query was expressed as follows: *security AND (training OR education) AND user*. Note that the query was modified to match the syntax of the databases used in the study. The search term was applied to titles, abstracts, and keywords to focus the results. This was motivated by the argument that papers that do provide important information concerning the aim of the study are focused on cybersecurity training of end-users and will therefore include all search words in the metadata. To increase the chance that the study includes all important papers on the topic, an inclusive mindset was applied in choosing databases resulting in the use of *Scopus, Web of Science (core collection), Science Direct, dblp, and Usenix.*

All identified papers were evaluated against inclusion criteria. As suggested by [48], the criteria were established before the search process started to avoid bias during the selection process. The criteria were first applied to the abstracts of the identified papers. Paper that clearly failed to meet the criteria were excluded before the criteria were applied to the full remaining papers. Papers written by the authors of this paper were also excluded from the study to minimize bias. The criteria for inclusion were the following:

1. Published 2015 or later.
2. Not a duplication of another included paper.
3. Published in peer-reviewed journal or conference.
4. Free to access for the author.
5. Written in English.
6. Discusses the topic of this study.
7. Reports on one or more evaluations of SAT methods.

The first five criteria were used to limit the body of included papers to recent high-quality research and were, to some extent, applied automatically during the search process where publication year, language, and outlet could be configured during the search. The last two criteria were included to ensure that identified papers specifically discussed end-user training in the cybersecurity context and that they reported on findings based on their own data rather than conclusions based on cited material or similar. The included papers were analyzed using thematic coding in an open fashion, as described by [5]. During the analysis process, the papers were read and categorized in three steps:

1. All papers were read and individual methods of cybersecurity training were identified.
2. The papers were reread with the focus of identifying individual ways of evaluating training methods.
3. The goal and outcome of the evaluations presented in the papers were analyzed. At this stage, the papers were positioned according to what method they evaluated and how with the intent of analyzing how various evaluation methods are used.

EndNote Desktop was used for the categorization and coding of included papers.

3   Results

The searches, conducted on 2020-09-07, resulted in a total of 3664 papers, distributed among the included databases as follows:

- Scopus: 1997 hits
- Web of science: 1495 hits
- Science Direct: 129 hits
- dblp: 13 hits
- Usenix: 30 hits

All papers and their abstracts were loaded into EndNote, and duplicate papers were removed automatically during this process. Next, the titles and abstracts of all papers were scanned, and papers that clearly failed to meet the inclusion criteria were removed from the study, leaving 106 candidate papers. The inclusion criteria were then applied to the full body of those papers, resulting in 28 papers that were included in this study. Those papers were analyzed using thematic coding as described throughout the rest of this section.

3.1   Initial Categorization of Included Papers

During the first analysis stage, the papers were first categorized according to what type of cybersecurity training they evaluated, resulting in an overview of what SAT methods have been evaluated in recent work. An overview and listing of papers included in the review are presented in Table 1. Included papers will from hereon be referenced by the label (Ax) provided in Table 1; the number in brackets point to the entry in the reference list that provides a full reference to the respective papers.

3.2   Identification of Evaluation Methods

Following the identification of cybersecurity training types, the papers were once again analyzed focusing on what kind of evaluations they contained. At this point, four distinct methods of evaluation were identified in the papers:

- Perception evaluations: Evaluations that focused on users' perception of a training method. This included usability studies and typically aimed to evaluate if users liked the proposed method.
- Knowledge evaluations: Evaluations that measured the knowledge gained by participants using a certain method of training.
- Simulation: Evaluations that measured security outcomes, such as phishing resilience or password behavior in a simulated scenario.
- Experimental: Evaluations that measured security outcomes, such as phishing resilience or password behavior in a naturalistic setting.

Table 1. List of included papers and initial categorization

Papers	Category	Category description
A1: [34], A2: [3], A3: [40], A4: [44], A5: [19]	Several	Papers evaluating several training categories
A6: [14], A7: [20], A8: [17], A9: [10], A10: [28], A11:[21], A12: [18], A13: [37], A14: [47]	Gamification	Papers evaluating gamified training
A15: [7], A16: [41]	Interactive online	Papers evaluating interactive material delivered online
A17: [45], A18: [25], A19: [42]	Lecture	Papers evaluating instructor-led lectures
A20: [26], A21: [49], A22: [11], A23: [51], A24: [24], A25: [9], A26: [50]	Situation aware	Papers evaluating training delivered in a situation where it is usable
A27: [29]	General_1	Evaluates the impact of progression in difficulty of material
A28: [33]	General_2	Evaluated how a variety of simultaneous methods affected phishing resilience in an organization

3.3   Analysis of Evaluation Methods

The included papers were analyzed once again, focusing on the methods the papers used for evaluation, the author's comments on the used evaluation methods, and the rationale for adopting certain methods. The result in this step is an overview of what research goals are addressed using the four distinct methods of evaluation. Table 2 provides an overview of which evaluation methods are discussed in the included papers, and the remainder of this section describes the evaluation methods in more detail.

Table 2. Overview of evaluation types presented in the included papers

Evaluation type	Papers
Perception	A3, A4, A6, A7, A8, A9, A10, A12, A16, A23
Knowledge	A5, A11, A16, A17, A19
Simulation	A1, A2, A3, A4, A7, A12, A14, A15, A18, A21, A23, A24, A27
Experiment	A4, A5, A6, A13, A20, A22, A25, A26, A28

Ten of the included papers report on evaluations based on assessing participants *perception* using interviews or surveys. Two main types of studies can be identified where one evaluates users' perception of their own skill or knowledge. In contrast, the other evaluates the users' perception of a SAT method often in terms of how enjoyable or usable it is. A rationale provided as a motivation for perception evaluations is that a more enjoyable SAT is more likely to be used by the intended users in a naturalistic setting. The most frequently discussed shortcoming is that it cannot assess the actual effect on user behavior.

A similar type of evaluation is *knowledge based evaluation* where the participants' knowledge is measured, often using a survey. The rationale is that knowledge about correct behavior is a pre-condition for correct behavior. Similar to perception evaluations, a shortcoming is that actual behavior is not assessed. However, a potential benefit compared to evaluation based on perception is that risk of response bias can be lesser.

Simulations measure the effect of SAT on security behavior but in a simulated environment. Simulations are presented in 13 of the included papers. The most commonly presented study type measures the participants' ability to distinguish between legitimate and fraudulent emails after being subjected to SAT. A few studies employ a pre-validated security awareness instrument to measure the SAT's effect on security awareness. A1 mentions that participants will likely be primed since they know that they participate in a study, and A21 argues that as a reason for why a simulation cannot fully mimic a natural scenario. However, the rationale for using simulations over naturalistic experiments is that simulations can provide insight into behavioral change without ethical and procedural difficulties that are often associated with experiments.

Experiments are used in nine of the included papers and measure security behavior in a naturalistic setting. Experiments are often performed using penetration testing techniques or by monitoring behavior in an organization after SAT is deployed. A rationale for using experiments is that the effect on actual behavior can be measured and observed, but several included papers demonstrate that experiments present ethical and procedural challenges. The ethical challenges stem from the fact that participants are often involved without explicit informed consent, or with informed consent that does not disclose the full extent of the experiment. The argument is that telling participants that their security behavior will be studied may influence their behavior (A11, A22, A26, A28). A workaround is to use limited informed consent and debrief participants upon study completion. Another workaround is to perform the study in an organizational setting and get permission from the organization. A practical difficulty involves that experiments with deceptive components need to consider ethical clearance.

In addition to the distinct evaluation types, the coding process identified several additional methodological considerations, and those are accounted for next. The first consideration relates to the study design, where the included papers demonstrate diversity. Between-group, pre-post, and one-shot case studies are present for all four evaluation methods. One-shot case studies report on the evaluation of a single SAT method, and an obvious drawback is that it cannot provide insight into how the SAT compares to other SAT methods. One-shot case studies are most prominently used when evaluating the users' perception of a single SAT method. Pre-post tests typically involve a study design where participants are subjected to a measure, then presented with SAT before they are again measured. The rationale is that the effect of the SAT is then isolated. Finally, the Between-group design includes subjecting different groups to different SAT methods to compare the effects, often including one group that is not subjected to any SAT method. A rationale for using a between-group design over a pre-post test is that the pre-post test design provides an increased risk of participation bias which is arguably especially risky in studies evaluating security awareness and behavior.

Another aspect discussed in several included papers (e.g., A6, A7, A14, A15, A18) is knowledge retention, but this is only evaluated in a few of the included studies. In relation to knowledge retention, studies report that the effect of several SAT methods seems to wear off after a certain amount of time (A6). A second aspect considered in some of the included papers is if the participants would have participated in SAT if it was voluntary (A8, A10). Assessing if participants would participate voluntarily is important since prospective users need to participate in SAT for the training to be able to provide its intended effect. The effect of user unwillingness to participate in SAT is hard to account for in evaluations. A related consideration mentioned in A18 is a possible bias stemming from the participants' participation itself. Participants who know that they participate in an awareness evaluation are likely to be more aware compared to when they are not informed about the evaluation.

3.4   Discussion on the Results

This paper reports on a structured literature review where 28 papers evaluating SAT methods were included. The evaluation methods used are classified as *Perception evaluations, knowledge evaluations, simulations, and experiments*. The analysis of how they are used and argued for demonstrates that they all have different benefits and shortcomings. While the end goal of any SAT is to improve user behavior, and experiments are arguably the only method that is fully capable of evaluating effects on behavior, they are practically and ethically challenging to perform. Simulations provide a less complicated alternative but are also argued to be less reliable [16,43]. A second benefit of simulations is that the controlled nature of them allows for follow-up interviews with participants. Further, voluntary user participation is argued to be an important aspect of SAT, and perhaps the only evaluation method that captures that is *perception evaluations*. As such, an insight from this SLR is that an extensive SAT development project should evaluate its outcomes using diverse evaluation methods.

The results further demonstrate that bias and ethics present tough challenges for the evaluation of SAT. In addition to sources of bias common to most research on human subjects, SAT evaluations essentially evaluate awareness. A participant who participates in an awareness evaluation is bound to be more aware than the regular user. The results demonstrate that the study design is of high importance and aligns with previous publications in research methodology [8].

Concerning research ethics, true experiments are likely to involve deception and can include handling sensitive data, which is ethically challenging and highlights the importance of ethical reviews and ongoing ethical discussions.

As for the limitations of this particular study, an SLR is dependant on its included papers and therefore on its search and selection process. The process in this study was designed to include research published from the past five years in five different databases. While a broader selection of papers could have generated a larger empirical base, we argue that the included 28 papers are enough to provide insight into the evaluation methods used in recent research in this domain. This was also demonstrated by saturation experienced by the researchers during the analysis. A second possible risk in qualitative research is researcher bias, given the researchers' heavy involvement in the analysis process. While difficult to minimize, researcher bias was handled in this study by ensuring that it was reported on in a way that enabled replication. The search, selection, and analysis process have been documented to ensure that it can be replicated and scrutinized by others.

4   Conclusions

This paper aimed to explore recently published work in the domain of end-user cybersecurity training to identify how such training methods are evaluated and outline considerations related to the identified evaluation methods. The paper identifies the four distinctive methods of *Perception evaluations, knowledge evaluations, simulations, and experiments* and shows that all are used in different evaluations of SAT with different challenges and benefits. As such, this study concludes that all identified evaluating types should ideally be used during the development of SAT methods. On this note, experiments and simulations are needed to provide empirical evidence as to how efficiently SAT methods can improve cybersecurity behavior while studying user perceptions of SAT methods is important in order to analyze the likelihood that users will opt to use the SAT voluntarily. The study further suggests that SAT evaluations should pay great attention to ethical challenges and bias stemming from mere participation in such studies, not least when deciding what study design to employ. This review also demonstrates that interactive and gamified training has received significant interest from researchers over the past five years.

The contribution of this paper is to the scientific community, where it provides an overview of evaluation methods used for the evaluation of SAT. The results can support future studies by providing insight into what results to expect from different evaluation methods and important considerations related to the use of the different methods. Consequently, the paper can contribute to the quality of future SAT development projects, and in the long run, to the practitioner community, which will receive even better guidelines for how to implement SAT.

This study identified participation bias and ethical challenges as two difficulties that are to be considered when evaluating SAT methods. A suggested direction for future work would be further studies into the design of ethically sound evaluation methodologies where bias is minimized. A second direction for future work is more studies concerning the retention of knowledge gained from SAT methods. While knowledge retention is mentioned in several of the papers included in this study, it is only evaluated in a few of those.

References

1. Al-Daeef, M.M., Basir, N., Saudi, M.M.: Security awareness training: a review. Proc. World Congress Eng. **1**, 5–7 (2017)
2. Alshaikh, M., Maynard, S.B., Ahmad, A., Chang, S.: An exploratory study of current information security training and awareness practices in organizations. In: Proceedings of the 51st Hawaii International Conference on System Sciences (2018)
3. Ayyagari, R., Figueroa, N.: Is seeing believing? training users on information security: evidence from java applets. J. Inf. Syst. Educ. **28**(2), 115–120 (2017)
4. Boss, S., Galletta, D., Lowry, P.B., Moody, G.D., Polak, P.: What do systems users have to fear? using fear appeals to engender threats and fear that motivate protective security behaviors. MIS Q. (MISQ) **39**(4), 837–864 (2015)
5. Braun, V., Clarke, V.: Using thematic analysis in psychology. Qualitative Res. Psychol. **3**(2), 77–101 (2006)
6. Bulgurcu, B., Cavusoglu, H., Benbasat, I.: Information security policy compliance: an empirical study of rationality-based beliefs and information security awareness. MIS Quarterly **34**(3), 523–548 (2010)
7. Burris, J., Deneke, W., Maulding, B.: Activity simulation for experiential learning in cybersecurity workforce development. In: Nah, F.F.-H., Xiao, B.S. (eds.) HCIBGO 2018. LNCS, vol. 10923, pp. 17–25. Springer, Cham (2018). https://doi.org/10.1007/978-3-319-91716-0_2
8. Campbell, D.T.: Factors relevant to the validity of experiments in social settings. Psychol. Bull. **54**(4), 297 (1957)
9. Choi, K.H., Lee, D.H.: A study on strengthening security awareness programs based on an rfid access control system for inside information leakage prevention. Multimed. Tools Appl. **74**(20), 8927–8937
10. Cole, J.R., Pence, T., Cummings, J., Baker, E.: Gamifying security awareness: a new prototype. In: Moallem, A. (ed.) HCII 2019. LNCS, vol. 11594, pp. 115–133. Springer, Cham (2019). https://doi.org/10.1007/978-3-030-22351-9_8
11. Cuchta, T., et al.: Human risk factors in cybersecurity, pp. 87–92
12. Cybint: (2020) https://www.cybintsolutions.com/cyber-security-facts-stats/
13. Desman, M.B.: The ten commandments of information security awareness training. Inf. Secur. J. A Glob. Perspect. **11**(6), 39–44 (2003)
14. Dincelli, E., Chengalur-Smith, I.: Choose your own training adventure: designing a gamified seta artefact for improving information security and privacy through interactive storytelling. European Journal of Information Systems
15. EC-Council: (2019). https://blog.eccouncil.org/the-top-types-of-cybersecurity-attacks-of-2019-till-date/
16. Eck, J.E., Liu, L.: Contrasting simulated and empirical experiments in crime prevention. J. Exp. Criminol. **4**(3), 195–213 (2008)
17. Gjertsen, E.G.B., Gjaere, E.A., Bartnes, M., Flores, W.R.: Gamification of Information Security Awareness and Training. Icissp (2017)

18. Gokul, C.J., Pandit, S., Vaddepalli, S., Tupsamudre, H., Banahatti, V., Lodha, S., Acm: PHISHY - a serious game to train enterprise users on phishing awareness. In: Proceedings of the 2018 Annual Symposium on Computer-Human Interaction in Play Companion Extended Abstracts (2018)

19. Gundu, T.: Acknowledging and Reducing the Knowing and Doing gap in Employee Cybersecurity Compliance, pp. 94–102. International Conference on Cyber Warfare and Security (2019)

20. Huynh, D., Luong, P., Iida, H., Beuran, R.: Design and evaluation of a cybersecurity awareness training game. In: Munekata, N., Kunita, I., Hoshino, J. (eds.) ICEC 2017. LNCS, vol. 10507, pp. 183–188. Springer, Cham (2017). https://doi.org/10.1007/978-3-319-66715-7_19

21. Jayakrishnan, G.C., Sirigireddy, G.R., Vaddepalli, S., Banahatti, V., Lodha, S.P., Pandit, S.S.: Passworld: a serious game to promote password awareness and diversity in an enterprise. In: (SOUPS 2020), pp. 1–18 (2020)

22. Jesson, J., Matheson, L., Lacey, F.M.: Doing your literature review: Traditional and systematic techniques. Sage (2011)

23. Joinson, A., van Steen, T.: Human aspects of cyber security: behaviour or culture change? Cyber Secur. Peer-Reviewed J. 1(4), 351–360 (2018)

24. Kunz, A., Volkamer, M., Stockhardt, S., Palberg, S., Lottermann, T., Piegert, E.: Nophish: evaluation of a web application that teaches people being aware of phishing attacks, vol. P-259, pp. 509–518 (2016)

25. Lastdrager, E., Gallardo, I.C., Hartel, P., Junger, M.: How effective is anti-phishing training for children? pp. 229–239 (2017)

26. Lim, I.K., Park, Y.G., Lee, J.K.: Design of security training system for individual users. Wirel. Personal Commun. 90(3), 1105–1120 (2016)

27. Meline, T.: Selecting studies for systematic review: inclusion and exclusion criteria. Contemporary Issues in Communication Science and Disorders 33(21–27) (2006)

28. Micallef, N., Arachchilage, N.A.G.: Involving users in the design of a serious game for security questions education. arXiv preprint arXiv:1710.03888 (2017)

29. Moreno-Fernández, M.M., Blanco, F., Garaizar, P., Matute, H.: Fishing for phishers. improving internet users' sensitivity to visual deception cues to prevent electronic fraud. Comput. Hum. Behav. 69, 421–436 (2017)

30. Paré, G., Kitsiou, S.: Methods for literature reviews. In: Handbook of eHealth Evaluation: An Evidence-based Approach [Internet]. University of Victoria (2017)

31. Parsons, K., Butavicius, M.A., Lillie, M., Calic, D., McCormac, A., Pattinson, M.R.: Which individual, cultural, organisational and interventional factors explain phishing resilience? In: HAISA, pp. 1–11 (2018)

32. Puhakainen, P., Siponen, M.: Improving employees' compliance through information systems security training: an action research study. MIS quarterly, pp. 757–778 (2010)

33. Rastenis, J., Ramanauskaitė, S., Janulevičius, J., Čenys, A.: Impact of information security training on recognition of phishing attacks: A case study of vilnius gediminas technical university. vol. 1243. CCIS, pp. 311–324

34. Reinheimer, B., et al.: An investigation of phishing awareness and education over time: when and how to best remind users. In: (SOUPS 2020), pp. 259–284 (2020)

35. Renaud, K., Zimmermann, V.: Ethical guidelines for nudging in information security & privacy. Int. J. Hum. Comput. Stud. 120, 22–35 (2018)

36. Safa, N.S., Von Solms, R.: An information security knowledge sharing model in organizations. Comput. Hum. Behav. 57, 442–451 (2016)

37. Silic, M., Lowry, P.B.: Using design-science based gamification to improve organizational security training and compliance. J. Manage. Inf. Syst. **37**(1), 129–161 (2020)
38. Siponen, M.T.: A conceptual foundation for organizational information security awareness. Information Management & Computer Security (2000)
39. Soare, B.: (2020). https://heimdalsecurity.com/blog/vectors-of-attack/
40. Stockhardt, Simon, et al.: Teaching phishing-security: which way is best? In: Hoepman, Jaap-Henk., Katzenbeisser, Stefan (eds.) SEC 2016. IAICT, vol. 471, pp. 135–149. Springer, Cham (2016). https://doi.org/10.1007/978-3-319-33630-5_10
41. Takata, T., Ogura, K., IEEE: Confront Phishing Attacks - from a Perspective of Security Education, pp. 10–13. International Conference on Awareness Science and Technology (2019)
42. Taneski, V., Heričko, M., Brumen, B.: Impact of security education on password change, pp. 1350–1355 (2015)
43. Tichy, W.F.: Should computer scientists experiment more? Computer **31**(5), 32–40 (1998)
44. Tschakert, K.F., Ngamsuriyaroj, S.: Effectiveness of and user preferences for security awareness training methodologies. Heliyon **5**(6), e02010 (2019)
45. Van Rensburg, W.J., Thomson, K.L., Futcher, L.: An educational intervention towards safe smartphone usage. In: HAISA 2018 (2018)
46. Vroom, C., Von Solms, R.: Towards information security behavioural compliance. Comput. Secur. **23**(3), 191–198 (2004)
47. Wen, Z.A., Lin, Z.Q., Chen, R., Andersen, E.: What. Hack: engaging anti-phishing training through a role-playing phishing simulation game. In: Chi 2019 (2019)
48. Wohlin, C., Runeson, P., Höst, M., Ohlsson, M.C., Regnell, B., Wesslén, A.: Experimentation in software engineering. Springer Science & Business Media (2012)
49. Xiong, A.P., Proctor, R.W., Yang, W.N., Li, N.H.: Embedding training within warnings improves skills of identifying phishing webpages. Human Factors **61**(4), 577–595 (2019)
50. Yang, W., Xiong, A., Chen, J., Proctor, R.W., Li, N.: Use of phishing training to improve security warning compliance: Evidence from a field experiment. vol. Part F127186, pp. 52–61 (2017)
51. Zhou, L.M., Parmanto, B., Alfikri, Z., Bao, J.: A mobile app for assisting users to make informed selections in security settings for protecting personal health data: Development and feasibility study. Jmir Mhealth and Uhealth **6**(12), e11210 (2018)

People and Technology

When Googling It Doesn't Work: The Challenge of Finding Security Advice for Smart Home Devices

Sarah Turner(✉)⬥, Jason Nurse⬥, and Shujun Li

Institute of Cyber Security for Society (iCSS), University of Kent, Canterbury, UK
{slt41,j.r.c.nurse,s.j.li}@kent.ac.uk

Abstract. As users increasingly introduce Internet-connected devices into their homes, having access to accurate and relevant cyber security information is a fundamental means of ensuring safe use. Given the paucity of information provided with many devices at the time of purchase, this paper engages in a critical study of the type of advice that home Internet of Things (IoT) or smart device users might be presented with on the Internet to inform their cyber security practices. We base our research on an analysis of 427 web pages from 234 organisations that present information on security threats and relevant cyber security advice. The results show that users searching online for information are subject to an enormous range of advice and news from various sources with differing levels of credibility and relevance. With no clear explanation of how a user may assess the threats as they are pertinent to them, it becomes difficult to understand which pieces of advice would be the most effective in their situation. Recommendations are made to improve the clarity, consistency and availability of guidance from recognised sources to improve user access and understanding.

Keywords: Internet of Things · Cyber security · Smart home · Cyber security advice · Information · Online search · Connected home

1 Introduction

Home Internet of Things (IoT) devices[1] create different risks to their users than more traditional Internet-connected devices, such as personal computers. At an individual level, these include threats to physical safety, home security, personal control and privacy [20], and at a societal level, facilitating botnets and other Internet-based crime [1]. As these devices may come with little in-built security, these risks can quite quickly spread further than the individual device; as such the user must also understand how to manage the appropriate security of their entire home network. Home IoT devices are typically marketed on their minimal interfaces [9], leaving the user to search elsewhere for guidance on issues

---

[1] The phrase "home IoT devices" here aligns with the list of devices found in [3].

© IFIP International Federation for Information Processing 2021
Published by Springer Nature Switzerland AG 2021
S. Furnell and N. Clarke (Eds.): HAISA 2021, IFIP AICT 613, pp. 115–126, 2021.
https://doi.org/10.1007/978-3-030-81111-2_10

such as cyber security. The availability of good quality, consistent and actionable information is crucial for keeping users safe and confident in their device use. Appropriately targeted levels of guidance for users is particularly necessary as cyber security is broadly considered a difficult topic for individuals to manage, despite there being a general acceptance of individual accountability for personal device use [17]. This is increasingly important for users, manufacturers, Internet Service Providers (ISPs) and policy-making bodies to understand and attempt to mitigate as sales in home IoT devices continue to grow apace, with users seemingly undeterred by frequent media stories of data breaches and other security risks.

This paper provides a review of cyber security information available on the Internet in relation to home IoT devices. It is driven by three primary research questions: what information is made available about cyber security threats posed to individuals using home IoT devices, what information is given around how to mitigate those threats, and what type of organisations or entities provide that information. Using search methods that a typical user might undertake, we find that advice that users are presented with is typically generalised and not sufficiently specific to act upon immediately, that the advice returned is often contradictory between sources, and that organisations that users would reasonably expect to have most responsibility for providing accurate content (manufacturers, governmental bodies, and ISPs) are not as prominently featured as they should be.

Following a brief literature review in Sect. 2, and methodology in Sect. 3, we report our findings in Sect. 4. Section 5 considers the ways in which advice may need to be better tailored and managed to bolster users' understanding and willingness to act. Section 6 considers limitations of the research, and how this could be addressed with future work. Section 7 concludes the paper.

2 Literature Review

Previous research has looked at how users understand, evaluate and use cyber security methods. Cost, effort to set up and perceived inefficacy have been shown to stop individuals from adopting security tools such as anti-malware or password managers [4]. Tabassum et al. [19] found that some home IoT device owners applied security knowledge learned from other contexts (such as from using computers and the Internet) when securing their home devices, despite the differences in threats posed and potential mitigating actions required. It is widely recognised that this action, in part, arises from a wide-spread lack of accurate mental models about these devices [24], unless the user is already very technically minded [12].

Even if individuals do act to implement cyber security measures at home, they could be overwhelmed with the number of actions that are deemed to be essential: Redmiles et al. [15] found 374 pieces of actionable advice in reviewing publicly available documentation, and argued that what is needed is effective prioritisation of that advice. Prior to purchase, users rarely look for security and privacy information, but note that it is impossible to find if they do [7]. Gcaza argued that security awareness is a necessary requirement for communities to consider themselves "smart" [8]: enhanced levels of clarity have been called for in both governmental and manufacturer's advice, to promote tangible steps to security [18], a better understanding of how the technology works [23], and how the user is affected in the case of a breach [25]. This clarity should extend to the practices of the manufacturer, in particular in relation to privacy and security concerns [11]. There is a clear benefit to this: users will pay a premium for devices that have prominent details about security features [2].

3   Methodology

In order to understand what a home IoT device user might encounter when searching for information about how to secure devices that they may have, the decision was taken to search the Internet for cyber security guidance. This was done both in relation to general devices, using general search terms and reviewing the results that mentioned home IoT devices specifically, as well as for the most popular devices in the UK at this time: smart TVs (and streaming devices), and smart home assistants [21]. This decision was made because of the proportion of individuals voluntarily using these devices; findings for these specific types of devices may offer more value by virtue of their ubiquity than other device types. Recent research has used similar practices in relation to posted user reviews [13] to understand what type of information users may encounter online on specific topics.

Table 1. Generalised search queries

Search terms	
Cyber security information	Cyber security charities
Cyber security awareness	Internet of Things cyber security help
Cyber security knowledge	Cyber security help
Cyber security education	Cyber security support
Cyber security learning	Smart devices cyber security help
Cyber security training	How to stop being hacked
Cyber security organisations	How to secure my devices

The general device resources were sought through search terms listed in Table 1, and reflect a final list after researcher experimentation with various similar terms. Using these general search terms, pages in the results that had references to home IoT devices were captured for analysis. Search terms relating to specific devices took the form "How to secure my smart TV/streaming device/smart speaker" along with "[manufacturer name] [device name] security" (e.g., "Amazon Echo security"). Specific brands were chosen based upon lists of "Top devices for 2020" focused on UK consumers.[2] Having logged out of all browser accounts, cleared user history and using a VPN connection to a different IP address in the UK, the search terms were entered into three search engines: Google, Bing and Duck Duck Go,[3] and non-paid search results from the first two pages of each search query were captured, on the understanding that less than one in ten users are likely to go to the second page of search results [14]. The pages were retrieved between August and December 2020. For both results from the generalised search and specific devices searches, each page was then reviewed, and those that had content referring to home IoT devices were then taken forward for analysis. Following methodology from [1] and [22], a number of predefined criteria were captured from each page, including who produced the information and when, the type of devices considered, and the threats and advice given.

4   Results

4.1   Sources of Information

The prominence of news and opinion outlets is clear in the results. 125 sources (53.41%) of the 234 organisations with web pages considered in the review were either recognised news organisations (such as The Guardian, Wired, CNet) or websites offering news and opinion pieces of varying levels of specialty and expertise, ranging from personal blogs to user-facing technology sites (such as PC Mag, ZD Net). The search also returned a volunteer-run cyber security helpline,[4] offering help across a wide range of cyber security issues. We also found that the favourable rankings of more traditional news sites acted to suppress sources of advice and information about device security in favour of prior security and data breaches: notably, a 2014 breach relating to Philips' smart TV range still dominated the first two pages of results, even in Google's Featured Snippets,[5] despite the age of the story. Although the majority of individual web pages returned were dated 2019 and 2020 (228 web pages, 53.40%, of 427 total web pages), 91 were undated, and 2 websites (from a retailer, and anti-malware provider) had content dating from 2011 (from the date given in the body of the article).

Only nine information sources of the 234 organisations were affiliated with global governmental departments; there were three consumer protection bodies (such as Which? and Consumer Reports) and five additional not-for-profit or charitable bodies. Conversely, bodies that may have been trying to sell a

---

[2] https://www.techradar.com/uk/news/best-smart-speakers,   https://www.techra dar.com/uk/news/best-tv,   https://www.techadvisor.co.uk/test-centre/digital-home/best-media-streaming-box-3580569/.

[3] These account for nearly 97% of all UK search engine traffic as of July 2020 [10].

[4] https://www.thecyberhelpline.com.

[5] For more on Google's Featured Snippets, see https://support.google.com/websearch/answer/9351707.

service related to security were much more common: there were nine anti-malware providers (such as Malwarebytes and Kaspersky), and firms offering cyber security services (such as BullGuard, Digital Guardian and Cytelligence) accounted for 21 pages. There were 13 forum sites, both third-party (Reddit, Stack Exchange) and manufacturer community pages. There were no sites from ISPs returned in the results.

Table 2. Advice and Threat Types

(a) Top five: threat types

Type of threat	Count
Unauthorised access	144
Malware	22
Data theft	13
Botnet	9
Ransomware	8

(b) Top five: advice types

Type of advice	Count
Strong password management	149
Limit data access	145
Better home network security	143
Turn off features/devices	117
Update software	113

4.2 Reported Threats

Discussions about cyber security typically arise from the need to secure something from a specific and meaningful threat. In the review, 57 individual types of threats were raised; for the top five, see Table 2a. 144 websites referred to some form of unauthorised access to devices, most typically "hacking", without further explanation (Table 3, #1). 39 web pages focused on either how to manage after you have been hacked or avoiding being hacked, typically presenting reactive advice rather than explaining why it may be necessary to take proactive measures ahead of an event (Table 3, #2). Malware and ransomware were mentioned a total of 30 times, with theft of personal data being mentioned 13 times. Botnets were referenced nine times. It is noticeable how many types of threat were referenced only once or twice throughout the review. 26 types of threat came up only once (examples ranging from domestic abuse, to ghostware and hacktivism). Lack of personal knowledge was framed as a threat (rather than a potential vulnerability) in five instances (Table 3, #3). In some cases, the publication of specific academic or industry reports were reflected in the reporting of several news sources (Table 3, #4). In these cases, the threats reported upon are typically accompanied by the researchers' views on how to mitigate the risk, albeit at a high level, often without accompanying links to manufacturer guidance for specific devices.

4.3 Types of Advice Needed and Provided

In total, there were 1,342 pieces of advice counted in the reviewed web pages, which, when coded for advice type provided a total of 54 unique topics. The top five advice types are listed in Table 2b.

Table 3. Examples of advice given (as referenced throughout text)

	Source	Advice given	URL
1	IoT for All (2020) (IoT blog)	Generic threat explanation: "...they leave us vulnerable to cyber crime... [IoT devices] are top targets for hackers."	https://www.iotforall.com/iot-cyber-security-2
2	Lifewire (2019) (consumer technology blog)	Reactive security guidance - things to do after you have been "hacked": "no matter how you were hacked, you're feeling vulnerable."	https://www.lifewire.com/securing-your-home-network-and-pc-after-a-hack-2487231
3	IoT Wiki (2019) (IoT enthusiast blog)	Lack of knowledge a threat: "many individual users...still lack information about the risk"	https://internetofthingswiki.com/biggest-security-issues-iot-devices-face/1344/
4	Tech Crunch (2019)	Report of FBI advice on smart TV security	https://techcrunch.com/2019/12/01/fbi-smart-tv-security/
5	Now TV (undated) (streaming devices)	Password guidance: "DON'T use a word that's found in the dictionary"	https://help.nowtv.com/article/tips-to-help-you-keep-your-account-secure
6	Comparitech (2020) (consumer technology blog)	Password guidance: "Make changing the router password part of your monthly routine"	https://www.comparitech.com/blog/information-security/secure-home-wireless-network/
7	CSO Online (2016) (technology risk news site)	Don't use devices as intended: "Don't connect your devices unless you need to... turn off UPnP...be wary of cloud services"	https://www.csoonline.com/article/3085607/8-tips-to-secure-those-iot-devices.html
8	Lifehacker (2018) (consumer blog)	Not-specific advice: "If you're lucky, your router can broadcast a 'guest network' ..."	https://lifehacker.com/how-to-keep-your-friends-from-trolling-your-chromecast-1828605478
9	Cytelligence (undated) (cybersecurity service)	Non-specific advice: 10 ten list with no further details (e.g. "Stick with protected unnecessary features...Secure your network fully")	https://cytelligence.com/cyber-security-and-smart-devices/
10	Digital Trends (2021) (consumer technology blog)	How to secure your Alexa device (with 12 suggestions)	https://www.digitaltrends.com/home/how-to-secure-your-alexa-device/
11	Wired (2020) (technology magazine)	Guest networks: "grant your you guests access to a Wi-Fi connection without letting them get at the rest of your network your Sonos speakers, the shared folders on your laptop..."	https://www.wired.com/story/secure-your-wi-fi-router/
12	Kaspersky (undated) (anti-malware software)	Guest networks: "[set] up guest networks for your IoT home devices"	https://www.kaspersky.com/resource-center/threats/how-safe-is-your-smart-home
13	How-To Geek (2020) (consumer technology blog)	Guest networks: "you would connect all your IoT devices... and actual guests to the guest network"	https://www.howtogeek.com/659084/how-secure-is-your-home-wi-fi/
14	Google (undated) (Android devices)	How to log your child into their Android device	https://support.google.com/families/answer/7158477?hl=en
15	Help Cloud (undated) (consumer security service)	Buy a more secure router: "[invest] in a sound WiFi router"	https://www.helpcloud.com/blog/cybersecurity-experts-and-iot-smart-devices-and-smart-homes/
16	Ready.gov (undated) (US governmental resource)	Implication of need to buy more security: "[use] a password manager...use antivirus solutions...use a VPN..."	https://www.ready.gov/cybersecurity
17	PCWorld (2019) (technology news site)	Implication of need to buy more security: "Our favourite password manager is xxxx...you'll need to pay an annual fee, but it's worth it."	https://www.pcworld.com/article/3332211/secure-android-phone.html
18	Real Simple (2020) (consumer blog)	Buy reputable devices: "If you want to have IoT devices around...a wiser route is going to be by shopping in Apple or Google's walled gardens..."	https://www.realsimple.com/work-life/technology/safety-family/smart-home-cyber-security
19	Norton (undated) (anti-malware software)	Choose based on privacy and data policies: "What are the privacy policies? Will the provider store your data or sell it to a third party? How are updates enabled?"	https://us.norton.com/internetsecurity-iot-smart-home-cyber-security
20	The Guardian (2020) (news site)	Coverage of Sonos' decision to stop software updates for old devices	https://www.theguardian.com/technology/2020/jan/23/sonos-to-deny-software-updates-to-owners-of-older-equipment
21	eBuyer (2018) (consumer technology blog)	Software updates:"You should always update your smart devices...as soon as it becomes available"	https://www.ebuyer.com/blog/2018/10/smart-devices-and-security/
22	National Cyber Security Centre (2019) (UK government body)	Wiping device of data: "you should first perform a factory reset."	https://www.ncsc.gov.uk/guidance/smart-devices-in-the-home

There were 149 separate instances of recommended strong password management (11.10% of the total pieces advice given), many of which gave advice contrary to the current guidance from the UK's National Cyber Security Centre (NCSC) to use three random words to create a strong password. For example, two manufacturers explicitly suggested that words found in the dictionary should not be used (Table 3, #5), and suggestions to change passwords frequently were also common (Table 3, #6).

Limiting the access services have to personal data was the second most frequent type of advice given in the reviewed web pages (145 instances; 10.80%), although precise guidance as to what this means for specific devices was not generally explained. Disabling some features (such as Universal Plug and Play) or turning off the device (or router, or WiFi) altogether was the fourth most common (117; 8.71%). The trade-offs of doing these actions were again, largely unexplored (Table 3, #7). Specificity of advice was a common problem—the heterogeneity of devices left some pages assuming that devices had particular functionality as the premise of their advice (Table 3, #8), or providing a list of things to do with no guidance at all (Table 3, #9). Other pages gave so much advice as to run the risk of seeming overwhelming (Table 3, #10).

There were 143 instances of advice around improving the strength of home networks. Advice around improving the strength of the user's home network is particularly difficult to follow, as the exact, typically relatively technical, steps vary upon the router in the house. In the general searches returned, there was no guidance about smart home security provided by ISPs. Without further searching in relation to the router owned by the individual, at first glance it is impossible for the reader to know which pieces of advice (such as "use a VPN" or "set up a guest network") would be feasible for their current router. Setting up a guest network, in particular, was recommended, but the specifics of doing so were varied: some pages suggested putting all the user's devices on one network and anyone external on the other (Table 3, #11); others suggested keeping home IoT devices on one network, and the users' other devices and guests on the second (Table 3, #12); and there was also suggestion to keep your personal non-IoT devices on one, and your home IoT devices and guests on the other (Table 3, #13).

When manufacturer's pages were returned in the reviewed web pages they were typically in a wiki-format, for a very specific topic—focusing how to change a specific setting rather than why you might do this—with minimal visual guidance: a checklist of steps to perform a specific activity on a specific device (Table 3, #14). In contrast, sites not affiliated with manufacturers offer more generic advice. Not only did they provide little to specific device guidance or explanation as to what that would protect against, but they frequently suggested additional products that come at additional costs. Some are explicit: buying a more secure router (Table 3, #15), or, less clearly, products and services that can come with a cost, such as anti-malware, VPNs or password managers (Table 3, #16, #17). Other advice given includes to be choosy with home IoT device providers (even at a risk of becoming locked into a single provider) (Table 3,

#18), and performing pre-purchase checks such as reading privacy and data sharing/selling policies (Table 3, #19).

There was a striking lack of information about end of life device management, with the exception of the negative press relating to Sonos' decision to stop supporting older models in early 2020 (Table 3, #20), and general advice to "update software" (but not explicitly to be aware of the end of the supported life of your device) (Table 3, #21). Only the NCSC discussed wiping a device at the point of reselling or throwing away (Table 3, #22).

5   Discussion

A significant proportion of the guidance discovered in the reviewed web pages was not actionable for home IoT devices without further understanding or learning by the reader. The heterogeneity of home IoT devices, and the situations in which they are used, means that there may be best practices that are specific to the device and its use. Different designs mean that users cannot guarantee that they will be able to follow steps to disable settings, for example, to adhere to best security practices, assuming the specific device they have has the functionality to allow the user to access and alter security settings. Different threats mean that some users may be best off following different advice for the same device, but without an ability to accurately assess the threats and risks that the device poses to them, users are likely to fall back to behaviours that have worked for them before, which may not be appropriate in this case [19].

Furthermore, the most appropriate point to modify security settings may be at the home network, and not device, level. Calls to alter router settings, for example, are assuming that users have the technical confidence, sufficient access to the controls within the home setting, and that their routers have the functionality to do so, none of which may be the case [24]. Additional suggestions to use more software—ideally, purchase software—is problematic: it introduces another barrier to effective cyber security for those who cannot afford it, and it is unclear how to apply such software across all devices in the home, if it is even possible to do so. The attrition rates for use of such software is likely to be high, particularly if its value in protecting devices is not visible or obvious [4].

Governmental and consumer awareness resources did appear, often low down in results. Despite their relative trustworthiness and validity as relevant and impartial cyber security information, such resources are often indistinguishable from other sources in search results. These other sources may have financial interests in the framing of their advice (such as anti-malware providers), or the guidance may be from irrelevant or out of date sources. Users would benefit from higher placement in search results of official guidance from governmental agencies and manufacturers to try and provide up to date, specific information; inspiration could be taken from the work done to place prominent information from recognised expert bodies at the top of search results relating to COVID-19.

Advice to choose devices based upon more agreeable privacy policies or calls to do research before purchase and buy "more secure devices" highlight a lack of congruence between the advice and real life. Privacy policies are notoriously hard to read and comprehend [16], and offer no ability for the user to negotiate the terms of their use. Calling upon users to research devices prior to purchase suggests that sufficient information is available to make a useful comparison of security features—not only is it hard to find this information, it may not be meaningful or useful when found [7].

Providing standardised labels on packaging to provide information on fundamental security features may be helpful to help users determine what is important to them at the time of purchase [6], however manufacturers need to help users to assess and review their security settings throughout the life of their devices. This could take the form of periodic notifications on the device or associated app, reminding users to check key risk areas for a given device. This, of course, may be device specific, but manufacturers could use the opportunity to target common areas of concern based upon market intelligence or user research to ensure that users are given an opportunity to secure the most pressing risks. Manufacturers should avoid confusion by only providing guidance that is in line with the regional governmental cyber security agency, or in the case of international manufacturers, picking advice from respected agencies or bodies, and referencing and linking back to those bodies so that users can see the underlying guidance themselves. As the results of the website review show, conflicting advice is abundant as a result of the number of expert opinions in the field, and so manufacturers can help users understand why they are promoting the security practices that they are. This also provides users an opportunity to learn about the evolving nature of cyber security information, and promotes the need for periodic reviews of the user's security setup. Making users aware that guidance is dynamically evolving, and explaining how they will receive updated advice, is crucial, and facilitates user learning.

Before being able to manage risks effectively, however, users need to have more meaningful guidance about the types of threats that their devices may pose, so that they can appropriately evaluate what risk management means to them. This is a complex area, given the potential for misuse, abuse, and power imbalances [5]. However, manufacturers of devices could produce and point users to common device use cases, for example, with different permutations of household device use (including how children and visitors may use the device). These use cases could explain the potential threats to the device in the situation, the implications of those threats, and how to mitigate those risks based upon the security features of the device. This would also be beneficial for ISPs to offer their customers in relation to home router setup, to ensure insecure devices do not pose unexpected threats, both inside and outside of the home.

6   Limitations and Future Work

This work was an exploratory piece of research, to determine what the Internet offered users when a number of generalised queries, and searches based upon the most popular devices reported in a recent survey were undertaken. The queries were researcher-generated, meaning that they may not exactly reflect the types of queries typical home users would perform. Decisions to limit the pages used in the search may also not reflect a user's behaviour when looking for a specific answer. While we did our best to mirror a reasonable keyword selection process and user-oriented approach to pages viewed, future work should involve users to generate these search terms, and use a more precise understanding of when users might stop looking for answers on a page. It may also be useful to do a wider review, as limiting the research to a handful of specific devices may ignore advice that is necessary for the security of other types of devices. The search results also point to the complex role that routers have in the smart home. Repeating the work with routers included as a specifically searched-for device may be beneficial.

7 Conclusions

Through a review of web pages, this research has shown that finding reputable, actionable and coherent guidance on how to approach securing home IoT device against cyber security threats is challenging. Users are confronted by an overwhelming number of resources, often with little direct credibility or specific actionable advice. We consider that improvements could be made by device manufacturers in particular in creating clearer, more actionable content, as well as a need for search engine results to reflect more prominently those resources from relevant organisations (notably manufacturers and governmental bodies) to ensure users find the most specific advice for their situation.

References

1. Blythe, J.M., Johnson, S.D., Manning, M.: What is security worth to consumers? investigating willingness to pay for secure Internet of Things devices. Crime Sci. **9**(1), 1–9 (2020). https://doi.org/10.1186/s40163-019-0110-3
2. Blythe, J.M., Sombatruang, N., Johnson, S.D.: What security features and crime prevention advice is communicated in consumer IoT device manuals and support pages? J. Cybersecur. **5**(1), tyz005:1-tyz005:10 (2019). https://doi.org/10.1093/cybsec/tyz005
3. Department for Digital: Culture, Media and Sport: Code of practice for consumer IoT security. Tech. rep, Department for Digital, Culture, Media and Sport (2018)
4. Dupuis, M., Geiger, T., Slayton, M., Dewing, F.: The use and non-use of cybersecurity tools among consumers: Do they want help? In: Proceedings of the 20th Annual SIG Conference on Information Technology Education, pp. 81–86. ACM (2019). https://doi.org/10.1145/3349266.3351419
5. Ehrenberg, N., Keinonen, T.: The technology is enemy for me at the moment: How smart home technologies assert control beyond intent. In: Proceedings of the 2021 CHI Conference on Human Factors in Computing Systems. No. 401. ACM, New York (2021). https://doi.org/10.1145/3411764.3445058
6. Emami-Naeini, P., Agarwal, Y., Faith Cranor, L., Hibshi, H.: Ask the Experts: What Should Be on an IoT Privacy and Security Label? In: 2020 IEEE Symposium on Security and Privacy (SP), pp. 447–464 (2020). https://doi.org/10.1109/SP40000.2020.00043

7. Emami-Naeini, P., Dixon, H., Agarwal, Y., Cranor, L.F.: Exploring how privacy and security factor into IoT device purchase behavior. In: Proceedings of the 2019 CHI Conference on Human Factors in Computing Systems, pp. 534:1–534:12. ACM (2019). https://doi.org/10.1145/3290605.3300764
8. Gcaza, N.: Cybersecurity awareness and education: a necessary parameter for smart communities. In: Proceedings of the Twelfth International Symposium on Human Aspects of Information Security & Assurance (HAISA 2018), pp. 80–90. University of Plymouth (2018)
9. Geeng, C., Roesner, F.: Who's in control? interactions in multi-user smart homes. In: Proceedings of the 2019 CHI Conference on Human Factors in Computing Systems. p. 268:1–268:13. ACM (2019). https://doi.org/10.1145/3290605.3300498
10. Johnson, J.: Market share held by the leading search engines in the United Kingdom (UK) as of June 2020. Market research report, Statista (2020). https://www.statista.com/statistics/280269/market-share-held-by-search-engines-in-the-united-kingdom/
11. Kulyk, O., Milanovic, K., Pitt, J.: Does my smart device provider care about my privacy? investigating trust factors and user attitudes in IoT systems. In: Proceedings of the 11th Nordic Conference on Human-Computer Interaction: Shaping Experiences, Shaping Society. ACM (2020)
12. Luger, E., Sellen, A.: "Like having a really bad PA": The gulf between user expectation and experience of conversational agents. In: Proceedings of the 2016 CHI Conference on Human Factors in Computing Systems, pp. 5286–5297. ACM (2016). https://doi.org/10.1145/2858036.2858288
13. Oygür, I., Epstein, D.A., Chen, Y.: Raising the responsible child: Collaborative work in the use of activity trackers for children. Proc. ACM Hum.-Comput. Interact. 4(CSCW2) (Oct 2020). DOI: 10.1145/3415228
14. Ray, L.: We surveyed 1,400 searchers about Google - here's what we learned. Blog article (2019). https://moz.com/blog/new-google-survey-results
15. Redmiles, E., et al.: A comprehensive quality evaluation of security and privacy advice on the Web. In: Proceedings of 29th USENIX Security Symposium, pp. 89–108. USENIX Association (2020). https://www.usenix.org/conference/usenixsecurity20/presentation/redmiles
16. Renaud, K., Shepherd, L.A.: How to make privacy policies both GDPR-compliant and usable. In: Proceedings of 2018 International Conference On Cyber Situational Awareness, Data Analytics And Assessment, pp. 1–8 (2018)
17. Renaud, K., Flowerday, S., Warkentin, M., Cockshott, P., Orgeron, C.: Is the responsibilization of the cyber security risk reasonable and judicious? Comput. Secur. **78**, 198–211 (2018). https://doi.org/10.1016/j.cose.2018.06.006
18. van Steen, T., Norris, E., Atha, K., Joinson, A.: What (if any) behaviour change techniques do government-led cybersecurity awareness campaigns use? J. Cybersecur. **6**(1) (2020)
19. Tabassum, M., Kosinski, T., Lipford, H.R.: "I don't own the data": End user perceptions of smart home device data practices and risks. In: Fifteenth Symposium on Usable Privacy and Security (SOUPS 2019), pp. 435–450. USENIX Association, Santa Clara, CA, August 2019. https://www.usenix.org/conference/soups2019/presentation/tabassum
20. Tanczer, L.M., Steenmans, I., Elsden, M., Blackstock, J., Carr, M.: Emerging risks in the IoT ecosystem: Who's afraid of the big bad smart fridge? In: Living in the Internet of Things: Cybersecurity of the IoT - 2018, pp. 1–9. IET (2018)

21. techUK and GfK: The state of the connected home 2020. Industry report, techUK (2020). https://www.techuk.org/resource/the-state-of-the-connected-home-2020-report-edition-4.html
22. Turner, S., Quintero, J.G., Turner, S., Lis, J., Tanczer, L.M.: The exercisability of the right to data portability in the emerging Internet of Things (IoT) environment. New Media & Society 0(0) (0). https://doi.org/10.1177/1461444820934033
23. Voit, A., Niess, J., Eckerth, C., Ernst, M., Weingärtner, H., Woundefinedniak, P.W.: 'It's not a romantic relationship': stories of adoption and abandonment of smart speakers at home. In: Proceedings of the 19th International Conference on Mobile and Ubiquitous Multimedia, pp. 71–82. ACM (2020). https://doi.org/10.1145/3428361.3428469
24. Zeng, E., Mare, S., Roesner, F.: End user security and privacy concerns with smart homes. In: Thirteenth Symposium on Usable Privacy and Security (SOUPS 2017), pp. 65–80. USENIX Association, Santa Clara, CA, July 2017. https://www.usenix.org/conference/soups2017/technical-sessions/presentation/zeng
25. Zou, Y., Danino, S., Sun, K., Schaub, F.: You 'might' be affected: An empirical analysis of readability and usability issues in data breach notifications. In: Proceedings of the 2019 CHI Conference on Human Factors in Computing Systems, pp. 194:1–194:14. ACM (2019). https://doi.org/10.1145/3290605.3300424

Making Access Control Easy in IoT

Vafa Andalibi[1]($\boxtimes$), Jayati Dev[1], DongInn Kim[1], Eliot Lear[2],
and L. Jean Camp[1]

[1] Indiana University, Bloomington, IN, USA
{vafandal,jdev,dikim,ljcamp}@indiana.edu
[2] Cisco Systems, Zurich, Switzerland
lear@cisco.com

Abstract. Secure installation of Internet of Things (IoT) devices requires configuring access control correctly for each device. In order to enable correct configuration Manufacturer Usage Description (MUD) has been developed by Internet Engineering Task Force (IETF) to automate the protection of IoT devices by micro-segmentation using dynamic access control lists. The protocol defines a conceptually straightforward method to implement access control upon installation by providing a list of every authorized access for each device. This access control list may contain a few rules or hundreds of rules for each device. As a result, validating these rules is a challenge. In order to make the MUD standard more usable for developers, system integrators, and network operators, we report on an interactive system called MUD-Visualizer that visualizes the files containing these access control rules. We show that, unlike manual analysis, the level of the knowledge and experience does not affect the accuracy of the analysis when MUD-Visualizer is used, indicating that the tool is effective for all participants in our study across knowledge and experience levels.

Keywords: Usable security · Internet of Things · Network security · Usable access control · IoT · MUD · Manufacturer Usage Description

1 Introduction

The forecast for the number of connected IoT devices in 2025 is now raised to 30.9 billion [13], yet their (in)security is still a major concern [16]. There is a need for secure onboarding meaning that the device is secured as soon as it is connected to the network. One major component of secure onboarding both for cyber-physical systems and IoT is firewall configuration. Without access control, IoT devices are susceptible to participate in DDoS attacks [10], are vulnerable to ransomware [24], and enable information exfiltration from within networks [6]. It is the nature of botnets that the subverted devices need to be controlled by the attackers' command and control (C2) infrastructure [3]. Secure onboarding that implements allow-list access control limits exposure of devices to attacks

© IFIP International Federation for Information Processing 2021
Published by Springer Nature Switzerland AG 2021
S. Furnell and N. Clarke (Eds.): HAISA 2021, IFIP AICT 613, pp. 127–137, 2021.
https://doi.org/10.1007/978-3-030-81111-2_11

and prevents any subverted device from connecting to the attackers' C2 points. Unlike traditional botnets, the control servers in IoT are highly dynamic so the typical response of identifying then block-listing is infeasible [21].

To this end, the Internet Engineering Task Force (IETF) has developed the Manufacturer Usage Description (MUD); a standard that provides an isolation-based defense for IoT devices using dynamic access control [12]. The urgency and scale of the need for such a solution are shown by the fact that MUD is also a part of the National Institute of Standard and Technology (NIST) security for IoT initiatives [5]. In addition, the Department of Commerce has a working group to integrate the Software Bill of Materials (SBoM) initiative with MUD[1] and the IETF has a proposed standard integrating SBoM with MUD[2]. MUD can also be used for mitigating DDoS attacks in the Fog [1].

MUD relies on manufacturers for an Access Control List (ACL) in the form of a MUD-File. A MUD-File defines the allowed and expected behaviors of the associated device. The clear implication is that developers must be able to write clear and correct MUD-Files and network operators must be able to read and validate the MUD-Files to ensure that unnecessary communications, either locally or over the Internet, are not allowed. These are difficult problems, and like many security tasks, are not well aligned with human cognitive abilities [15].

In this work, we report on the usability analysis of the MUD-Visualizer [2]; a tool that is intended to support developers and network operators in evaluating overlaps, duplication, and possible conflicts in MUD-Files. We report on the design and results of our human subjects research that we conducted to investigate the following research questions:

RQ1: How does **security knowledge** affect the accuracy of the analysis of the MUD-Files?
RQ2: How does **security experience** affect the accuracy of the analysis of the MUD-Files?
RQ3: To what extent does **level of knowledge and experience** affect the accuracy of the analysis of the MUD-Files?

2   The MUD Standard

In this section, we briefly review the MUD standard for those readers who are unfamiliar with MUD. MUD is comprised of six main components: **MUD-File** which is a YANG-based JSON file (RFC 7951) created and digitally signed by the manufacturer. It embeds the behavioral profile of the IoT device in an access control list. MUD-Files should be hosted on manufacturer's **MUD file server**. The location of these files on the Internet is the **MUD-URI** which is stored on the IoT device. Upon connection of the device to a MUD-compliant network, the device sends the embedded MUD-URI to the Authentication, Authorization,

---

[1] https://www.ntia.doc.gov/files/ntia/publications/ntia_practices_model_and_summary_19-02-20_0.pdf.
[2] https://tools.ietf.org/html/draft-lear-opsawg-mud-sbom-00.

and Accounting, i.e., **AAA server**. The **MUD-Manager** is the core of MUD architecture. After receiving the MUD-URI, it will retrieve the MUD-File from the manufacturer's MUD file server and communicates the MUD-File rules to the AAA server [12]. The **Network Access Device (NAD)** (i.e., the router) is equipped with an internal firewall that is configured by the AAA server. MUD provides seven abstractions that can be used to define the behavior of and constraints on an IoT device in a MUD-File. The **domain-name** abstraction is used to enforce restrictions on cloud access. The **local-networks** abstraction defines the communication of a device with other devices on the network. With the **manufacturer** abstraction, the authority component (i.e., domain name) of a device is matched against the MUD-URI of another node which restricts devices' access to specific manufacturers. Similarly, the **same-manufacturer** abstraction defines when devices built by one manufacturer can communicate with each other but not with devices built by other manufacturers. Both of the **controller** and **my-controller** abstraction are used when devices use a controller to communicate. Lastly, the **model** abstraction constrains a device to communicate only with other instances of the same device (e.g., only lightbulbs interact) [12].

To address the human factors challenges in the analysis of the MUD-Files, Andalibi et al. [2] proposed and implemented MUD-Visualizer with the goal of 1) protocol checking to avoid formatting errors in the MUD-File to prevent coding errors 2) identifying internal inconsistencies and inefficiencies to prevent logic errors 3) enabling both manufacturers and sysadmins to review and validate the MUD-Files by processing the abstractions' access control rules and visualizing them. This processing is performed by encoding the merged Access Control Entries (ACEs) into a tree (i.e., ACE Tree) followed by pruning that tree to remove the duplicate ACEs that are generated by merging the MUD abstractions in two or more MUD-Files [2]. MUD-Visualizer can be deployed either as a standalone app or as a web app. It is scalable, open-source, and publicly available online on GitHub [2].

3   Related Work

Currently there are five implementations of MUD: Cisco MUD[3], NIST MUD[4], osMUD[5], Masterpeace MUD (closed-source), and CableLabs Micronets MUD[6]. NIST details the efficacy of these implementations against network-based attacks [5]. Regarding the MUD-Files, mudmaker[7] is a web app specifically for creating MUD-Files. For devices that are not MUD-compliant, Hamza et al. created MUDgee that uses the network traffic of the target IoT device to generate its MUD-File [8]. Beside MUD-Visualizer, which is the focus of this paper, mudpp[8]

---

[3] https://github.com/CiscoDevNet/MUD-Manager.

[4] https://tsapps.nist.gov/publication/get_pdf.cfm?pub_id=927289.

[5] https://github.com/osmud/osmud.

[6] https://github.com/cablelabs/micronets-mud-tools.

[7] https://www.mudmaker.org.

[8] https://github.com/iot-onboarding/mudpp.

(MUD Pretty Printer) is another tool that is developed for summarizing the ACL in the MUD-File. However, since it does not perform any analysis on the interaction between the MUD-Files we did not consider it for our study.

Usable access control has long been a challenge in usable security. An early study on the mitigation of human error in access control management was done by Maxion and Reeder [14]. They found that visualization improves the rate of completing the assigned task by a factor of three. The error in these completed tasks was also reduced by up to 94%. This study is particularly relevant to our work here because, like Maxion and Reeder, we selected computer and network science students with significant expertise.

The study conducted by Vaniea et al. [22] also investigated the difficulty of translating policy rules into access control rules where they recommend visual feedback. They implemented SPARCLE [22] to present the data in a table as a commonly used method of information visualization. The Expandable Grid developed by Reeder et al. [18] for improving file permissions in Windows XP is another example in this category.

Graph Visualization was previously used by [11] which is more similar to MUD-Visualizer's flow-based visualization [2]. Another study that concludes the importance of visualization is the work by Xu and colleagues [23]. They investigate the uncertainties in access control decisions and found that a lack of feedback forced the administrators who intend to resolve access control conflicts into a trial and error mode. Moreover, Smetters et al. [20] found that limitations in the UI would lead to the reluctance to change the access control settings which applies to MUD deployment as well; manual evaluation of the interaction between multiple MUD-Files is a difficult and time-consuming task for system administrators.

Erbenich et al. [7] studied the efficacy of the link visualization to better protect the end-users against phishing. They break down the URL and only visualize the most critical part of it for successful phishing detection. The same concept was used in MUD-Visualizer where only the summary of the MUD-Files was presented to the users. In another work, Scott and Ophoff [19] conducted a user study to study the effectiveness of information security knowledge in decision making. By analyzing the knowledge-behavior gap, they found that a deeper technical understanding of cyber threats will help the user to effectively derive a more cautious and preventing behavior. This motivates one of our goals; to find out whether MUD-Visualizer can help the users with higher knowledge and expertise in the analysis of the MUD-Files.

4   Method

Our survey incorporated two groups of participants: the first group used MUD-Visualizer for the analysis and the second group directly analyzed plain-text MUD-Files (hereinafter referred to as mudviz and plain groups respectively). The plain group acted as a control group to measure the efficacy of the mudviz group. We asked a total of 81 questions, including three screening questions, five demographic questions, twenty-three questions related to the analysis of the MUD-Files (main experiment), forty expertise questions, and ten usability questions from the participants.

Our **screening questionnaire and recruitment** were designed to ensure that the participants have the required knowledge for analyzing a MUD-File. Before inclusion, participants had to show the knowledge of fundamentals of computer networking (i.e., understanding IP, Port, and access control) through manual parsing of components of a MUD-File. We focused on recruitment in an advanced computer networking course.

The **demographic questions** contained questions about age, gender, education, employment status, and income motivated from the study about the privacy for WEIRD populations [9].

The core of the **experiment design** was 23 questions about the analysis of the MUD-Files. We first asked the participants about the remote servers or local devices allowed for a specific device given its MUD-File. This included two questions about the number of nodes devices allow-listed, seven questions about the name of these allowed nodes, and one question about between-node communication. We also included thirteen questions about the Transport and Network layer protocols that are allow-listed for use, e.g. IP version, Port number, TCP vs UDP.

The **post-experiment** questions comprised 50 questions in two categories: forty expertise questions incorporating a set of computer expertise questions from [17] and ten usability questions from the System Usability Scale (SUS) [4].

5   Results

31% of our screening survey respondents (24 out of 76) failed to answer one or more of the screening questions and were not considered for the main study. The **participants** in our study were skewed with respect to gender (84.6% male, 15.4% female). Out of the total of 52 participants, 41 were below the age of 30 years. Over 70% were students, with 50 participants having at least a technical Bachelors's degree. This includes only the participants who passed the screening questions. Participants were split equally between the two groups, `mudviz` and `plain`.

In order to evaluate **participants' security and computer expertise**, they were presented with a set of 13 question categories. These questions were obtained from the set of computer expertise questions from [17]. For measures of `knowledge`, these were knowledge-based questions on (i) phishing (`Kphish`) (ii) certificates (`Kcert`) (iii) SQL commands (`Ksql`) (iv) intrusion detection systems (`Kids`) (v) port 80 (`K80`) (vi) Website markers for security (`Kweb`) (vii) defining IoT (`Kiot`) and (viii) access control (`Kac`). For single response questions, if the participants' answers matched the correct responses, these variables were coded as 1, otherwise 0. For multiple response questions (`Kphish` and `Kcert`), if the participants' got a sum of correct values above the median in each category, the variables were coded as 1, otherwise 0. Since, all participants got responses to

`Kiot` correct, these responses were removed in calculating the covariance matrix for factor analysis.

We then performed a factor analysis on the remaining seven variables to create a `TotalKnowledge` variable. A scree plot and a test of hypothesis showed that a factor of one was sufficient to measure knowledge. This factor, `TotalKnowledge`, was a combination of four factors, calculated by the equation below:

$$TotalKnowledge \leftarrow (-0.5 * Kcert) + (0.6 * Ksql) + (0.6 * Kids) + (0.7 * K80)$$

`TotalExperience` was similarly a combination of weighted factors, given by the equation below:

$$TotalExperience \leftarrow (0.5 * Eyears) + (0.4 * Elang) + (0.4 * Efreq)$$

That is, for the measure of experience, the remaining five questions on experience were evaluated - (i) prior computer expertise (`Eexp`) (ii) prior security expertise (`Etech`) (iii) programming languages known (`Elang`) (iv) years of experience working in security (`Eyears`) and (v) frequency of dealing with security problems (`Efreq`). Since the answers to these questions cannot be evaluated as correct/incorrect, we normalized each of the five variables and performed a second-factor analysis to create a `TotalExperience` variable. A scree plot and a test of hypothesis showed that a factor of one was sufficient to measure knowledge.

We then evaluated the **Effect of Knowledge on Accuracy** by first calculating `TotalKnowledge` and `TotalExperience`. Accuracy was measured as a summation of the correct answer to the 23 questions in the experiment, providing a raw accuracy percentage for each participant.

In order to answer **RQ1**, we first performed a linear regression to measure the effect of the independent variable `TotalKnowledge` on the dependent variable `Accuracy` for both groups (Fig. 1a and 1b). Unsurprisingly, knowledge has a positive effect on the accuracy of the analysis of the MUD-Files. We also found that the effect of `TotalKnowledge` on `Accuracy` is significant in the `plain` group ($b = 7.689, p - value = 0.0164$) but not for the `mudviz` group ($b = 2.148, p - value = 0.406$). Thus, participants in the `mudviz` group seemed to have the same level of accuracy across computer and security knowledge levels. However, this is not the case for plain text files. Participants with greater `TotalKnowledge` seemed to have significantly high `Accuracy` in the `plain` group. This suggests that normally a high level of security expertise is needed to understand textual MUD-Files, but that an effective visualization can result in accuracy by moderate experts indistinguishable from that of the most expert.

The results of a linear regression conducted on each of the factors indicate that none of the factors in the `mudviz` have a significant effect on `Accuracy`, but some factors in the `plain` group are significant. Table 1 shows the regression of individual knowledge factors for both groups. We see that the `Kphish`, `Kids`, `K80`, and, `Ksql` are more strongly significant than the other factors in contributing to `Accuracy`.

To answer the first part of **RQ3**, we analyzed whether `TotalKnowledge` can be divided into sub-groups of knowledge and expertise respectively; and how these interact with `Accuracy`. We sorted the participants from each of the

Table 1. Regression analysis for individual knowledge factors versus accuracy in MUD analysis (showing significant components only).

Factors	Mudviz		Plain	
	coefficient	p-value	coefficient	p-value
Kphish	7.412	0.136	**12.847**	**0.0445** *
Kids	1.967	0.624	**11.594**	**0.0413** *
K80	3.370	0.411	**9.576**	**0.0968** .
Ksql	1.733	0.701	**11.957**	**0.0348** *
TotalKnowledge	2.148	0.406	**7.689**	**0.0164** *

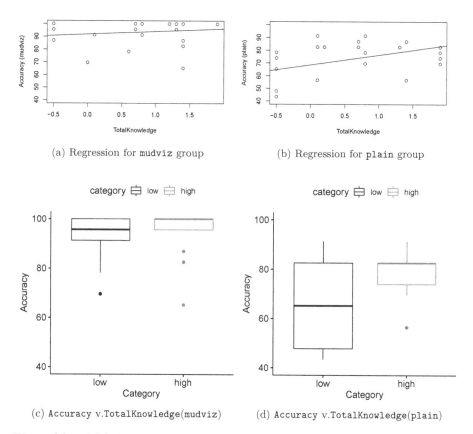

(a) Regression for `mudviz` group

(b) Regression for `plain` group

(c) `Accuracy v.TotalKnowledge(mudviz)`

(d) `Accuracy v.TotalKnowledge(plain)`

Fig. 1. (a) and (b) show the scatter plot of `Accuracy` against `TotalKnowledge`. (c) and (d) show `Accuracy` for four groups, indicating that the effect of the MUD-Visualizer is consistently positive across knowledge groups.

mudviz and plain groups in ascending order based on their TotalKnowledge with 13 participants in each sub-group. A signed Wilcoxon Rank-sum test indicated significant difference between the four sub-group categories, with p-values between the low and high groups of less than 0.001. We conducted an ordinal logistic regression between the two categories (low and high) for each of the two groups for TotalKnowledge against Accuracy, (a) Mudviz and (b) Plain. As seen in Fig. 1c, the accuracy in correct interpretation of the MUD-Files did not vary significantly between high and low knowledge categories in the Mudviz group ($b = -0.018, p - value = 0.663$). However, in case of the plain group (Fig. 1d) TotalKnowledge played a significant role in increasing the accuracy ($b = -0.066, p - value = 0.054$). The accuracy was consistently higher in the mudviz group compared to the plain group in all cases.

To investigate the **Effect of Experience on Accuracy (RQ2)** we began with a linear regression to measure the effect of independent variable TotalExperience on Accuracy for the both groups. Figure 2a and 2b show the scatterplot and the regression lines for each of the mudviz and plain groups respectively. Unsurprisingly, experience has a positive effect on Accuracy in case of mudviz.

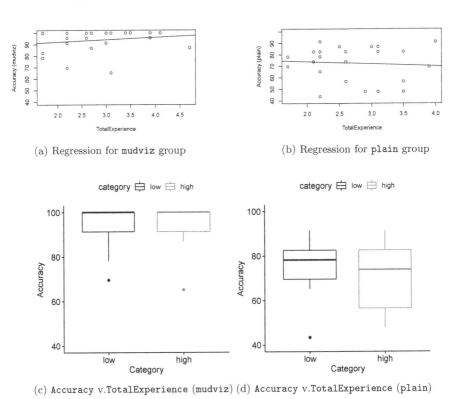

(a) Regression for mudviz group   (b) Regression for plain group

(c) Accuracy v.TotalExperience (mudviz) (d) Accuracy v.TotalExperience (plain)

Fig. 2. (a) and (b) show the scatter plot of Accuracy against TotalExperience. (c) and (d) show Accuracy for four groups, indicating that the effect of the MUD-Visualizer is consistently positive across all experience groups.

Yet there appears to a weak negative effect on `Accuracy` in case of `plain` in Fig. 2d, which we delve into in Table 2 below.

`TotalExperience` is not significant for `Accuracy` in either case of the `plain` group ($b = -1.879, p - value = 0.687$) or the `mudviz` group ($b = 2.018, p-value = 0.425$); although differences in the distribution of the `plain` are apparent. Thus, participants in the group that were presented with the MUD-Visualizer seemed to have the same level of accuracy across computer and security experience levels.

Table 2. Regression analysis for individual experience factors versus accuracy in MUD analysis.

Factors	Mudviz		Plain	
	coefficient	p-value	coefficient	p-value
Eexp	1.187	0.393	**6.505**	**0.00299 ****
Efreq	1.789	0.259	−4.797	0.18
Eyears	0.345	0.899	−0.050	0.989
TotalExperience	2.018	0.425	−1.879	0.687

Taking a closer look at the experience factors by conducting a linear regression for each of the factors, we see that none of the factors in the `mudviz` group affect `Accuracy` significantly, but the `Eexp` factor in the `plain` group does. In that case, `Eexp` is significant and positive. Table 2 shows the regression of individual experience factors for both groups. `Eexp` is a set of Booleans from querying if participants had experience with any of the following: designing a website, registering a domain name, using SSH, configuring a firewall, creating a database, installing a computer program, and writing a computing program. The intriguing but not significant negative effect on `Accuracy` is due to `Efreq` (frequency of handling security incidents) and `Eyears` (years of experience working in the security field). It is possible that this may result from less experienced people defining security incidents (e.g., spam vs. an intrusion) or being in the security field differently (e.g., total years in coursework vs. years in incident response not DevOps).

To answer the second part of the **RQ3**, we analyzed whether `TotalExperience` can be divided into sub-groups of knowledge and expertise respectively, and how they affect the `Accuracy`. We sorted the participants from each of the `mudviz` and `plain` groups in ascending order based on their `TotalExperience`. Again, we considered 13 participants in each sub-group. A signed Wilcoxon Rank-sum test showed that the four sub-group categories are significantly different, with $p-values$ between each of the low versus high groups being less than 0.001. We conducted an ordinal logistic regression between the two categories (low and high) for each of the two groups of `TotalExperience` against `Accuracy`, (a) `Mudviz` (b) `Plain`. The results illustrated that for `Mudviz` ($b = 2.018, p - value = 0.425$), the accuracy in interpreting the MUD-File correctly was the nearly the same for low and high `TotalExperience` (Similar to `TotalKnowledge`).

6 Conclusions

In this work, we sought to evaluate the efficacy of MUD-Visualizer for correct evaluation of MUD-File by participants with some expertise. We report on the increase in efficacy among all participants, showing that the difference in the performance of network engineers with and without knowledge of security or security expertise was significant. More-so, accuracy of participants using the MUD-Visualizer showed knowledge of security to be insignificant (among these participants). Given the difficulty of providing network engineers with security expertise, having a visualization that decreases the cost of inexperience argues for the importance of human factors in standards. Beyond that we found evidence that interpretation of security questions may be having a subtle impact on the results; those with less experience may not be reporting experience with the same baseline as those with more. This phenomena is worthy of additional research, although in this case any impact would strengthen the results.

Acknowledgements. This research was supported in part by the National Science Foundation awards CNS 1565375 and CNS 1814518, as well as the grant #H8230-19-1-0310, Cisco Research Support, Google Research, and the Comcast Innovation Fund. Any opinions, findings, and conclusions, or recommendations expressed in this material are those of the author(s) and do not necessarily reflect the views of the National Science Foundation, Cisco, Comcast, Google, nor Indiana University.

References

1. Andalibi, V., Kim, D., Camp, L.J.: Throwing MUD into the FOG: defending IoT and fog by expanding MUD to fog network. In: 2nd USENIX Workshop on Hot Topics in Edge Computing (HotEdge 19) (2019)
2. Andalibi, V., Lear, E., Kim, D., Camp, J.: On the Analysis of MUD-Files' Interactions, Conflicts, and Configuration Requirements Before Deployment. In: 5th EAI International Conference on Safety and Security in Internet of Things, SaSeIoT. Springer (2021)
3. Bailey, M., Cooke, E., Jahanian, F., Xu, Y., Karir, M.: A survey of botnet technology and defenses. In: 2009 Cybersecurity Applications & Technology Conference for Homeland Security, pp. 299–304. IEEE (2009)
4. Brooke, J.: SUS: A "Quick and Dirty" Usability. CRC Press (1996)
5. Dodson, D., et al.: Securing Small Business and Home Internet of Things (IoT) Devices: Mitigating Network-Based Attacks Using Manufacturer Usage Description (MUD). Tech. rep, National Institute of Standards and Technology (2019)
6. D'Orazio, C.J., Choo, K.K.R., Yang, L.T.: Data exfiltration from internet of things devices: iOS devices as case studies. IEEE Internet Things J. **4**(2), 524–535 (2016)
7. Erbenich, V.I.P., Träder, D., Heinemann, A., Nural, M.: Phishing attack recognition by end-users: concepts for URL visualization and implementation. In: HAISA, pp. 179–188 (2019)
8. Hamza, A., Ranathunga, D., Gharakheili, H.H., Roughan, M., Sivaraman, V.: Clear as MUD: generating, validating and applying IoT behavioral profiles. In: Proceedings of the 2018 Workshop on IoT Security and Privacy, pp. 8–14. ACM (2018)

9. Henrich, J., Heine, S.J., Norenzayan, A.: Most people are not WEIRD. Nature **466**(7302), 29–29 (2010)
10. Kolias, C., Kambourakis, G., Stavrou, A., Voas, J.: DDoS in the IoT: mirai and other botnets. Computer **50**(7), 80–84 (2017)
11. Kolomeets, M., Chechulin, A., Kotenko, I., Saenko, I.: Access control visualization using triangular matrices. In: 2019 27th Euromicro International Conference on Parallel, Distributed and Network-Based Processing (PDP), pp. 348–355 (2019). https://doi.org/10.1109/EMPDP.2019.8671578
12. Lear, E., Droms, R., Romascanu, D.: Manufacturer Usage Description Specification. RFC 8520 (2019). 10.17487/RFC8520. https://rfc-editor.org/rfc/rfc8520.txt
13. Lueth, K.L.: State of the IoT 2020: 12 billion IoT Connections, Surpassing non-IoT for the First Time. https://iot-analytics.com/state-of-the-iot-2020-12-billion-iot-connections-surpassing-non-iot-for-the-first-time
14. Maxion, R.A., Reeder, R.W.: Improving user-interface dependability through mitigation of human error. Int. J. Hum. Comput. Stud. **63**(1–2), 25–50 (2005)
15. Oliveira, D., Rosenthal, M., Morin, N., Yeh, K.C., Cappos, J., Zhuang, Y.: It's the psychology stupid: how heuristics explain software vulnerabilities and how priming can illuminate developer's blind spots. In: Proceedings of the 30th Annual Computer Security Applications Conference, pp. 296–305 (2014)
16. O'Neill, M., et al.: Insecurity by design: today's IoT device security problem. Engineering **2**(1), 48–49 (2016)
17. Rajivan, P., Moriano, P., Kelley, T., Camp, L.J.: Factors in an End User Security Expertise Instrument. Information & Computer Security (2017)
18. Reeder, R.W., et al.: Expandable grids for visualizing and authoring computer security policies. In: Proceedings of the SIGCHI Conference on Human Factors in Computing Systems, pp. 1473–1482 (2008)
19. Scott, J., Ophoff, J.: Investigating the knowledge-behaviour gap in mitigating personal information compromise. In: HAISA, pp. 236–245 (2018)
20. Smetters, D.K., Good, N.: How users use access control. In: Proceedings of the 5th Symposium on Usable Privacy and Security, pp. 1–12 (2009)
21. Tanabe, R., et al.: Disposable botnets: examining the anatomy of IoT botnet infrastructure. In: Proceedings of the 15th International Conference on Availability, Reliability and Security, pp. 1–10 (2020)
22. Vaniea, K., Ni, Q., Cranor, L., Bertino, E.: Access control policy analysis and visualization tools for security professionals. In: SOUPS Workshop (USM), pp. 7–15 (2008)
23. Xu, T., Naing, H.M., Lu, L., Zhou, Y.: How do system administrators resolve access-denied issues in the real world? In: Proceedings of the 2017 CHI Conference on Human Factors in Computing Systems, pp. 348–361 (2017)
24. Yaqoob, I., et al.: The rise of ransomware and emerging security challenges in the internet of things. Comput. Networks **129**, 444–458 (2017)

The Development of a Multidisciplinary Cybersecurity Workforce: An Investigation

Daniel Hulatt⬤ and Eliana Stavrou(✉)⬤

Applied Cybersecurity Research Laboratory, University of Central Lancashire Cyprus, Larnaka, Cyprus
estavrou@uclan.ac.uk

Abstract. The unexpected digital transformation that was forced due to COVID-19 found many citizens and organizations unprepared to deal with the relevant technological advances and the cyber threat landscape. This outcome highlighted once more the cybersecurity skills shortage and the necessity to address this gap. A solution to this, is to consider a multidisciplinary cybersecurity workforce with professionals originating from different backgrounds, beyond the traditional ones such as computing and IT. To be able to engage people though, they need to be aware of the possibilities that exist in cybersecurity for those that originate from non-traditional disciplines. Moreover, cybersecurity professionals need to be aware of the added value when collaborating with these professionals. These are aspects that need to be extensively investigated to provide insights to academia and industry, to develop education and training curricula towards building a multidisciplinary cybersecurity workforce. This paper investigated these aspects in a Further Education and Higher Education College in the UK, where 88 students from 5 disciplines were surveyed, providing valuable observations as to the interest of students, and future professionals, to work in cybersecurity industry and their perception on the subject disciplines relevant to cybersecurity jobs.

Keywords: Cybersecurity education · Multidisciplinary cybersecurity workforce · Cybersecurity skills shortage

1 Introduction

COVID-19 has reformed how citizens and organizations communicate and do business. This new societal reality expanded the attack surface [1] and gave opportunities to attackers to get even more creative and attack every aspect of society. Unfortunately, not all organizations have been prepared to deal with the digital transformation that resulted due to COVID-19, in terms of security technologies, procedures, human resources and relevant expertise. This had impacted their operations severely, and on many occasions, putting them out of business.

Although demand for cybersecurity professionals is rising the last few years, there is a huge skills shortage that the industry is trying to address [2]. To do so, the industry needs to explore a diverse range of solutions to narrow the ever-increasing cybersecurity

© IFIP International Federation for Information Processing 2021
Published by Springer Nature Switzerland AG 2021
S. Furnell and N. Clarke (Eds.): HAISA 2021, IFIP AICT 613, pp. 138–147, 2021.
https://doi.org/10.1007/978-3-030-81111-2_12

skills shortage. One approach is to consider a diverse workforce that will complement the competencies of people that are developed in the context of different disciplines. Traditional disciplines that have a direct link with cybersecurity include Computing and IT. The challenge here is to be able to engage people originating from a range of disciplines, beyond the traditional ones, and build the necessary workforce faster. To be able to engage people though, they need to be aware of the possibilities that exist in cybersecurity for those that originate from non-traditional backgrounds. Also, it is essential for cyber professionals to be aware of complementary disciplines and how professionals from these disciplines can offer an added value when included in a cyber team. These are aspects that are not extensively investigated. However, at a time where cyber professionals are struggling to keep up with their responsibilities that expand due to the dynamic threat landscape, expanding the cyber teams with professionals from other disciplines to offer support, can assist in balancing the amount of responsibility with the cyber roles undertaken. In this way, cybersecurity talents will be retained and grow by expanding the cyber teams.

The objective of this work was twofold. First to identify potential cybersecurity roles that can benefit from the skills offered by people outside of the traditional routes such as computing and IT. These cybersecurity roles were extracted from the leading cybersecurity workforce framework proposed by NIST [10, 11]. Then, this work investigated the awareness level and the interest of students studying in non-computing disciplines in a vocational college in UK, to work within the cybersecurity industry. To this end, the perception of students studying towards Computing subjects was also investigated, providing an insight as to whether they identify that professionals from other disciplines have a fit in cybersecurity and can complement existing cybersecurity teams. The outcome of this work is expected to provide an insight to both education providers and the industry as to the efforts that need to be placed to engage people, from different disciplines, with cybersecurity and address the skills shortage. Section 2 discusses related work. Section 3 presents the cybersecurity roles that have a cross-over with different disciplines. Section 4 analyses the results from the investigations performed in a vocational college in UK. Finally, Sect. 5 concludes the work and provides future directions.

2   Related Work

In a 2020 study [3] conducted by the Department for Digital, Culture, Media & Sport (DCMS) in the UK, it was identified that 48% of UK organisations have a basic cybersecurity skills gap. Whilst over the last few years this has improved, a continued skills shortage has contributed to an ever-increasing number of successful cyberattacks on organisations. With the supply of suitable candidates for cybersecurity roles failing to meet industry demand, the cybersecurity industry needs to look at other recruitment strategies alongside its educational focus to meet its demand. Specifically, there is a need for the cybersecurity industry to consider the role of other disciplines. This is particularly important as they could contribute to the industry in ways that had not previously been considered, which in turn could have an impact when trying to manage and close the cybersecurity skills gap [4]. According to Hoffman et al. [5], by focusing on the holistic development of a cybersecurity workforce, it is possible for an organisation to benefit from a much greater level of collaboration.

One of the problems with recruiting into a cybersecurity role is the perception that this is a technical area that is associated with computing-related studies and expertise. In a survey performed by ISC2 [4], it was discovered that amongst those questioned, 71% reported that their view of cybersecurity professionals working within the industry is that they are "smart, technically skilled individuals". The perception of cybersecurity being only for technically minded individuals will ultimately limit those interested in pursuing the subject from the outset. Currently, this stereotype has contributed to the narrow pipeline of new recruits, from different disciplines, into the subject of cybersecurity. It is for this reason that Javidi and Sheybani [6] explored in their project ways to encourage more students from a younger age to consider the role of cybersecurity in their daily life. They focused on providing cybersecurity educational training to teachers in all disciplines, to better prepare them to incorporate the subject, wherever possible, into the educational curriculums.

Even though studies, e.g. [4], indicate a strong perception regarding cybersecurity being a technically field, a shift to this mindset is required to address the cybersecurity skills shortage as indicated in a report published by Gartner [7], where it is concluded that we have passed the point in which a purely technical approach is needed. To this end, Blair et al. [8], have presented their vision on the multidisciplinary cybersecurity teams of the future, identifying a range of disciplines that have a role in the cybersecurity industry such as computing, operations research, artificial intelligence and data science, electrical and computing engineering, cognitive science and psychology, law, political science and international relations, and business. The work performed by Parrish et al. [9] also analyses a broad range of disciplines, e.g., computer science, information systems, information technology, computer engineering, software engineering, etc., that can be integrated into cybersecurity curricula and discusses how to build cybersecurity competencies for 2030 using an interdisciplinary approach. The value of building teams with complementary skills and experience, to allow organizations to manage risks effectively and holistically, is also highlighted in the latest version of the NIST Cybersecurity Workforce Framework (NICE) [11].

3 Cybersecurity Roles, Subject Disciplines, and Knowledge Areas Mapping

This work explored the links between the job roles defined in the NIST NICE Cybersecurity Workforce Framework [10, 11] and the vocational training offered by a Further Education (FE) and Higher Education (HE) College in the UK. The aim of NICE framework is to develop a common language for use in education and training, highlighting the interdisciplinary nature of working within the cybersecurity workspace as well as driving workforce structure and development planning [12]. The framework defines 32 areas of specialty which exist within the cybersecurity industry and are further broken down into 52 work roles.

Initially, the skills and knowledge attributes required by the job roles defined in the NIST NICE Cybersecurity Workforce Framework [10] have been analyzed. By comparing these attributes to the skills and knowledge developed in vocational training curriculums of a Further Education (FE) and Higher Education (HE) College in the UK, it was possible to identify cybersecurity roles where the skills and knowledge crossed into a range of different (non-traditional) disciplines. The identified NICE cybersecurity roles which could benefit from working alongside others with a greater variety of skills and knowledge across multiple subject domains included: Security Architect, Technical Support Specialist, Cyber Policy and Strategy Planner and Cyber Instructional Curriculum Developer. From the analysis, 8 non-traditional disciplines have been identified that present a crossover of knowledge and skills to perform the identified cybersecurity roles: Media, Art & Design, Teacher Education, Political Science, Psychology, Business, Law and Engineering.

Table 1. Cybersecurity roles, subject disciplines, and knowledge areas mapping

	Media	Art & Design	Teacher Education	Political Science	Psychology	Business	Law	Engineering
Security Architect						K0002, K0008, K0026, K0052, K0214, K0287	K0003, K0004, K0260, K0261	K0010, K0011, K0030, K0035, K0055, K0057, K0093, K0102, K0170, K0322
Technical Support Specialist						K0002, K0114, K0287, K0292, K0317	K0003, K0004, K0260, K0261	K0109, K0114, K0294
Cyber Policy and Strategy Planner				K0127, K0248, K0313		K0002, K0006, K0146, K0311, K0313	K0003, K0004, K0168, K0313	
Cyber Instructional Curriculum Developer	K0239	K0239	K0204, K0208, K0213, K0216, K0217, K0220, K0243, K0245, K0250, K0252		K0124	K002, K006, K0146, K0287	K003, K004	

Table 1 highlights the knowledge areas required for specific cybersecurity roles which can be developed in the context of the identified disciplines. The listed work roles and knowledge areas are extracted from NICE Cybersecurity Workforce framework (version 2017). The NICE knowledge areas IDs (Kxxxx) are retained.

Professionals with a Media, Art & Design background can advise on alternative ways to promote information via written, oral, and visual media, assist in the development of media-related cyber material for education and training purposes, and communicate complex information, concepts, or ideas to different audiences. Such knowledge can

benefit the role of a Cyber Instructional Curriculum Developer. This role can also benefit from the knowledge of professionals with a Teacher Education background. Teacher
Education studies develop knowledge on topics such as learning levels, learning modes
and assessment techniques, education processes and educational technologies. All these
topics are relevant to the Cyber Instructional Curriculum Developer role as it is expected
to develop, plan, coordinate, and evaluate cyber training/education courses based on
instructional needs. Political Science curriculums can build knowledge on aspects such
as strategic theory, cyberspace policy and doctrine, political factors that can influence
regulations and the nature and function of a National Information Infrastructure, etc.
A professional with such knowledge can support a Cyber Policy and Strategy Planner.
Moreover, Psychology studies build knowledge on cognitive domains and on methods applicable for learning in each domain. Professionals with a cognitive psychology
background can advise a Cyber Instructional Curriculum Developer, creating effective
training curricula by adapting appropriate learning methods for audiences with different
abilities.

As it can be observed from Table 1, professionals originating from Business backgrounds have a wider cross coverage of knowledge with cyber roles. Specifically, all
roles listed on Table 1 can benefit from this discipline as people build knowledge on
key cyber aspects such as risk management, customer operations, business continuity
and disaster recovery processes, operational impacts, etc. Another important aspect that
is essential to all roles listed on Table 1 covers knowledge of laws, regulations, policies, and ethics as they relate to cybersecurity and privacy. These topics are covered in
detail by relevant Law curriculums. Finally, a discipline that can be considered technically closer to cybersecurity aspects is engineering. This can also be justified from the
knowledge coverage presented on Table 1 that concerns more technical roles (Security
Architect, Technical Support Specialist). People with an engineering background have a
good understanding of how systems work, they can configure, integrate and troubleshoot
software and hardware and are aware of relevant security threats and vulnerabilities. An
overall observation stemming from Table 1, is that a significant percentage of knowledge
areas can be covered from the listed disciplines.

4   Investigations

In the context of this work, a questionnaire was prepared to investigate the interest and
the perception of students in a FE and HE UK college regarding the disciplines which
could complement and support the work carried out by specific cybersecurity jobs. Based
on the college offered degrees, 4 non-traditional disciplines (Media, Art & Design, Business, Teacher Education) from the ones listed on Table 1 have been considered, plus a
traditional discipline (Computing). Ethical approval was obtained prior delivering the
questionnaire. Initially, 88 participants engaged with the investigations. Specifically, 8
participants were studying towards Media, 3 towards Art & Design studies, and 20 participants were studying towards Business and Teacher Education subjects, respectively.
Finally, 37 Computing students, were engaged to investigate if they can envision collaborating with people from other disciplines to fulfill cybersecurity tasks. Participation was
on a volunteer basis. The low number of participants from specific subjects, provided an

initial observation as to the interest in this topic. The following section presents results coupled with relevant discussion points.

4.1 Results

Familiarity with Cybersecurity and Interest to Work in This Area. The study began by acquiring an initial view of participants' familiarity with cybersecurity. Approximately 50% of responders reported hearing about cybersecurity from their school/college, 46% listed social media, while other sources of information included news articles (39%), family (19%), and friends (22%).

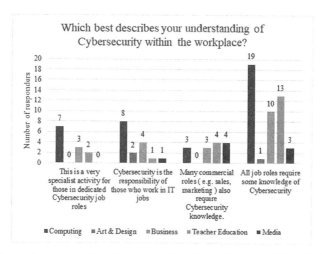

Fig. 1. Perceptions on relation of cybersecurity with workplace within each discipline

The increase in cybersecurity awareness is supported by the results shown in Fig. 1, which indicate that only 14% believe that "Cybersecurity is a specialist activity limited to dedicated Cybersecurity job roles". A high percentage (52%) of responders listed that "All job roles require some knowledge of Cybersecurity". This perception indicates that there is a growing acceptance that cybersecurity aspects touch upon job roles across industries. It is therefore critical for everyone to be involved in the topic as the current cyber threat landscape can impact people's ability to conduct their day-to-day role to a great extent. An interesting observation though is the higher percentage of students (approx. 31%) engaged with non-Computing curriculums that have this perception compared to the percentage (21%) of students following Computing studies. Investigating this observation further, one can derive from Fig. 1 more insight. There is a high percentage (approx. 40%) within people currently following a Computing curriculum who believe that cybersecurity is limited to specialist roles or it is the responsibility of those who work in IT jobs. The same perception is reported by approximately 27% of responders from non-computing disciplines. This could indicate that the way the topic is taught outside of Computing leads to a much more rounded and generalised understanding of the subject, whereas the teaching in the Computing programs focuses more on the specialist skills and knowledge that it neglects to highlight the role of other disciplines. These initial findings would indicate that cybersecurity programs within Computing curricula need to highlight the need to work with professionals having different backgrounds.

Students were also asked to "Rate on a scale of 1 (extremely unlikely) to 10 (extremely likely), how likely are you to consider a job in Cybersecurity?". Computing students indicated that they would be 'Somewhat likely' to consider a job in this industry (Mean = 7.49). Students from the Media (Mean = 3.13), Art & Design (Mean = 3) and Teacher Education (Mean = 3.7) disciplines reported that they would be 'Very unlikely' to consider a job in this industry. Business students appeared to have a 'neutral' feeling towards the idea of working in this industry (Mean = 5.05), further investigations though indicated that there were 2 clusters, one interested and one not that interested in working in cybersecurity. Also, a few students from Teacher Education reported their strong interest in working in this area, which was an encouraging observation even though the majority reported otherwise. Overall, the interest of non-computing disciplines was low, highlighting the need to make more efforts to engage these disciplines with cybersecurity. Note that this aspect was measured before any clarity was provided to students as to how their skills can be utilized in cybersecurity.

Perceptions on Subject Disciplines Relevant to Cybersecurity Jobs. An important aspect of this work was to investigate whether students can identify potential aspects of collaboration between people originating from different disciplines. The study required the students to read the brief job descriptions of the 4 NICE cybersecurity job roles listed on Table 1, and select all the disciplines (Fig. 2) they believed would have some crossover with the cybersecurity jobs described. Figure 2 demonstrates that most participants saw an important role for IT and Business professionals in supporting the job functions described, with a significant number of participants also suggesting a role for those who have studied Criminology, Law and Media. However, it is noted that participants saw less of a role for Art & Design, Psychology, Political Science and Electrical Engineering within the Cybersecurity industry. This may be due to a lack of insight into the value that these disciplines may bring in cybersecurity. The role of other disciplines should be addressed as part of cyber awareness programs, highlighting how they could support cybersecurity, and addressing issues such as human error, message delivery and systems design and installation.

Figure 3 shows a breakdown of job titles related to the disciplines listed in Fig. 2. Students had to select the jobs which could work as part of a cybersecurity team. Interestingly, the results show a similar response to the results in Fig. 2, in that the highest rated jobs relate to IT, Business, Criminology and Law. However, it was surprising to observe that Media roles, e.g., social media manager, game designer, etc., received less attention compared to the higher number of responses reported in Fig. 2 and acknowledging this discipline. Moreover, participants provided low responses related to Curriculum Designer and Lecturer roles, even though more participants listed Educational Studies as a discipline that can complement cybersecurity. This could indicate a general misunderstanding about the type of roles different programs of study could lead to. Another surprising observation is that the Training and Development Officer received more responses compared to relevant roles such as a Curriculum Designer and Lecturer.

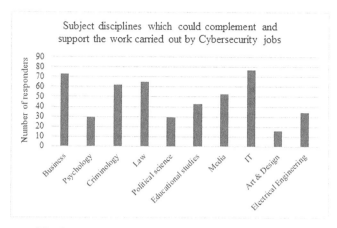

Fig. 2. Subject disciplines relevant to cybersecurity jobs

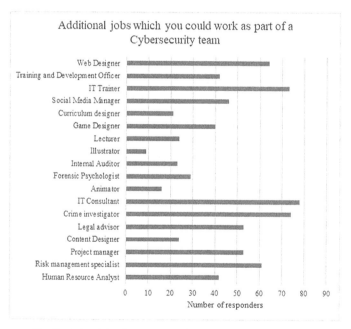

Fig. 3. Other jobs that can complement a cybersecurity team

This could also indicate lack of knowledge as to how these roles are related and how they can completement cybersecurity teams.

Current Competencies in Cybersecurity. Moving on, participants were asked about their competencies developed in their programme of study and whether they can help them work in cybersecurity (Fig. 4).

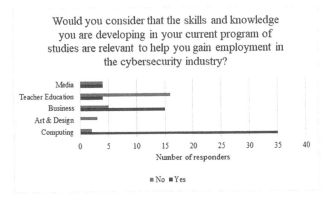

Fig. 4. Students' perception on current skill set and relevance to cybersecurity

Figure 4 demonstrates that most of the Computing and Business students feel that the skills and knowledge developed would help them to gain employment in the Cybersecurity industry. To some level, this was expected due to relevant cybersecurity topics that are typically taught in these curriculums. The surprise result came from the other discipline students, especially those in the Teacher Education that did not feel that the skills and knowledge developed in their studies complement Cybersecurity roles. This observation contrasts the strong indication from Fig. 2 that Educational Studies would complement Cybersecurity roles. A positive note, when students were asked whether they are interested in learning more about cybersecurity and relevant roles within their current studies, the majority (approx. 86%) of students answered positively.

5   Conclusions and Future Directions

With the cybersecurity industry continuing to grow at a pace faster than the skills gap can be addressed, developing multidisciplinary teams can assist in addressing this issue and empower organizations to better defend and keep up with a dynamic cyber threat landscape. The initial investigations from this work, indicated that there seems to be very little interest from students outside of those currently studying a Computing course, to work in cybersecurity. In addition, this work established that there was a lack of clarity on how the skills and knowledge developed in vocational courses across a range of disciplines can be translated into a career in the cybersecurity industry. To address these findings, it is recommended that educational facilities start to explore projects between the departments identified in this report to foster a better understanding of the relationship between the different disciplines and cybersecurity. An example of this could be the creation of a cybersecurity awareness campaign, with the cybersecurity content being co-authored by students from Business and Computing and the key content being converted into graphics by students in Media and Art and Design for use on social media. By exploring the topic together in this way, it would have the benefit of providing practical demonstrations about how the disciplines could work together. By building cybersecurity synergies between different disciplines, this approach will assist over time in identifying opportunities for those studying in alternative disciplines to enter an industry where there is a significant skills shortage, with fantastic career opportunities.

References

1. Hakak, S., Khan, W.Z., Imran, M., Choo, K.R., Shoaib, M.: Have you been a victim of COVID-19-related cyber incidents? Survey, taxonomy, and mitigation strategies. IEEE Access **8**, 124134–124144 (2020)
2. Muncaster, P.: Two-thirds of CISOs struggling with skills shortages (2020). https://www.inf osecurity-magazine.com/news/twothirds-of-cisos-struggling/
3. Department for Digital, Culture, Media & Sport: Cyber security skills in the UK labour market (2020). https://www.gov.uk/government/publications/cyber-security-skills-in-the-uk-labour-market-2020/cyber-security-skills-in-the-uk-labour-market-2020
4. ISC2: how views on cybersecurity professionals are changing and what hiring organizations need to know (2020). https://www.isc2.org/-/media/ISC2/Research/2020/Perception-Study/2020ISC2CybersecurityPerceptionStudy.ashx. Accessed 25 Apr 2021
5. Hoffman, L., Burley, D., Toregas, C.: Holistically building the cybersecurity workforce. IEEE Secur. Priv. **10**(2), 33–39 (2012)
6. Javidi, G., Sheybani, E.: K-12 Cybersecurity education, research, and outreach. In: IEEE Frontiers in Education Conference (FIE), pp. 1–5 (2018)
7. Gartner: The urgency to treat cybersecurity as a business decision (2020)
8. Blair, J.R.S., Hall, A.O., Sobiesk, E.: Educating future multidisciplinary cybersecurity teams. Computer **52**(3), 58–66 (2019)
9. Parrish, A., et al.: Global perspectives on cybersecurity education for 2030: a case for a meta-discipline. In: Proceedings of 23rd Annual ACM Conference on Innovation and Technology in Computer Science Education, Larnaca, Cyprus (2018)
10. Newhouse, W., Keith, S., Scribner, B., Witte, G.: National initiative for cybersecurity education cybersecurity workforce framework. NIST Special publication 800–181 (2017)
11. Petersen, R., Santos, D., Wetzel, K., Smith, M., Witte, G.: Workforce framework for cybersecurity (NICE framework). NIST Special publication 800–181, Rev. 1 (2020)
12. Paulsen, C., McDuffie, E., Newhouse, W., Toth, P.: NICE: creating a cybersecurity workforce and aware public. IEEE Secur. Priv. **10**(3), 76–79 (2012)

Friend or Foe: An Investigation into Recipient Identification of SMS-Based Phishing

Max Clasen, Fudong Li[✉], and David Williams

School of Computing, University of Portsmouth, Portsmouth, UK
{Fudong.Li,David.Williams2}@port.ac.uk

Abstract. Short Message Service (SMS) messaging plays a key role in many people's lives, allowing communication between friends, family and businesses through the convenient use of a mobile phone. At the same time, criminals are able to utilise this technology to their own benefit, such as by sending phishing messages that convince their victims into sharing sensitive information or installing dangerous software on their devices. Indeed, Proofpoint's State of the Phish report found 81% of surveyed US organisations had faced smishing attacks – which is a type phishing attack via SMS message in 2020.

Although phishing is well studied, the amount of research in SMS-based phishing is somewhat limited. Therefore, this study addresses the lack of SMS-based phishing insight, investigating which techniques/tactics are used by malicious senders and honest recipients to disguise/identify SMS-based phishing. By using an online questionnaire, a total of 576 participants' options upon 20 text messages (10 genuine and 10 phishing) were gathered. The result shows 73.4% of the SMS messages were categorised correctly; also a number of factors such as shortened URLs, inconsistent metadata/content, urgency cue, and age play a positive role in identifying phishing attacks.

Keywords: Short Message Service (SMS) · Phishing · Text message · Mobile phishing

1 Introduction

Smartphone ownership and usage continues to increase; 88% of people in the United Kingdom in 2019 own at least one smartphone, up from 52% in 2012 (Deliotte 2019). Smartphones are not just used to communicate with individuals they are used to access data sensitive services such as mobile banking, managing healthcare data and appointments and conducting business. This creates both a complex environment for users to manage and a data rich environment presenting malicious actors additional vectors of attack, including for socially engineering and phishing.

SMS messaging, social media and email are the top three distribution methods for mobile phishing (Wandera 2018), with 17.3%, 16.4% and 15.4% of the share respectively. Wandrera's Mobile Threat Landscape Report found over half of surveyed organisations to have experienced at least one mobile phishing incident in 2019 (Wandera 2020);

© IFIP International Federation for Information Processing 2021
Published by Springer Nature Switzerland AG 2021
S. Furnell and N. Clarke (Eds.): HAISA 2021, IFIP AICT 613, pp. 148–163, 2021.
https://doi.org/10.1007/978-3-030-81111-2_13

more alarmingly, Proofpoint's State of the Phish report found 81% of surveyed US organisations had faced smishing attacks – which is a type phishing attack via SMS message (Proofpoint 2021).

Consequences of phishing attacks can be damaging to both individuals and businesses. According to Verizon's 2020 Data Breach Investigation report, 22% of data breaches in 2020 involved phishing (Verizon 2020) and phishing was involved in 78% of cyber-espionage incidents 2019 (Verizon 2019). Cyber incidents, such as these, lead to direct monetary loss, operational costs and brand damage (Wardman 2016).

In order to detect phishing attacks, a wide range of methods have been investigated. For instance, Ho et al. (2019) investigated characteristics of phishing based upon a dataset of 113 million employee-sent emails from 92 organisations; their results demonstrate latest state of enterprise phishing attacks. Sahingoz et al. (2019) proposed machine learning based phishing detection from URLs with a 97.98% accuracy rate on a dataset containing 36,400 legitimate and 37,175 phishing links. In addition, a number of studies were proposed for investigating the issues for Smishing specifically, such as Balim and Gunal (2019), Mishra and Soni (2019), and Sonowal and Kuppusamy (2018). Nonetheless, those proposed were mainly focused upon the detection of smishing attacks by using machine learning techniques rather than from users' point of view. It is well known that users are the weakest link in the security chain. Indeed, 97% of people around the world cannot identify a sophisticated phishing email (Inspired eLearning 2017). To this end, this paper presents a survey study which investigates the accuracy with which individuals can differentiate between phishing and legitimate SMS messages as well as the methods used to differentiate them.

The remainder of the paper is structured as: Sect. 2 reviews related academic literature; Sect. 3 provides the research methodology; Sect. 4 presents key results; and Sect. 5 draws conclusions and highlights future research directions.

2   Literature Review

This literature review explores the techniques and tactics used by attackers when constructing SMS phishing messages and external factors that influence the capability of recipients to detect phishing.

2.1   Phishing Techniques and Tactics

Techniques used to hide the malicious intent of the message and exploit the trust recipients have in known websites include spoofing URLs to appear similar to the genuine website (Patel and Lou, 2007; Kim et al. 2011). By using URL shortening services, attackers can obfuscate the destination of malicious links in **shortened URLs**. This helps attackers to visually deceive the recipient; it also allows them to bypass URL blacklisting software (Le Page et al. 2018; Joo et al. 2017). Other message elements used to deceive include the use of security components like HTTPS to trick victims into believing it is a legitimate website (Dong et al. 2008). According to the APWG (2019, p. 10), this has become increasingly common, providing a possible indication to its effectiveness. It follows that the presence of HTTPS in SMS messages with a URL may have some influence on how the recipient determines the legitimacy of the message.

Harrison et al. (2016) explain how phishing messages rely on a sense of urgency to reduce the recipient's ability to make rational decisions by acting quickly. Two types of **urgency cues** should be considered: fear-based and reward-based. Fear-based cues use some form of threat, such as imminent account closure if action is not taken; while reward-based cues attempt to offer something of value, but within a limited time. In an experiment with 194 participants, Harrison et al. (2016) investigated whether fear-based cues were more successful than reward-based cues, but no solid evidence to prove this hypothesis was obtained. It may be that young people (the mean age of the experiment's participants was 20 years) are less influenced by the difference between fear-based and reward-based messages.

From the recipient's perspective, Nicho et al. (2018) believe a sense of urgency in an email presents an easy indicator of a phishing attack; nonetheless, victims still fall for them because vigilance of phishing is often not a priority. Jensen et al. (2017) agree as determining whether a message is a threat is often an "ancillary task". They advocate the use of mindful training techniques to promote recipients into thinking about the message request (including whether the message invokes a feeling of urgency).

Abroshan et al. (2018) suggest that part of the phishing process on the recipient-side involves two steps of decision making: whether to trust the sender and then whether to share information with them. A commonly accepted method for gaining trust is to exploit trust imparted by third-parties by masquerading as them (APWG 2019; Abroshan et al. 2018; Whittaker et al. 2010). Attackers seek to acquire trust by making their messages mirror legitimate ones, e.g., by spoofing the sender ID and making the implication of being from a legitimate service in the body of the message (Jensen et al. 2017). Dong et al. (2008) state that **metadata/content inconsistencies**, i.e., differences between metadata (e.g., the sender ID) and content data (i.e., the text message), can lead to detection of phishing, so harmonising these two factors is to the attacker's benefit.

Harrison et al. (2016) mention leakage cues, such as grammar and spelling mistakes in the message impact trust, leading to increased attention by the recipient and thereby reduce phishing success. This is intuitive as one might expect genuine messages from services to have limited mistakes. Nonetheless, Jakobsson (2018) argues that it is easier to fake an SMS text message due to its simplicity, as it consists mostly of just a sender ID, plain text message and a timestamp.

2.2 External Factors

While evidence suggests **age** may be a factor in how susceptible one is to phishing, there is disagreement over gender being a factor. Siadati et al. (2017) found that older people fall for phishing less frequently than younger people. This is consistent with the demographic study on phishing susceptibility conducted by Sheng et al. (2010); their study suggests that people between 18–25 years were more likely to fall victim than other age groups due to a lack of sufficient technical knowledge and experience. Sheng et al. (2010) also suggest that females are more prone to phishing attacks as they clicked on links more often than males, but Siadati et al. (2017) contradict this having found no significant difference in verification code phishing susceptibility by **gender**.

In their experiment to compare the more common rule-based training techniques against mindfulness techniques, Jensen et al. (2017) found that many participants reported a high level of **confidence and expertise** in identifying phishing messages. They also discovered that those trained to use mindfulness techniques, such as thinking about the request and whether the message felt rushed, were more successful than those who had received rule-based training, where elements like an unusual sender ID or the appearance of embedded links are used. It is generally considered that training users to understand and become more familiar with phishing attacks increases their ability to correctly identify phishing and non-phishing messages (Khonji et al. 2013; Jensen et al. 2017; Jain and Gupta 2018).

According to Harrison et al. (2016, p. 270), participants who are **study aware** (i.e., participants are aware they are being tested on phishing detection) exhibit increased cognitive processing of messages. However, it is unlikely that users scrutinise every message in real life; as a result, it is more likely that users make a rapid decision based on straightforward cues found in the message. Jackson et al. (2007) found that aware participants are more likely to categorise both real and fake messages as phishing.

2.3 Summary

As demonstrated earlier, visual elements in phishing messages that may be influenced by attackers can be used to trick recipients; also a number of external factors should be considered on whether an individual can detect a phishing message through these elements. Nonetheless, the influence of these elements has not been wholly investigated in terms of the SMS communication medium. Therefore further work is required to investigate those elements within the domain of phishing via SMS.

3 Methodology

To investigate which factors are used to identify SMS-based phishing, a questionnaire that can be used to test the participant's ability to distinguish genuine SMS messages from phishing messages was designed; also, several factors, including: suspicious requests, urgency cues, leakage cues and inauthentic URLs, were considered when messages were selected. For each chosen SMS message, a screenshot was presented, asking participants to judge whether the message was phishing, not phishing, or if they did not know, and (optionally) to justify their answer (Harrison et al. 2016). In addition to the chosen messages, the following were asked from participants: their age, gender, their experience in phishing, and their ability to identify phishing attempts.

With the aim of harvesting phishing emails, five managed phone numbers were exposed within publicly viewable spaces at 30 of the most visited websites as rated by Alexa.com and Quantcast (Balduzzi et al. 2016). Phishing messages were determined as such if they were unsolicited and attempted to convince the recipient to do something that would likely result in harming them. Other factors within the message could also be examined, such as analysing any provided URLs via sandboxing tools and seeking information on the sender phone number in known "bad number" lists. Logical factors in the message content were also used, such as attempting to request information from an iPhone user despite being received on an Android phone, or supposed banks requesting recipients to share information that they would not ask for through SMS. By using this method, a total of six SMS-based phishing messages were obtained; another four phishing messages that had been shared publicly on social media were collected. Also, ten genuine SMS-based messages were included; most of the genuine messages were received via those five managed phones and they were related to verification code. The total of 20 SMS messages is inline with the work of Siadati et al. (2017) which had a total of 18 messages. Examples of both phishing and genuine SMS messages are presented in Figs. 1 and 2 below; also, the rest of the messages are available in the Appendix.

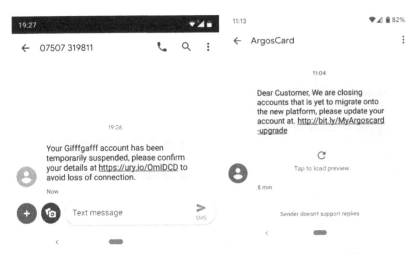

Fig. 1. Example of two phishing messages (Messages 1 and 2)

3.1 Data Collection

The primary research was collected using an online questionnaire via Google Forms due to its popularity, ease of use and accessibility. The questionnaire was distributed via a post on the "r/SampleSize" page of a popular social media website Reddit.com on Friday 24th January 2020. Also, it was shared to all students within the authors' department on Wednesday 29th January 2020. The questionnaire was closed to further responses on Friday 31st January 2020 after receiving 576 responses (around 500 responses were gathered via Reddit). Amongst those 576 participants, 50% were males, 45% were females and the rest (5%) were classified as others. The majority (i.e. 86.4%) of the participants were younger people with 40.5%, 27.9% and 18% for age groups of 18–21, 22–25 and 26–30 respectively. Also, the proportions for age groups 31–40 and 40+ are 9.2% and 4.3% respectively. 3 participants of the total 576 did not select an age group.

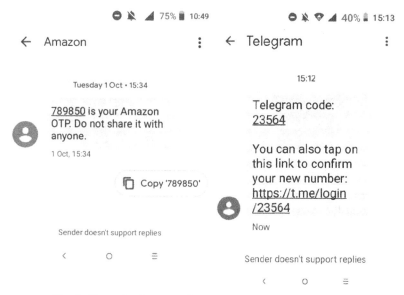

Fig. 2. Example of two genuine messages (Messages 3 and 20)

4 Survey Findings

The 576 survey participants correctly **categorised** SMS messages 73.4% of the time. Messages were incorrectly categorised 14.8% of the time and stating they did not know if the message was phishing or not at a rate of 11.8%. The correct categorisation rate for the phishing messages (87.6%) was significantly higher than that for the genuine messages (59.2%). The genuine messages received an overall incorrect categorisation rate of 23.3% (where participants stated the message was phishing when in fact it was not), with the remaining 17.5% accounting for occasions when participants responded that they did not know whether or not it was phishing. Phishing messages were incorrectly categorised 6.3% of the time and were unknown 6.1% of the time (see Fig. 3).

Messages that appeared later in the questionnaire gradually received fewer responses than those nearer to the beginning. For example, M1 received 351 responses out of the 576 participants (61.8% of participants) while M20 received 151 responses (26.2%). The reduced response rate for later messages may be attributed to response fatigue. Randomising the message order may have equalised the response rate. The total number of responses to the optional open-ended questions was 6531, averaging to 227.8 per message (39.5%).

Table 1 breaks down the accuracy of responses for each message. The accuracy rates are conditionally formatted to display a different background colour. Higher percentages have a green background, while lower percentages have a red background.

4.1 Phishing Messages

As shown in Table 1, the phishing messages M1, M10, M14 and M17 were accurately categorised more than any other message, each having a correct identification rate of over

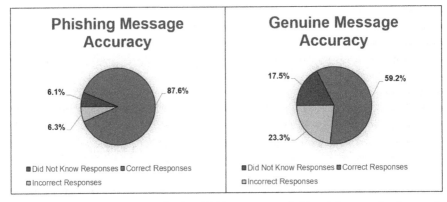

Fig. 3. The overall accuracy rate for the phishing messages (left) and the same for the genuine messages (right).

Table 1. Accuracies for individual messages

Individual Message Accuracy										
Phishing Messages	M1	M2	M4	M8	M10	M12	M13	M14	M16	M17
I don't know	12	44	37	29	5	74	84	15	41	12
No - This is NOT a phishing message	6	42	28	19	5	98	105	7	46	7
Yes - This is a phishing message	558	490	511	528	566	404	387	554	489	557
I don't know rate	2.1%	7.6%	6.4%	5.0%	0.9%	12.8%	14.6%	2.6%	7.1%	2.1%
Incorrect rate ("No" answers)	1.0%	7.3%	4.9%	3.3%	0.9%	17.0%	18.2%	1.2%	8.0%	1.2%
Correct rate ("Yes" answers)	96.9%	85.1%	88.7%	91.7%	98.3%	70.1%	67.2%	96.2%	84.9%	96.7%
Genuine Messages	M3	M5	M6	M7	M9	M11	M15	M18	M19	M20
I don't know	42	72	107	102	111	54	164	165	47	144
No - This is NOT a phishing message	514	415	269	376	210	463	191	185	478	310
Yes - This is a phishing message	20	89	200	98	255	59	221	226	51	122
I don't know rate	7.3%	12.5%	18.6%	17.7%	19.3%	9.4%	28.5%	28.6%	8.2%	25.0%
Correct rate ("No" answers)	89.2%	72.0%	46.7%	65.3%	36.5%	80.4%	33.2%	32.1%	83.0%	53.8%
Incorrect rate ("Yes" answers)	3.5%	15.5%	34.7%	17.0%	44.3%	10.2%	38.4%	39.2%	8.9%	21.2%

95%. Messages M2, M4, M8 and M16 were also all correctly categorised relatively often, with success rates of between 91.7% and 84.9%. In contrast, M12 (70.1% accurately categorised) and M13 (67.2%) were correctly categorised the least of all the phishing messages.

Shortened URLs are apparently one reason for the high correct response rate for the phishing messages M1, M14 and M17. Shortened URLs within these three messages were cited as cause for suspicion by 13.4%, 16.4% and 32.1% of responses, respectively. Outside of these three messages, only M2 had a comparatively high rate for this point as well, at 15.0%, with the other messages being 4.0% and below.

The messages most frequently described as a suspicious request were M1, M10 and M17 (10.4%, 6.0% and 6.4% of responses respectively stating as such). By contrast, M14 had one of the lowest rates for this, with only 0.3% stating that it seemed unusual. The message itself did not contain a request, instead using a reward-based **urgency cue** notifying the recipient that they had won a sum of money. This was noticed by respondents; 13.9% indicated that the reward was "too good to be true" and 16.4% stated there was a clear attempt to entice the user with a reward.

Urgency cues in M10 were picked up frequently, with the sense of fear or other threat being mentioned in 9.6% of its responses, more than any other message. It was also the message for which leakage cues were mentioned most frequently, with 42% of responses pointing out the spelling and grammar mistakes in the text. The lack of urgency cues in M12 and M13 may have been behind them being the most miscategorised. Only 0.4% of responses to M13 mentioned any sense of fear or threat from the message, lower than any other except M12, which received no responses that indicated a sense of urgency.

For M12, 28.6% noticed the **metadata/content inconsistency**, mentioning that it appeared that the URL was not for the service provider claimed in the message, higher than any other phishing message with the next closest comparison being M16 at 21.2%. Relating the appearance of the URL to the supposed service the message was often used to help categorise the messages, as witnessed in the responses to M4 (19.7% of responses made this observation), M10 (16.3%) and M12 (19.6%).

M13 was the only message that lacked a URL. Interestingly, this was mentioned as a sign of legitimacy in 3.6% of responses. However, 31.1% successfully recognised that the message was an attempt to obtain a verification code. One respondent noted:

> "This requires you to be a little savvy. When you get a verification code you should never share it with anyone. Sometimes the company tells you that when they send the code, and sometimes they don't. This is the most sophisticated attempt on this survey so far."

4.2 Genuine Messages

The genuine messages most frequently categorised correctly were M3 (correctly categorised in 89.2% of responses), M11 (80.4%) and M19 (83%); also mostly categorised correctly were M5 (72.0%) and M7 (65.3%), respectively. The remainder of the genuine messages were accurately categorised only between 53.8% and 32.1% of cases. M9 (36.5%), M15 (33.2%) and M18 (32.1%) were correctly categorised as genuine the least frequently.

The most correctly categorised genuine messages M3, M11 and M19, were often simply considered legitimate second-factor authentication code messages, as mentioned in 28.2%, 32.6% and 34.2% of responses for each message, respectively – higher than any other message. Responses for M3 (13.2% of responses), M11 (18.7%) and M19 (24.8%) noted that the message lacked any request for information or a foreseeable way to acquire information.

In contrast, M9, M15 and M18, were correctly categorised the least. None of these messages used an authentication code, instead asking the recipient to respond to an application installation request via a web link. Respondents were sceptical of the request, especially in M9 where 14.4% mentioned that it was inherently suspicious. In both 9.5% of M15 responses and 9.0% of M18 responses, the use of an in-house URL shortening service rather than a public one was considered an indication of legitimacy.

4.3 Analysis of External Factors

Participants were asked to indicate their age; there was a significant imbalance in representation across age ranges, reflective of the demographics of Reddit. Participants aged 18–21 years comprised the overall majority at 40.5%, followed by 27.9% for 22–25, 18% for 26–30, 9.2% for 31–40 and 4.4% for 41+. Table 2 combines data across the age groups of 41–50, 51–60 and 61+ into a 41+ age group to compensate for the small number of participants above the age of 40. The percentage of responses that correctly categorised phishing messages marginally increased with age before dropping off at 41+ (see Table 2). For example, participants aged 18–21 years correctly categorised phishing messages 87.4% of the time, while participants aged 31–40 correctly categorised 90%. At 41–50 this dropped to 79.3%; all those 41+ collectively categorised phishing messages at a rate 79.6%. The categorisation of genuine messages revealed an opposite trend where younger participants correctly categorised them at a higher rate than for older participants.

Table 2. Accuracy by age groups

Accuracy by Age Group								
Age Group	Phishing			Genuine			Overall		
	Correct	Incorrect	Did not know	Correct	Incorrect	Did not know	Correct	Incorrect	Did not know
18-21	87.4%	7.7%	4.9%	62.0%	25.3%	12.7%	74.7%	16.5%	8.8%
22-25	87.9%	5.2%	6.9%	59.9%	20.7%	19.4%	73.9%	12.9%	13.2%
26-30	88.0%	6.4%	5.6%	58.3%	20.9%	20.9%	73.1%	13.6%	13.3%
31-40	90.0%	3.8%	6.2%	54.9%	24.5%	20.6%	72.5%	14.2%	13.4%
41+	79.6%	6.0%	14.4%	42.0%	26.8%	31.2%	60.8%	16.4%	22.8%

Each participant was also asked to rate their **confidence** in identifying phishing messages on a scale of 1 to 5, with 1 being lowest and 5 being highest, the vast majority of participants rated themselves highly. 31.9% rated themselves a 5, while 51% rated themselves a 4. This drops significantly at 14.6% for a 3, 2.1% for a 2 and just 0.3% for a 1. Those that rated themselves with a 5 accurately categorised phishing messages 90.8% of the time. This gradually decreased with those rating themselves a 4 (accurately categorising phishing messages 87.2% of the time) and those rating themselves a 3 (82.4%). However, the 2 (resp. 12) participants that rated themselves as a 1 (resp. 2) accurately identified phishing messages 90% (resp. 84.2%) of the time. The extent to which conclusions could be drawn from any apparent correlation between confidence rating provided and accurate categorisation of phishing and genuine SMS messages is limited by the significant under-representation of the lower confidence ratings.

No significant differences based upon **gender** were witnessed. The 288 participants that identified as male accurately categorised messages 74.8% of the time, in comparison to 71.9% for the 259 participants that identified as female and 74.7% for the 29 participants that identified as other.

5 Conclusion

Phishing has been used widely to attack the users, who are the weakest point of the cyber security system. Also, phishing attack can be distributed across many platforms (e.g. SMS message). The result of this research demonstrates that still a significant amount of users cannot differentiate between phishing and genuine SMS messages. Also, a number of factors (e.g. age and urgency cue) that can be used to identify phishing messages are investigated and the outcome is positive. In future, additional factors that may affect user's ability in identifying the legitimacy of a message should be investigated; this would provide a better understanding in training users to spot malicious messages.

Appendix

Genuine messages.

Phishing messages.

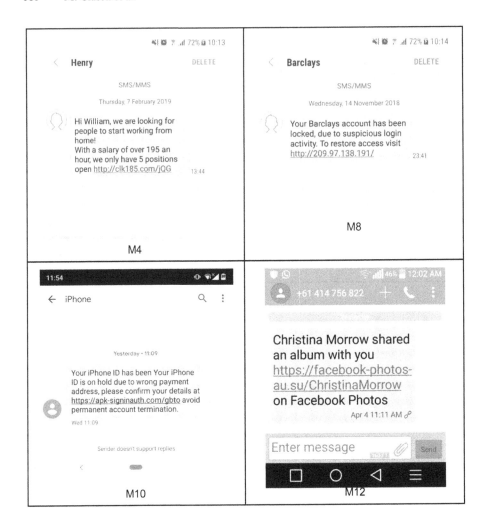

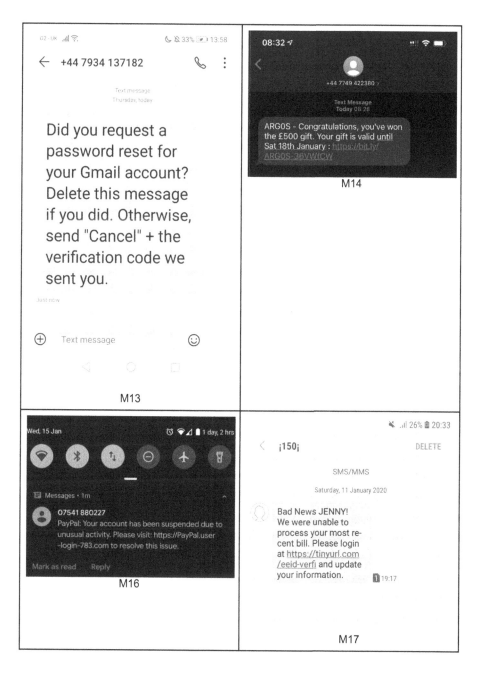

References

Abroshan, H., Devos, J., Poels, G., Laermans, E.: Phishing attacks root causes. In: Cuppens, N., Cuppens, F., Lanet, J.-L., Legay, A., Garcia-Alfaro, J. (eds.) CRiSIS 2017. LNCS, vol. 10694, pp. 187–202. Springer, Cham (2018). https://doi.org/10.1007/978-3-319-76687-4_13

Anti-Phishing Working Group [APWG]: APWG Phishing Activity Trends Report 3rd Quarter 2019 (2019). https://docs.apwg.org/reports/apwg_trends_report_q3_2019.pdf

Balduzzi, M., Gupta, P., Gu, L., Gao, D., Ahamad, M.: MobiPot: understanding mobile telephony threats with honeycards. In: Proceedings of the 11th ACM on Asia Conference on Computer and Communications Security, pp. 723–734 (2016). https://doi.org/10.1145/2897845.2897890

Balim, C., Gunal, E.S.: Automatic detection of smishing attacks by machine learning methods. In: 2019 1st International Informatics and Software Engineering Conference (UBMYK), Ankara, Turkey (2019).https://doi.org/10.1109/UBMYK48245.2019.8965429

Deloitte: Smartphone accessories market to ring up revenues of £1.9bn in 2020 as UK reaches 'peak' handset ownership (2019). https://www2.deloitte.com/uk/en/pages/press-releases/articles/smartphone-accessories-market-to-ring-up-revenues-of-1-point-9-billion-pounds-in-2020.html

Dong, X., Clark, J.A., Jacob, J.: Modelling user-phishing interaction. In: 2008 Conference on Human System Interactions, Human System Interactions, pp. 627–632 (2008). https://doi.org/10.1109/HSI.2008.4581513

Harrison, B., Svetieva, E., Vishwanath, A.: Individual processing of phishing emails. Online Inf. Rev. **40**(2), 265–281 (2016)

Ho, G., et al.: Detecting and characterizing lateral phishing at scale. In: 28th USENIX Security Symposium, USENIX Security 2019, pp. 1273–1290 (2019). ISBN 978-1-939133-06-9

Inspired eLearning: Phishing Statistics – The Rising Threat to Business (2017). https://inspiredelearning.com/blog/phishing-statistics-facts/

Jackson, C., Simon, D.R., Tan, D.S., Barth, A.: An evaluation of extended validation and picture-in-picture phishing attacks. In: Dietrich, S., Dhamija, R. (eds.) FC 2007. LNCS, vol. 4886, pp. 281–293. Springer, Heidelberg (2007). https://doi.org/10.1007/978-3-540-77366-5_27

Jain, A.K., Gupta, B.B.: Rule-Based Framework for detection of smishing messages in mobile environment. Proc. Comput. Sci. **125**, 617–623 (2018). https://doi.org/10.1016/j.procs.2017.12.079

Jakobsson, M.: Two-factor in authentication – the rise in SMS phishing attacks. Comput. Fraud Secur. **2018**(6), 6–8 (2018). https://doi.org/10.1016/S1361-3723(18)30052-6

Jensen, M.L., Dinger, M., Wright, R.T., Thatcher, J.B.: Training to mitigate phishing attacks using mindfulness techniques. J. Manag. Inf. Syst. **34**(2), 597–626 (2017). https://doi.org/10.1080/07421222.2017.1334499

Joo, J.W., Moon, S.Y., Singh, S., Park, J.H.: S-Detector: an enhanced security model for detecting smishing attack for mobile computing. Telecommun. Syst. **66**(1), 29–38 (2017). https://doi.org/10.1007/s11235-016-0269-9

Khonji, M., Iraqi, Y., Jones, A.: Phishing detection: a literature survey. IEEE Commun. Surv. Tutor. **15**(4), 2091–2121 (2013). https://doi.org/10.1109/SURV.2013.032213.00009

Kim, W., Jeong, O.-R., Kim, C., So, J.: The dark side of the internet: attacks, costs and responses. Inf. Syst. **36**(3), 675–705 (2011). https://doi.org/10.1016/j.is.2010.11.003

Le Page, S., Jourdan, G.V., Bochmann, G.V., Flood, J., Onut, I.V.: Using URL shorteners to compare phishing and malware attacks. In: eCrime Researchers Summit 2018, May, pp. 1–13 (2018). https://doi.org/10.1109/ECRIME.2018.8376215

Mishra, S., Soni, D.: A content-based approach for detecting smishing in mobile environment. In: Proceedings of International Conference on Sustainable Computing in Science, Technology and Management (SUSCOM), Amity University Rajasthan, Jaipur, India, 26–28 February 2019 (2019)

Nicho, M., Fakhry, H., Egbue, U.: When spear phishers craft contextually convincing emails. In: Proceedings of the IADIS International Conference on WWW/Internet, pp. 313–320 (2018)

Patel, D., Luo, X.: Take a close look at phishing. In: Proceedings of the 4th Annual Conference on Information Security Curriculum Development, Kennesaw, GA, USA (2007)

Proofpoint: 2021 State of the Phish - An In-Depth Look at User Awareness, Vulnerability and Resilience (2021). https://www.proofpoint.com/sites/default/files/threat-reports/gtd-pfpt-uk-a4-r-state-of-the-phish-2021.pdf

Sahingoz, O.K., Buber, E., Demir, O., Diri, B.: Machine learning based phishing detection from URLs. Exp. Syst. Appl. **117**, 345–357 (2019). ISSN 0957-4174. https://doi.org/10.1016/j.eswa.2018.09.029

Sheng, S., Holbrook, M., Kumaraguru, P., Cranor, L., Downs, J.: Who falls for phish? A demographic analysis of phishing susceptibility and effectiveness of interventions. In: Proceedings of the SIGCHI Conference on Human Factors in Computing Systems, CHI 2010, pp. 373–382. Association for Computing Machinery, New York (2010). https://doi.org/10.1145/1753326.1753383

Siadati, H., Nguyen, T., Gupta, P., Jakobsson, M., Memon, N.: Mind your SMSes: mitigating social engineering in second factor authentication. Comput. Secur. **65**, 14–28 (2017). https://doi.org/10.1016/j.cose.2016.09.009

Sonowal, G., Kuppusamy, K.S.: SmiDCA: an anti-smishing model with machine learning approach. Comput. J. **61**(8), 1143–1157 (2018). https://doi.org/10.1093/comjnl/bxy039

Verizon: 2019 Data Breach Investigations Report (2019). https://enterprise.verizon.com/resources/executivebriefs/2019-dbir-executive-brief.pdf

Verizon: 2020 Data Breach Investigations Report (2020). https://enterprise.verizon.com/resources/reports/dbir/

Wandera: Mobile Phishing Report (2018). http://go.wandera.com/rs/988-EGM-040/images/mobile-phishing-report.pdf

Wandera: Understanding the key trends in mobile enterprise security in 2020 (2020). http://go.wandera.com/rs/988-EGM-040/images/Mobile%20Threat%20Landscape%202020.pdf

Wardman, B.: Assessing the gap: measure the impact of phishing on an organization. In: Annual ADFSL Conference on Digital Forensics, Security and Law. 2 (2016). https://commons.erau.edu/adfsl/2016/thursday/2

Whittaker, C., Ryner, B., Nazif, M.: Large-scale automatic classification of phishing pages (2010)

Towards a Risk Assessment Matrix
for Information Security Workarounds

Eugene Slabbert[(✉)] [iD], Kerry-Lynn Thomson[iD], and Lynn Futcher[iD]

Nelson Mandela University, Port Elizabeth, South Africa
{s215028333,kerry-lynn.thomson,lynn.futcher}@mandela.ac.za

Abstract. Workarounds are often a necessary response to obstructions or inefficiencies within organisations. Their utilisation could, however, introduce information security risk into an organisation. It is, therefore, important for organisations to firstly identify, then determine the reasons for information security workarounds, and how to assess the potential risk they pose to the organisation. Workarounds are generally triggered by human factors which can be explained with the Protection Motivation Theory, as well as environmental influences that exist within an organisation. This is shown in the paper using a flowchart to illustrate the decision-making process of employees regarding information security workarounds. Having understood why workarounds occur within a particular organisation, the value of their information security risk can be determined using a Risk Assessment Matrix for information security workarounds and an accompanying Information Security Workaround Risk Index. Using the tools proposed in this paper, information security officers can respond appropriately to information security workarounds and, where necessary, make modifications to their information security policies, depending on the potential risk associated with the identified information security workarounds.

Keywords: Information security policy · Information Security Workaround Risk · Risk assessment

1 Introduction

Information security is a major concern for modern organisations, all organisations rely on vast numbers of technologies and risk treatment methods, however, the human factor of information security in the form of non-compliance or resistance, remains the weakest link in the chain. One of these forms of non-compliance or resistance are workarounds. Workarounds exist everywhere and have the potential to introduce information security risk nearly every time they are used [2, 10]. Workarounds, therefore, need to be assessed to determine the level of risk introduced into an organisation. Ultimately, organisations should aim to eliminate information security workarounds. Workarounds are often employed by employees who feel that information security policies are irrational or inconvenient when considering their job expectations [10]. It should, however, be noted that policies should always be designed and contextualised to meet

S. Furnell and N. Clarke (Eds.): HAISA 2021, IFIP AICT 613, pp. 164–178, 2021.
https://doi.org/10.1007/978-3-030-81111-2_14

the needs of the employees who are expected to comply with them. Without contextualising these information security policies, employees are less likely to comply them [15]. This paper aims to investigate information security policy workarounds which are a form of non-conformity with organisational policies. Further, the paper will discuss these workarounds and the potential information security risk their use introduces. Furthermore, the paper addresses the influencing factors regarding the utilisation of workarounds. Section 2 discusses information security risk assessment and introduces employee information security behaviour. Section 3 follows by defining workarounds and the various factors that influence them, which include both Human Factors and Environmental Factors in Sect. 4. Section 5 covers Alter's Theory of Workarounds and relates this to an employee's decision-making process when utilising workarounds. Section 6 presents Workaround Classification and Risk Assessment, and Sect. 7 concludes the paper.

2 Information Security Risk Assessment

Information security policies, such as the Acceptable Use Policy, are typical organisational documents that should be used to influence employee's information security behaviour, and compliance with these policies is required to minimise potential information security risk in an organisation.

As seen in Fig. 1, Risk Management comprises Risk Assessment and Risk Treatment. Potential information security risks in an organisation should be assessed as part of overall organisational Risk Assessment [16].

Fig. 1. Risk management process (adapted from [16])

Risk Assessment is done by identifying all important assets within an organisation and determining what the assets are vulnerable to, and the frequency at which a threat may try to exploit the vulnerability [16]. A threat is an entity or natural occurrence, either internal or external to the organisation, that aims to take advantage of vulnerabilities that assets have. The vulnerability of an asset describes how likely an asset is to resist an attack from a threat. Assets are anything the organisation deems to be valuable to their operation. These assets are identified by the asset owner during the risk management process. An asset's impact value is determined by the importance of the asset to the organisation and the consequences of asset loss [16]. Asset impact value of an asset considers public reaction to a data breach, cost of fines and loss of the asset's value that it brought to the organisation. Asset impact value is not an exact value, but rather an organisationally relative value. An example of a risk assessment method can be found in ISO27005 [16].

As seen in Fig. 1, following Risk Assessment, various actions could be chosen in Risk Treatment to address the risks identified. These actions are Risk Modification, Risk Retention, Risk Avoidance, Risk Sharing and Risk Acceptance.

Risk Modification considers the financial, time and operational constraints of an organisation when implementing controls to reduce the risk to an asset or group of assets.

Risk Retention is the acceptance of risk in its form if the organisation's operating goals allow for the risk to exist without affecting the organisation negatively.

Risk Avoidance is the process of modifying processes, procedures, or activities to avoid a specific risk that would not be financially viable nor efficient to manage reasonably.

Risk Sharing takes place by splitting risk between parties, sharing the consequences between those parties, such as insurance coverage on assets.

Risk Acceptance is when the identified risk is accepted by an organisation. Accepting the risk may prove to be beneficial, as the risk may allow for operational benefits such as efficiency or the risk may simply not demand enough priority to require treatment [16].

After Risk Treatment there is always going to be residual risk, which is the remaining risk after the above actions have been implemented. Residual risk is accepted and monitored in subsequent rounds of risk assessment in case the priority of these risks changes [16].

The information assets of an organisation could be put at risk if employees do not comply with information security policies. An employee's willingness to comply with information security policies is reliant on many factors. One of those factors is related to employees and their attitude towards the policy itself. According to Beautement *et al.* [4], how useful an employee perceives an action to be and how easy the employee perceives an action is to perform plays a significant role in the employee's acceptance towards any related information security policies.

An employee's security behaviour is generally understood by considering their intention in the form of acceptance and resistance towards information security policies. When provided with full autonomy, an employee would be expected to be fully conformant and accepting of the organisation's policies, however, this is not always the case [3].

3 Workarounds Defined

Defined by Alter [2] a workaround is *"a goal-driven adaptation, improvisation, or other change to one or more aspects of an existing work system in order to overcome, bypass, or minimize the impact of obstacles, exceptions, anomalies, mishaps, established practices, management expectations, or structural constraints that are perceived as preventing that work system or its participants from achieving a desired level of efficiency, effectiveness, or other organizational or personal goals"* [2]. Therefore, a workaround is used to overcome an aspect of a system that they perceive to be a constraint or an obstruction to the workflow.

Patterson [12] adds to this definition stating that when policies and procedures are designed, procedures are '*work as imagined*' by management versus '*work as done*', which refers to the actual procedures performed by the employees. A further definition suggested by Kobayash *et al.* [9] states that workarounds are *"temporary, informal procedures implemented by employees to overcome workflow bottlenecks"*. Workarounds are often utilised to overcome technical malfunctions or perceived inefficient procedures. This is influenced directly by an employee's decision-making strategy and tacit technical knowledge which may be determined by their personal goals, the organisation's operational goals or their motivation to undermine working systems.

Workarounds are viewed as non-conformant and resistant behaviour [3]. They exist throughout all industries and are typically implemented in situations where a procedure may seem inefficient or inadequate by the employee expected to implement an organisation's procedures. Workarounds may develop as innovations, as well as a form of resistance to policies and procedures [8].

Section 4 highlights the main factors that influence employees' use of workarounds.

4 Factors that Influence Workarounds

Workarounds are products of their environments, the employees who exist within them, and the influences that these employees are exposed to. The factors influencing workarounds can therefore be categorised according to the employees and their decision-making processes [3, 11].

4.1 The Employee Decision-Making Process

All people are unique and are responsible for varying decisions when considering information security related actions. Many behavioral theories and models exist relating to information security behaviour, such as the Theory of Planned Behaviour [1], the Information Security Competency Model [18] and Agency Theory [17]. However, the Protection Motivation Theory will be used as it considers the Threat Appraisal that a person may use when deciding to use a workaround. The Protection Motivation Theory, which relies on a person's threat appraisal and coping appraisal, could provide an explanation for an employee's decision to use a workaround in a specific environment. Within the context of an organisation, threat appraisal is an employee's perception of environmental threats within the organisation.

Threat appraisal consists of *Perceived Vulnerability* and *Perceieved Severity*. *Perceived Vulnerability* is an employee's perception of the validity of the threats. *Perceived Severity* is the perception of the consequences of the threats being realised [12].

Coping appraisal consists of *Self-efficacy*, *Response Cost* and *Response Efficacy*. *Self-efficacy* is described as an employee's drive to implement procedures that would keep them safe and their belief in their ability to execute those procedures. Habits and personal biases towards activities, for example, may influence an employee's perception of *Self-efficacy*. *Response Cost* is the cost that the employee perceives from the implementation of a prescribed procedure, which may include related consequences for non-compliance. Lastly, *Response Efficacy* relates to the employee's perception of how effective a procedure might be in their environment [12]. The Protection Motivation Theory is shown in Fig. 2.

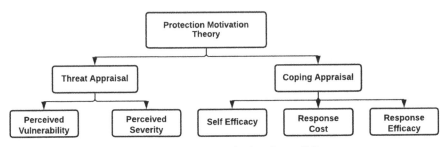

Fig. 2. Protection motivation theory [12]

Within the context of information security, employees would employ both threat appraisal and coping appraisal when deciding whether the procedures recommended by the information security policy are efficient and should be employed or not [7].

4.2 Environmental Factors

An organisation represents an environment within which various work activities and procedures exist. The employees of an organisation exist within this environment and their behaviour is influenced by this organisational environment [3].

Lalley and Malloch [11] present four environmental factors that may influence the need for workarounds, namely:

- **Block in Workflow:** These are hindrances to an employee's ability to work.
- **Additional Work Demands**: These may lead an employee to look for shortcuts to lighten their workload.
- **Poor System Design:** This influences the need for workarounds to overcome existing deficiencies.
- **Incompatible Policies:** These are policies that are incompatible with safety and system limitations.

These environmental factors may result in an employee considering the perceived information security vulnerability and perceived severity of threat to an information asset to be low enough to use a workaround. Furthermore, an employee lacking the *Self Efficacy* to execute information security procedures may use their own procedure, which may introduce risk. A lack of *Response Cost* in the form of consequences may also be a missing deterrent for utilising a workaround, resulting in non-conformance with the organisation's information security policies. The employee's *Response Efficacy* may also deem the risk from their workaround to be worth the benefit in efficiency gained. This all culminates in an employee utilising a workaround to meet their personal, perceived needs. The next section discusses Alter's [2] Theory of Workarounds, which provides a solid grounding in helping organisations understand employees' use of workarounds.

5 Alter's Theory of Workarounds

Alter's [2] Theory of Workarounds consists of seven steps associated with the use of workarounds. The original reasoning behind the Theory of Workarounds was to explain the use of workarounds to circumvent organisational processes. Table 1 presents these seven steps leading up to, during and upon utilisation of the workaround. Steps 1, 2 and 3 relate to the environmental factors and human decision-making process that may influence the use of a workaround. Steps 4, 5 and 6 focus on the workaround creation and utilisation, while Step 7 considers the consequences of such workarounds [2].

Figure 3 is a representation of the seven steps in Alter's [2] Theory of Workarounds - the number of each step is indicated in brackets. Figure 3 aims to show the *Work as Imagined* expectations of management and the designers of the policies and procedures (Steps 1 and 2). Next is the constraint or *Obstruction to Workflow* that may occur in a day-to-day work environment. At this point, an employee may or may not perceive the need for a workaround (Step 3). If an employee perceives no need for a workaround, work continues, and the *Expected Work Output* is achieved. However, if an employee perceives that there is a need for a workaround, the employee will then decide what type of workaround to utilise (Step 4). It is possible at this point, that an appropriate workaround does not exist or is not possible to execute and the employee would not be able to utilise a workaround. If, however, a workaround can be used and is decided upon (Step 5), the employee moves to the implementation of the workaround (Step 6). Upon implementation of the workaround, the local and broader consequences (Step 7) may be realised. It must be noted that *Work as Done* may not always equate to the *Work as Imagined*, as envisaged by management in Steps 1 and 2.

A hypothetical example takes place in Hospital AB, where a formal information security policy has been implemented and sufficiently supported. A workaround is performed daily in the reception area of Hospital AB, throughout the day and the employees interacts with information assets in the form of employee records and patient information. The information security policy specifies that employees should log out of their account when they are no longer at the computer. The workaround, in this example, allows for employees to remain logged in even when they are not there, as will be discussed in more detail below. Using Alter's [2] Theory of Workarounds as a guide, the decision-making process as to why an employee at Hospital AB may perceive a workaround as necessary can be understood:

- **Step 1** simply aims to add context, the employee is expected to conform with the information security policy of Hospital AB, represented as the Acceptable Use Policy (AUP).

Table 1. Steps in the theory of workarounds [2]

No.	Steps	Explanation
1	Intentions, Goals, and Interest	Understanding the goals of management is important for policy designers to create the procedures employees are expected to meet and the procedures to follow
2	Structure	The structure of policies and procedures, how they are designed, and the performance goals reward systems used, all influence the behaviour of those expected to comply with the procedures
3	Perceived need for workaround	This step is based on the performance goals of procedures, systems structure, constraints, as well as employee goals
4	Identification of possible workarounds	This step is triggered by the perceived need for a workaround. Employees consider costs, benefits, and risks when obstacles are encountered, and they perceive a need for a workaround
5	Selection of workaround to pursue, if any	In this step employees decide on the most appropriate workaround, if any, to utilise to overcome the perceived obstacle in their workflow
6	Development and execution of the workaround	This step can occur over a short to long period of time depending on the complexity of the situation presented to the employee
7	Local consequences and broader consequences	A workaround may yield local and broader consequences in its utilisation. These consequences may be either positive or negative depending on the risk introduced by the workaround

- **Step 2** indicates the work procedure within the AUP that states that employees should log out of their work account when not at their workstation, as an information security best practice, in Hospital AB. A backup automated logout system is implemented to log employees out after 10 idle minutes on the workstation.
- **Step 3** presents an opportunity for a *Block in Workflow* to occur. In this case, logging out and then having to log back into their work account is perceived by employees to take up a lot of time and may be viewed as tedious by the employees. For employees who do not perceive this requirement as being tedious, their work continues as normal and the employee logs in and out as required.
- **Step 4** occurs when an employee finds the logging in and out to be tedious or counterproductive to their workflow and seeks an alternative. The Protection Motivation Theory (Fig. 2) can be used to theorise the outcome of the decision. In this example, the

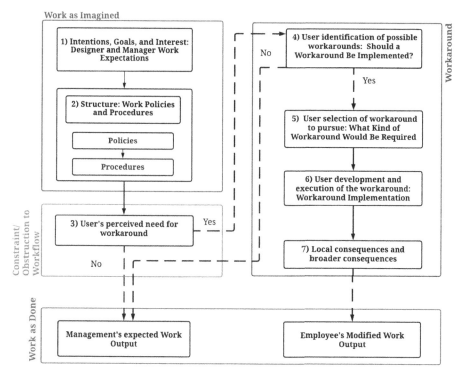

Fig. 3. An employee's decision-making process to utilise workarounds

threat appraisal of the employee considered the vulnerability of an unlocked computer as low, as well as a low severity if there were to be some type of associated breach. With regards to coping appraisal, an employee may be confident in their *Self-efficacy* for relogging onto their work account but may see more benefit in not complying. The *Response Cost* of not complying with the procedure may be high, as consequences are outlined in the AUP, but the employee may either not be aware of the AUP, and its contents, or may regard the workaround as more beneficial to them than following the correct procedure. Lastly, considering *Response Efficacy*, the employee does not feel that logging out of their account may result in a more significant information security risk than what they could possibly gain back in time when it comes to treating patients. In this example, the employee ultimately chooses to utilise the identified workaround.

- **Step 5** occurs when the workaround is chosen, and the employee decides that defeating the automatic logout system will be most effective. The employee does not log out of the workstation as this introduces too much delay into their work.
- **Step 6** is the actual utilisation of the workaround. The employee asks a co-worker to tap their computer's spacebar before the 10-min automatic logout has occurred, which would keep them logged in for longer periods of time. The computers, while still logged in, may be left unattended for a period of time.
- **Step 7** occurs when the employee has completed their work and logs out at the end of the day. The employee has 'got the job done' but has used a workaround of information

security procedures to achieve their goals. The risk introduced in this example is that leaving a logged-in computer unattended may give unauthorised access to patient information to someone who would not have had access if the correct procedure was followed.

A workaround is often viewed by employees as a necessity for quick reactions when changes occur in dynamic work environments or there are hindrances to the expected workflow [14]. When employees use workarounds, they may inadvertently introduce information security risk into the organisation. These workarounds need to be documented, understood and their risk assessed. Low risk workarounds should be viewed as an opportunity to improve existing information security policies and procedures. These workarounds are good candidates to incorporate into information security policies and procedures, as they are low risk and reflect what employees are doing. Medium to high risk workarounds, however, should be incorporated as examples of unacceptable behaviour and the related consequences clearly outlined.

Ultimately, workarounds need to be identified, assessed, and eradicated through their assimilation into the information security policies and procedures, either as adaptations of existing procedures or as unacceptable behaviour.

6   Workaround Classification and Risk Assessment

As discussed, a risk assessment of information security workarounds is needed to determine the risk employees may be introducing by not conforming to information security policies and procedures. Before a risk assessment for workarounds can be conducted, however, identification of the workarounds must occur. Information security workarounds may be identified through observation, reporting or in the aftermath of a security breach.

Burns *et al.* [5] present a workaround assessment method to be used by management to classify workarounds. Used together with the workaround descriptors of Friedman *et al.* [2], Burns *et al.* suggest both the classification and descriptions of workarounds as follows:

Workaround General Classifications:

- **Harmless:** These workarounds generally tend to be user-made procedures that allow for missing system features to be substituted by an employee's own creativity. These workarounds are generally *good*.
- **Essential:** The essential workaround is a user-made procedure that is used to accomplish *Work as Done* as close to imagined as possible. This is generally a *good* workaround.
- **Hindrance:** This serves the purpose of overcoming any procedures or work activities that employees may deem too difficult or time consuming. This workaround could be deemed *good* or *bad*, depending on the context.

Workaround General Descriptors:

- **Temporary/Routinised:** *Temporary* workarounds are short term solutions, whereas *routinised* workarounds are part of day-to-day routines. A *temporary* workaround example is an employee opening a secured door for another employee that left their key card at home, once. A *routinised* workaround is that staff member opening the secured door for the other staff member every day.
- **Avoidable/Unavoidable:** The *avoidable* workaround is a workaround that could have been solved with an acceptable solution. *Unavoidable* workarounds happen when an external force creates a situation that requires a workaround for continuation of work. An *avoidable* workaround example is when an employee introduces a workaround to save time on a task by skipping a few steps. An *unavoidable* workaround is where an employee needs to skip over steps in their work process as their capturing program is not functioning correctly and their job has a time requirement.
- **Deliberate/Unplanned:** *Deliberate* workarounds are purposefully put into place to address the limitations of existing systems or a deliberate act of non-compliance such as a malicious action. *Unplanned* workarounds tend to occur dynamically based on the tasks needing to be accomplished. A *deliberate* workaround is like an avoidable workaround; however, the intent is the major difference. A *deliberate* workaround example can be a workaround implemented maliciously by an employee such as leaving secured doors open as that employee may find the keypad system to be a nuisance or out of spite for their employers. An *unplanned* workaround example is when an employee notices a system does not have the functionality they require in that moment, and they take physical notes instead of recording the information on the computer program as prescribed.

These workaround classifications and descriptors are shown in a matrix format in Table 2. In the example used in Hospital AB, the workaround is performed due to the perceived inconvenience of repeatedly logging in and out of computers when not in use. Therefore, the *Hindrance* row will be selected to classify the workaround. Next, the workaround descriptors are addressed. In the Hospital AB example, the workaround is performed daily which leads to it being *Routinised*. The workaround is very much *Avoidable*, as it is not caused by an unexpected event. Finally, the workaround is *Deliberate*, as the employees have arranged to reset all the login timers whenever each of them enter the office.

Table 2. Workaround classification matrix

	Temporary or routinised	Avoidable or unavoidable	Deliberate or unplanned
Harmless			
Essential			
Hindrance	*Routinised*	*Avoidable*	*Deliberate*

While Table 2 categorises and describes a workaround, the potential risk introduced by a workaround is not taken into consideration at all and no objective way of determining the risk of a workaround is provided. Furthermore, another disadvantage of using this workaround classification method is that there is no final, singular output, it merely aims to classify the workaround.

Using the ISO27005 standard [16] as a guideline, a risk assessment matrix can be used for assessing the potential risk incurred through the utilisation of workarounds. The *Risk Assessment Matrix for Information Security Workarounds* requires the selection of three workaround aspects:

- *Frequency of Workaround Utilisation* is how often a particular workaround is utilised by employees.
- *Workaround Vulnerability* refers to the information security vulnerability that the workaround introduces to the associated assets. *Asset Impact Value* is determined by the cost of an information security breach being realised for a specific information asset [14]. The asset value is relative to an organisation.

Based on the risk assessment matrix in ISO27005 [16], Table 3 presents the *Risk Assessment Matrix for Information Security Workarounds. Frequency of Workaround Utilisation* is the rate at which workarounds are implemented, *Low* being a once off, *Medium* being occasionally and if part of a daily routine, the frequency is *High*. The *Perceived Workaround Vulnerability* is determined by accounting for the vulnerability of the asset using the level of security considered when implementing the workaround. *Asset Impact Value* is determined by considering the intangible, relative impact cost of a threat being realised.

Table 3. Risk assessment matrix for Information Security Workarounds

		Frequency of workaround utilisation								
		Low (L)			Medium (M)			High (H)		
		Perceived workaround vulnerability			Perceived workaround vulnerability			Perceived workaround vulnerability		
		L	M	H	L	M	H	L	M	H
Asset impact value	0 - Negligible	0	1	2	1	2	3	2	3	4
	1 - Low	1	2	3	2	3	4	3	4	5
	2 - Medium	2	3	4	3	4	5	4	5	6
	3 - High	3	4	5	4	5	6	5	6	7
	4 - Very high	4	5	6	5	6	7	6	7	8

When using the Risk Assessment Matrix for Information Security Workarounds to assess the risk of the workaround used in Hospital AB, the Frequency of Workarounds Utilisation, the Workaround Vulnerability, as well as the Asset Impact Value must be determined by information security officers. In the workaround identified in the Hospital AB example, the Frequency of Workaround Utilisation is High, as the workaround is used in day-to-day operations. The Perceived Workaround Vulnerability in the example is determined to be Medium. While there may be technical measures in place to protect the patient information, the computers in question are located in the reception area of the hospital and are easily accessible. If no employees are present in the reception area and the computers are left logged in, nobody would be aware of unauthorised access, as security cameras are not monitored live. The Asset Impact Value in the example is determined to be Very High, as the information assets are patient records. Therefore, in the Hospital AB example, the result from the Risk Assessment Matrix for Information Security Workarounds is 7.

Once a resultant value has been calculated through the *Risk Assessment Matrix*, it can be referenced to the *Information Security Workaround Risk Index*, shown in Table 4, to determine the final risk level. In the Hospital AB example, the calculated value from the *Risk Assessment Matrix* is 7. Therefore, the Information Security Risk Index for the workaround example is determined to be *High*. The *Risk Assessment Matrix for Information Security Workarounds* can play an important role in identifying the risk exposure that a workaround may introduce in an organisation.

Table 4. Information Security Workaround Risk Index

Information Security Workaround Risk Value	
0–2	Low
3–5	Medium
6–8	High

Using the proposed *Risk Assessment Matrix for Information Security Workarounds* and the *Workaround Risk Index*, the risk associated with identified workarounds can be identified and appropriate action taken. Medium to high risk workarounds should be explicitly identified in information security policies and procedures as unacceptable behaviour, and the resultant consequences detailed. Low risk workarounds should be considered for incorporation into the information security policies and procedures by adapting the relevant procedures to reflect the way employees are actually working.

Therefore, as seen in Fig. 4, identified workarounds should be assessed for risk according to the *Risk Assessment Matrix for Information Security Workarounds*. The results of the Matrix should provide information security officers with the risk level associated with a workaround. Depending on the identified risk levels, information security workarounds should be addressed through the appropriate actions of *Risk Modification, Risk Retention, Risk Avoidance, Risk Sharing* or *Risk Acceptance*. Through these actions, the information security risk introduced through workarounds should be 'treated' and

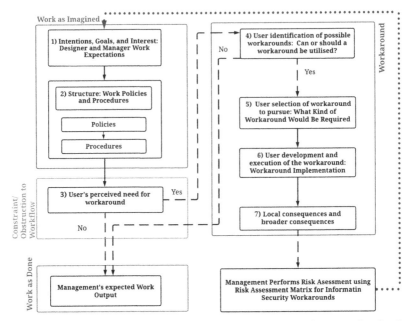

Fig. 4. An employee's decision-making process to utilise workarounds accounting for the risk assessment process.

result in workarounds being incorporated into information security policies, either as 'acceptable' or 'unacceptable' behaviour.

7   Conclusion

This paper proposes an objective *Risk Assessment Matrix for Information Security Workarounds* by assigning a *Frequency of Workaround Utilisation, Perceived Workaround Vulnerability*, and *Asset Impact Value* to an identified workaround. Risk assessment using the proposed *Risk Assessment Matrix for Information Security Workarounds* allows for understanding risk exposure of a workaround. The *Information Security Workaround Risk Index* then allows an associated risk value to be determined by comparing the *Risk Assessment Matrix for Information Security Workarounds* output to the *Information Security Workaround Risk Index*.

Using the *Risk Assessment Matrix for Information Security Workarounds* and the *Information Security Workaround Risk Index*, the *low risk* and *medium to high risk* workarounds can be distinguished. *Low risk* workarounds could be used to update and improve the existing policies and procedures. *Medium to high risk* workarounds could be used as examples of misuse and unacceptable use for future policy and procedure revisions.

Future research opportunities exist in researching the information security risk workarounds within various industries, as well as investigating the challenges of workaround identification.

References

1. Ajzen, I.: The theory of planned behavior. In: Handbook of Theories of Social Psychology, vol. 1, pp. 438–459 (2012). https://doi.org/10.4135/9781446249215.n22
2. Alter, S.: Theory of workarounds. Commun. Assoc. Inf. Syst. **34**(1), 1041–1066 (2014). https://doi.org/10.17705/1CAIS.03455
3. Bagayogo, F., Beaudry, A., Lapointe, L.: Impacts of IT acceptance and resistance behaviors: a novel framework. In: International Conference on Information System, ICIS 2013, vol. 3, pp. 2077–2095 (2013). Theme: Reshaping Society Through Information Systems Design
4. Beautement, A., Sasse, M.A., Wonham, M.: The compliance budget: Managing security behaviour in organisations. In: Proceedings of the New Security Paradigms Workshop, pp. 47–58 (2009). https://doi.org/10.1145/1595676.1595684
5. Burns, A.J., Young, J., Roberts, T., Courtney, J., Ellis, T.S.: Exploring the role of contextual integrity in electronic medical record (EMR) system workaround decisions: an information security and privacy perspective. AIS Trans. Hum. Comput. Interact. **7**(3), 142–165 (2015). https://doi.org/10.17705/1thci.00070
6. Friedman, A., et al.: A typology of electronic health record workarounds in small-to-medium size primary care practices. J. Am. Med. Inf. Assoc.**21**(E2) (2014). https://doi.org/10.1136/amiajnl-2013-001686
7. Ifinedo, P.: Understanding information systems security policy compliance: an integration of the theory of planned behavior and the protection motivation theory. Comput. Secur. **31**(1), 83–95 (2012). https://doi.org/10.1016/j.cose.2011.10.007
8. Ignatiadis, I., Nandhakumar, J.: The effect of ERP system workarounds on organizational control: an interpretivist case study. Scand. J. Inf. Syst. **21**(2), 59–90 (2009)
9. Kobayash, M., Fussell, S.R., Xiao, Y., Seagull, F.J.: Work coordination, workflow, and workarounds in a medical context. In: Conference on Human Factors in Computing Systems, pp. 1561–1564 (2005). https://doi.org/10.1145/1056808.1056966
10. Koppel, R., Smith, S., Blythe, J., Kothari, V.: Workarounds to computer access in healthcare organizations: you want my password or a dead patient? Stud. Health Technol. Inform. **208**, 215–220 (2015). https://doi.org/10.3233/978-1-61499-488-6-215
11. Lalley, C., Malloch, K.: Workarounds: the hidden pathway to excellence. Nurse Lead. **8**(4), 29–32 (2010). https://doi.org/10.1016/j.mnl.2010.05.009
12. Maddux, J.E., Rogers, R.W.: Protection motivation and self-efficacy: a revised theory of fear appeals and attitude change. J. Exp. Soc. Psychol. **19**(5), 469–479 (1983). https://doi.org/10.1016/0022-1031(83)90023-9
13. Patterson, E.S.: Workarounds to Intended use of health information technology: a narrative review of the human factors engineering literature. Hum. Factors **60**(3), 281–292 (2018). https://doi.org/10.1177/0018720818762546
14. Röder, N., Wiesche, M., Schermann, M., Krcmar, H.: Why managers tolerate workarounds - the role of information systems. In: 20th Americas Conference on Information Systems, AMCIS 2014, pp. 1–13 (2014)
15. Sadok, M., Alter, S., Bednar, P.: It is not my job: exploring the disconnect between corporate security policies and actual security practices in SMEs. Inf. Comput. Secur. **28**(3), 467–483 (2020). https://doi.org/10.1108/ICS-01-2019-0010
16. ISO/IEC: ISO/IEC 27005: 2012 International Organization for Standardization—Information technology—Security techniques—Information security risk management, International Organization for Standardization (2012)

17. Shapiro, S.P.: Agency theory. Ann. Rev. Sociol. **31**, 263–284 (2005). https://doi.org/10.1146/annurev.soc.31.041304.122159
18. Thomson, K.L., von Solms, R.: Towards an information security competence maturity model. Comput. Fraud Secur. **2006**(5), 11–15 (2006). https://doi.org/10.1016/S1361-3723(06)70356-6

A Theoretical Underpinning for Examining Insider Attacks Leveraging the Fraud Pentagon

Keshnee Padayachee[(✉)] [iD]

College of Science, Engineering and Technology, University of South Africa,
Pretoria, South Africa
padayk@unisa.ac.za

Abstract. The problem of the insider threat is extremely challenging to manage as it involves trusted entities who have legitimate authorization to the information infrastructure of an organization. It has been reasoned that the framing of the Fraud Pentagon may assist in predicting and preventing white collar crimes such as fraud. The Fraud Pentagon considers the elements of motivation, capability, rationalization, opportunity and arrogance which converge in a crime scenario. The current study considers the value of using the Fraud Pentagon in examining insider attacks. This paper evaluates this theoretical framing from an insider threat perspective, thereby assisting researchers, organizations and information security practitioners in understanding its complexity and its application to the insider threat problem.

Keywords: Insider threat · Fraud pentagon · Fraud triangle · Fraud diamond

1 Introduction

The insider threat problem is extremely challenging to address as it involves trusted users. A survey of cybersecurity professionals (n = 472) found that 90% of organizations feel susceptible to insider attacks [1]. This study is limited to malicious insiders who are users that use their legitimate access to an organization's Information Technology (IT) infrastructure to intentionally compromise the confidentiality, integrity, and availability of the organizations IT assets [2]. Malicious insiders typically respond to deterrents such as reducing motivations and removing opportunities [3]. The elements of motivation and opportunity form the basis of several models proposed to mitigate the insider threat. The Capability-Motivation-Opportunity (CMO) framing [4] is most commonly used toward managing the insider threat [5] while it has been reported that most practitioners use the Fraud Triangle [3] (originally proposed by [6]) which considers the elements of opportunity, motivation and rationalization, to manage the insider threat. The Fraud Diamond extends the Fraud Triangle to include capability [7]. The Fraud Diamond has been explored towards mitigating the insider threat problem [8, 9]. The insider threat problem is considered to be a "moral grey area" as it "allows insiders to undervalue their actions and to resort to rationalizations" [10]. It may be contended that character

© IFIP International Federation for Information Processing 2021
Published by Springer Nature Switzerland AG 2021
S. Furnell and N. Clarke (Eds.): HAISA 2021, IFIP AICT 613, pp. 179–188, 2021.
https://doi.org/10.1007/978-3-030-81111-2_15

traits could be a factor in influencing these rationalizations [11]. The Fraud Pentagon is the next evolution in understanding the constructs underpinning fraud, as it extends the Fraud Diamond with the trait of arrogance – it deals with the "why" element of crime [12]. The aim of this paper is to explore the interaction and the indicators of the elements of motivation, opportunity, rationalization, capability and arrogance on an insider in a criminogenic event.

A strategy to mitigate the insider threat cannot view the aforementioned constructs in isolation. Studies suggest that these constructs are not discrete but may have interdependencies [13–16]. For instance, it has been shown that in some contexts that opportunities combined with occupational status may be a greater driver than motivation and rationalization [17]. Further it has been shown in financial crime, that individuals who are considered predators, do not need the motivation nor the rationalization to engage in maleficence, they merely require the opportunity to be lured into crime [18].

However, there appears to be a dearth of studies that consider the interdependencies between the Fraud Pentagon and the insider threat problem. A related study by [19] who considered internal and external fraud, did not probe the interdependencies as a primary objective. Therefore, this study is a preliminary step in developing a theory for examining the insider attacks based on the vertexes of the Fraud Pentagon. This paper contributes to the cybersecurity domain in two cogent ways. First, the current elucidation will be useful to cybersecurity practitioners and researchers in generating solutions to the insider threat problem. Second, a presentation of the framing of the theoretical underpinning will assist cybersecurity practitioners in leveraging theories from criminology to manage insider threat problems. The rest of the paper is organized as follows – Sect. 2 presents related work; Sect. 3 explicates the theoretical framework; Sect. 4 presents the implications for practice and the paper concludes with Sect. 5.

2   Related Work

The review of the related work involved a preliminary systematic review which is summarized in Table 1, to identify the prevalence of the models based on fraud theories within insider threat literature.

Table 1. A preliminary systematic review

Database	CMO Model	Fraud triangle	Fraud diamond	Fraud pentagon
IEEE computer	1	1	1	0
ACM digital library	2	0	0	0
Science direct	3	4	1	0
Google scholar	37	78	31	3

This involved searching the most specialized databases for cybersecurity, that is, IEEE Computer, Science Direct, ACM Digital Library [20] and searching Google Scholar for additional grey literature. The terms used in the review were constructed using the following criteria: [All: "insider threat"] AND [All: "CMO Model"]; [All: "insider threat"] AND [All: "fraud triangle"]; [All: "insider threat"] AND [All: "fraud diamond"] AND [All: "insider threat"] AND [All: "fraud pentagon"]. A wider search with more generic search terms may have revealed a greater number of items, however, evidently there is a trend that the Fraud Pentagon has not been given due consideration in cybercrime. A generic search using only the term "fraud pentagon" found 2 unrelated records on Science Direct and 337 records on Google Scholar. A scan of the records found that the Fraud Pentagon is gaining momentum in other fields such as financial fraud and academic fraud.

The CMO model appears to be widely accepted toward managing the insider threat. Greitzer et al. [21] designed an ontology for an insider threat risk model based on the CMO model. Maasberg et al. [22] developed a model that considers the Dark Triad of personality traits based on the CMO model, however, they emphasized that further empirical research is required. Kandias et al. [23] proposed a model, which may be used to predict high-risk insiders based on the CMO model. It appears that the Fraud Triangle is also commonly referenced to manage the insider threat. Hoyer et al. [24] developed an architectural model to unify the fraud triangle to achieve better detection and prevention of the insider threat.

The Fraud Diamond is also commonly referenced in the literature. Goel et al. [9] considered a conceptual model that would provide probes to target the behavioral components of motivation, capability, opportunity, and rationalization in order to detect malicious insider threats. For example, a probe might present a pop-up message indicating "monitoring software is suspended" and the aim is to determine if the insiders will change their search behavior in response to this communication. The model proposed by [8] extended the CMO Model posed by Kandias et al. [23] in four cogent ways by including (1) the element of rationalization (2) prevention (3) contextual information and (4) privacy-preservation.

The Fraud Pentagon that was proposed by [12] and extends the Fraud Triangle with the elements competence and arrogance, is least cited. The paper by Ahmad et al. [19] is most comparable to this research, which considered the effect of digitization as an intervening variable between the elements of the Fraud Pentagon as associated with occupational fraud and external fraud in the telecoms industry. Ahmad et al. [19] reason that technology has helped to reduce some types of fraud by reducing opportunities for crime, however, there is a need to consider a holistic framing that includes organizational culture and processes. This work did not consider the interdependencies of the Fraud Diamond on occupational fraud. Evidently there is a need for more studies to demonstrate the viability of using the Fraud Pentagon for insider threat mitigation.

3 A Theoretical Underpinning for Insider Attacks

Pressure is also considered as the motive/incentive [13] for crime. The classification by Kassem and Higson [25] was extended to include elements that may provoke a motivated insider to commit maleficence [26]. Hence the indicators of pressure are – 1. personal pressure (i.e. financial as caused by gambling or debts); 2. organizational pressure (i.e. low salaries, unfair treatment, job dissatisfaction, job transfer); 3. external pressure (i.e. threats to financial stability, ego, image, and reputation, social engineering) and 4. provocations (i.e. frustration, stress, disputes, emotional arousal, peer pressure).

Poor security controls and poor management oversight create opportunities for cyber-crime [8]. Dellaportas [17] derived indicators suggesting that situations that create opportunities for crime include: lack of controls to prevent and detect maleficence, the ability to bypass controls that prevent and detect maleficence, failure to discipline perpetrators, lack of awareness, indifference, or an incapacity to detect maleficence and the lack of an audit trail.

Insider threats have a proclivity to justify their deeds [3]. Kaptein and Van Helvoort [27] explain that the term neutralization coined by Sykes and Matza [28] was intended to refer to the "justification given before the act instead of the term rationalization that refers to the justification given after the act". Criminals may prepare their rationalizations using a "vocabulary of adjustment" before they act, these verbalizations are intrinsically linked to their motivations for criminality [6]. For an in-depth commentary on the relationship between neutralization techniques and the insider threat, see [29] and [30]. Siponen and Vance [29] proposed a number of neutralization techniques that would be appropriate for the information security domain based on the techniques advanced by Sykes and Matza [28] and Minor [31]. Indicators of neutralization include – "denial of injury"; "defense of necessity"; "condemnation of the condemners" (i.e. attacking those who "disapprove of his/her violations" by denigrating them as "hypocrites" [28]); "appeal to higher authorities" (i.e. disregarding principles of the "larger society for the demands of the smaller social groups" to which the offender belongs [28]); "metaphor of the ledger" [32] (i.e. claiming entitlement to indiscretion as they are mostly good [31]) and "denial of responsibility".

A consideration of the knowledge and skills of insiders to address the insider threat problem [33] should be accorded significance. Capability consists of traits such as knowledge and power; intellect; strong ego; confidence and arrogance; ability to conceal fraud and coerce others [7]. Huff et al. [34] proposed a model for end user sophistication consisting of three facets of capability – breadth (knowledge and skill), depth (background and mastery), and finesse (creativity). However, competence (as designated by the Fraud Pentagon) is a variation of capability as it involves the ability to bypass internal controls, develop a concealment strategy and control social situations via manipulation [35]. To some extent the Fraud Pentagon splits the capability element derived by [7] into competence and arrogance. The distinction of the personality trait of arrogance which effects the ability of the person to see the cost-benefit analysis of crime [7] is highly significant as it underscores the human element in a crime scenario. Maasberg et al. [22] who chronicled the characteristics of insider threats found the following similarities among the cases – "unusual need for attention" a "sense of entitlement/above the rules", arrogance, "compensatory behaviors for self-esteem", "lack of impulse control", "lack of conscience" and "chronic rule violations". Indicators of 'arrogance' (described in [35]) can be detected in individuals with the following characteristics – large ego; suppressive attitude (i.e. a bully) "autocratic management style" and fear of losing power [36]. Further arrogance is indicated by individuals who assume that they are above controls, policies and regulations and assume they have immunity against them [16].

While the theoretical underpinning of the Fraud Pentagon suggests that all elements converge unilaterally in a crime scenario, studies suggest otherwise. For instance, if an insider is unable to rationalize an act of misconduct, then the misconduct is not considered to be an appropriate opportunity [14]. As the studies within the cybersecurity domain are limited, we will now consider studies from other domains in this discourse.

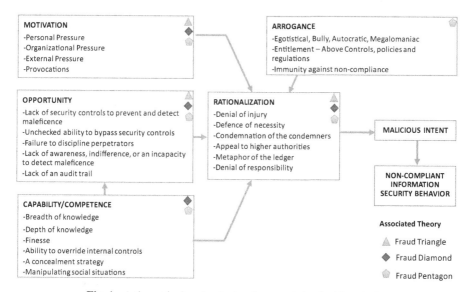

Fig. 1. A theoretical underpinning for examining insider attacks

Several studies found that arrogance was not a significant determinant for deviances [36–38]. However, Christian et al. [39] concluded that all five elements including arrogance influenced corporate fraud while [16] found that the work environment acts as an intervening variable between arrogance and unethical behavior in the workplace. The study by Harrison [15] based on the Fraud Diamond showed that the perception of opportunity is positively influenced by capability and that rationalization is influenced by motivation, opportunity and capability leveraging the Theory of Planned Behavior (TPB) [40]. The constructs of TPB considers one's intention in attaining a goal, in this case non-compliant information security behavior. Maasberg et al. [22] also argued for using TPB when considering the relationship between capability, motive and opportunity and the Dark Triad of Traits with respect to the insider threat. Evidently, an individual who is invoking techniques of neutralization (i.e. rationalizations) shows evidence of maladaptive behavior [41], and this suggests that personality is a mediating factor in the process [42]. Thus, arrogance influences the rationalization construct. Appropriating from the propositions of Harrison [15] and Maasberg et al. [22], the theoretical underpinning shows how the elements of the fraud pentagon result in non-compliant information security behavior in Fig. 1.

4 Implications for Practice

There is an overlap between cybercrime and white-collar crime as it relates to occupational crime. There is a conceptual overlap between cybercrime as technology is used in the perpetration of white-collar crime [43]. Clearly insider threat crime is subsumed within this definition of white-collar cybercrime. Insider threat crime is characteristically committed within the course of the insider's typical duties at work [2]. The categories of cybercrime that this theoretical framework would have as implications include – insider sabotage (i.e. using an organization's IT infrastructure to cause harm to the organization or an individual); insider theft of intellectual property (IP), insider fraud (i.e. unauthorized modification, addition or deletion of data) [2].

As the insider threat problem shares many similarities with white-collar crime it would be sensible to consider mitigation strategies from well-established criminology theories [44]. For example, several researchers applied the Situation Crime Prevention (SCP) theory [26] to cybercrime ([45–47]). SCP has been applied to the insider threat problem [47, 48]. The theory considers five categories (and 25 subcategories) of opportunity-reducing measures – increase effort, increase risks, reduce rewards, reduce provocations and remove excuses. These techniques were given digital analogies [44–46]. Some of the categories of the SCP theory may be mapped as a mitigation strategy towards curbing the manifestation of the Fraud Pentagon elements.

Some techniques that could be used to increase the effort and thus make an *opportunity less appealing* could be access controls, key splitting [44], segregation of duties [46], background checks [46], offsite storage of data [47], web access controls [44], filtering downloads [46], termination procedures [46], least privilege [44], file access permission [47] and periodic audits [47]. The increase the risks category involves increasing the perception that "the risk of detection, resistance and apprehension associated with maleficence [49] would be high". Techniques that could make an opportunity appear to be less appealing with respect to increasing the risk of being caught include: incident reporting [44], audit trails and event logging [46], a two-person sign-off [46] and resource usage monitoring [45].

The reduce provocations category involves removing "noxious stimuli from the environment" [49] that may precipitate a crime. This category considers situations that act as triggers or precipitators to an individual who is already *motivated* [50]. Strategies that have been suggested to reduce the insider from being provoked into maleficence include – dispute resolution and disciplinary processes [44]. The reduce the rewards category involves reducing the perception that the benefits of the crime [49] would be worthwhile. The reward for crime is a motivating factor. The strategies for reducing the benefit of cybercrime for insider threats include watermarking [45], digital signatures [46], encryption [46] and automatic data destruction mechanisms [45]. These strategies reduce the value of the information asset stolen (i.e. IP theft). Some insiders may gain satisfaction from damaging their employer's reputation (i.e. sabotage). This motivation can be minimized by continuity management [44] and incident management [44] which may reduce the desire for crime. It is challenging to determine the intrinsic forces involved in propelling an insider's motivation. Techniques involving conducting a linguistic analysis of mails [51], collecting information about computer usage and communication patterns [52] may be used as indicators of a motivated insider.

The remove excuses category involves *suppressing the rationalizations* of a criminal [49]. Therefore the remove excuses category can be used as a mechanism towards neutralization mitigation [49]. These techniques involve – setting rules (i.e. policies and procedures); posting instructions (for example e-mail disclaimers [45]), alerting conscience and assisting compliance.

Capability and arrogance cannot be mitigated, per se. However, these elements may be used to identify high risk individuals (i.e. background checks) who require targeted training. The capability of an insider to do irreparable damage to an organization's IT infrastructure can be diluted by using role-based access controls [53] where an individual's right to information and access is limited to their privileges. Arrogance also negatively impacts top management and it is suggested there should be leadership interventions to coach individuals on the nature of arrogance and its negative impacts [54].

5   Conclusion

The primary contribution of this paper is the propositions generated from the theoretical framing demonstrated that the constructs of the Fraud Pentagon may not act in synergy. This is significant as it would be of importance to determine the numerous permutations of the constructs that need to be mitigated or detected under specific scenarios. An added contribution of this work is the implications for practice which demonstrated how the vertexes of the Fraud Pentagon could be suppressed to overcome the insider threat. Appropriating the arguments from Lokanan [55] which were propositioned with respect to the limitations of the Fraud Triangle, we can extrapolate the following shortcomings of the framing. First, the framing does not consider collusion. Second, the rationalization, arrogance, and motivation legs of the framing are difficult to quantify. Third, not all constructs are present in a criminogenic event. This was also explored by Sorunke [56] who coincidently proposed an alternative Fraud Pentagon which includes a construct of personal ethics instead of arrogance. These shortcomings will be the objective of future research endeavors.

References

1. Cybersecurity Insiders: Insider Threat Report (2019). https://www.cybersecurity-insiders. com/portfolio/insider-threat-report/, Accessed 28 May 2021
2. Cappelli, D.M., Moore, A.P., Trzeciak, R.F.: The CERT Guide to Insider Threats: How to Prevent, Detect, and Respond to Information Technology Crimes (Theft, Sabotage, Fraud). Addison-Wesley, Upper Saddle River (2012)
3. Farahmand, F., Spafford, E.H.: Understanding insiders: an analysis of risk-taking behavior. Inf. Syst. Front. **15**(1), 5–15 (2013)
4. Schultz, E.E.: A framework for understanding and predicting insider attacks. Comput. Secur. **21**(6), 526–531 (2002)
5. Tan, S.-S., Na, J.-C., Duraisamy, S.: Unified psycholinguistic framework: an unobtrusive psychological analysis approach towards insider threat prevention and detection. J. Inf. Sci. Theory Pract. **7**, 52–71 (2019)

6. Cressey, D.R.: Other People's Money; A Study of the Social Psychology of Embezzlement. Free Press, New York (1953)
7. Wolfe, D.T., Hermanson, D.R.: The fraud diamond: Considering the four elements of fraud. CPA J. **2004**, 38–42 (2004)
8. Mekonnen, S., Padayachee, K., Meshesha, M.: A privacy preserving context-aware insider threat prediction and prevention model predicated on the components of the fraud diamond. In: Annual Global Online Conference on Information and Computer Technology (GOCICT), pp. 60–65. IEEE, Louisville (2015)
9. Goel, S., Williams, K.J., Zavoyskiy, S., Rizzo, N.S.: Using active probes to detect insiders before they steal data. In: 23rd Americas Conference on Information Systems, pp. 1–8. AIS, Boston, Massachusetts (2017)
10. Padayachee, K.: An insider threat neutralisation mitigation model predicated on cognitive dissonance (ITNMCD). South African Comput. J. **56**(1), 50–79 (2015)
11. Fagade, T., Tryfonas, T.: Hacking a bridge: an exploratory study of compliance-based information security management in banking organization. In: Callaos, N., Gaile-Sarkane, E., Hashimoto, S., Lace, N., Sánchez, B. (eds.) Proceedings of the 21st World Multi-Conference on Systemics, Cybernetics and Informatics (WMSCI 2017), pp. 94–99. International Institute of Informatics and Systemics, Orlando (2017)
12. Marks, J.: Fraud Pentagon – Enhancements to the Three Conditions Under Which Fraud May Occur (2020). https://boardandfraud.com/2020/05/21/fraud-pentagon-enhancements-to-the-fraud-triangle-and-under-which-fraud-may-occur/, Accessed 31 May 2021
13. Schuchter, A., Levi, M.: The fraud triangle revisited. Secur. J. **29**(2), 107–121 (2016)
14. Beebe, N.L., Roa, V.S.: Improving organizational information security strategy via meso-level application of situational crime prevention to the risk management process. Commun. Assoc. Inf. Syst. **26**(1), 329–358 (2010)
15. Harrison, A.J.: The Effects of Technology on Interpersonal Fraud. Iowa State University, Ames (2014)
16. Analisa, A.: Factors influencing unethical behaviour in banking industry. J. Contemp. Account. **2**(2), 97–107 (2020). https://doi.org/10.20885/jca.vol2.iss2.art4
17. Dellaportas, S.: Conversations with inmate accountants: motivation, opportunity and the fraud triangle. Account. Forum **37**(1), 29–39 (2013)
18. Dorminey, J.W., Fleming, A.S., Kranacher, M.-J., Riley, R.A., Jr.: Beyond the fraud triangle. CPA J. **80**(7), 17–23 (2010)
19. Ahmad, A.H., Masri, R., Zeh, C.M., Shamsudin, M.F., Fauzi, R.U.A.: The impact of digitalization on occupational fraud opportunity in telecommunication industry: a strategic review. PalArch's J. Archaeol. Egypt/Egyptol. **17**(9), 1308–1326 (2020)
20. Rea-Guaman, A., San Feliu, T., Calvo-Manzano, J., Sanchez-Garcia, I.: Systematic review: cybersecurity risk taxonomy. In: Mas, A., Mesquida, A., O'Connor, R.V., Rout, T., Dorling, A. (eds.) International Conference on Software Process Improvement, pp. 137–146. Springer, Cham, Switzerland (2017). https://doi.org/10.1007/978-3-319-69341-5_13
21. Greitzer, F., Purl, J., Becker, D., Sticha, P., Leong, Y.M.: Modeling expert judgments of insider threat using ontology structure: effects of individual indicator threat value and class membership. In: Bui, T.X. (ed.). Proceedings of the 52nd Hawaii International Conference on System Sciences, Grand Wailea, Maui, Hawaii, pp. 3202–3211 (2019).
22. Maasberg, M., Warren, J., Beebe, N.L.: The dark side of the insider: detecting the insider threat through examination of dark triad personality traits. In: Bui, T.X., Sprague, R.H. (eds.) 48th Hawaii International Conference on System Sciences (HICSS), pp. 3518–26. IEEE, Los Alamitos (2015)
23. Kandias, M., Mylonas, A., Virvilis, N., Theoharidou, M., Gritzalis, D.: An insider threat prediction model. In: Katsikas, S., Soriano, M., Lopez, J. (eds.) International Conference

on Trust, Privacy and Security in Digital Business, pp. 26–37. Springer, Heidelberg (2010). https://doi.org/10.1007/978-3-642-15152-1_3

24. Hoyer, S., Zakhariya, H., Sandner, T., Breitner, M.H.: Fraud prediction and the human factor: an approach to include human behavior in an automated fraud audit. In: 45th Hawaii International Conference on System Sciences, pp. 2382–2391. IEEE, Maui (2012)

25. Kassem, R., Higson, A.: The new fraud triangle model. J. Emerg. Trends Econ. Manag. Sci. **3**(3), 191–195 (2012)

26. Clarke, R.V.: Situational crime prevention: theory and practice. Br. J. Criminol. **20**(2), 136–147 (1980)

27. Kaptein, M., Van Helvoort, M.: A model of neutralization techniques. Deviant Behav. **40**(10), 1260–1285 (2019)

28. Sykes, G.M., Matza, D.: Techniques of neutralization: a theory of delinquency. Am. Sociol. Rev. **22**(6), 664–670 (1957)

29. Siponen, M., Vance, M.: Neutralization: new insights into the problem of employee information systems security policy violations. MIS Q. **34**(3), 487–502 (2010)

30. Willison, R., Warkentin, M.: Beyond deterrence: an expanded view of employee computer abuse. MIS Q. **37**(1), 1–20 (2013)

31. Minor, W.W.: Techniques of neutralization: a reconceptualization and empirical examination. J. Res. Crime Delinq. **18**(2), 295–318 (1981)

32. Klockars, C.: The Professional Fence. Free Press, New York (1974)

33. Magklaras, G.B., Furnell, S.M.: Insider threat prediction tool: evaluating the probability of IT misuse. Comput. Secur. **21**(1), 62–73 (2002)

34. Huff, S.L., Munro, M.C., Marcolin, B.: Modelling and measuring end user sophistication. In: Lederer, A.L. (ed.) Proceedings of the 1992 ACM SIGCPR conference on Computer personnel research, pp. 1–10. ACM, New York (1992)

35. Marks, J.: The Mind Behind The Fraudsters Crime: key Behavioral and Enviromental Elements, Crowe Holrath LLP (presentation) (2012). https://www.fraudconference.com/upl oadedFiles/Fraud_Conference/Content/Course-Materials/presentations/23rd/ppt/10C-Jon athan-Marks.pdf, Accessed 28 May 2021

36. Nindito, M.: Financial statement fraud: perspective of the Pentagon Fraud model in Indonesia. Acad. Account. Finan. Stud. J. **22**(3), 1–9 (2018)

37. Muhsin, K., Nurkhin, A.: What determinants of academic fraud behavior? from fraud triangle to fraud pentagon perspective. In: International Conference on Economics, Business and Economic Education, pp. 154–167. KnE Social Sciences, Dubai (2018)

38. Evana, E., Metalia, M., Mirfazli, E.: Business ethics in providing financial statements: the testing of fraud pentagon theory on the manufacturing sector in Indonesia. Bus. Ethics Leadersh. **3**(3), 68–77 (2019)

39. Christian, N., Basri, Y., Arafah, W.: Analysis of fraud triangle, fraud diamond and fraud pentagon theory to detecting corporate fraud in Indonesia. Int. J. Bus. Manag. Technol. **3**(4), 1–6 (2019)

40. Ajzen, I.: From intentions to actions: a theory of planned behavior. In: Kuhl, J., Beckmann, J. (eds.) Action control. SSSSP, pp. 11–39. Springer, Heidelberg (1985). https://doi.org/10. 1007/978-3-642-69746-3_2

41. Padayachee, K.: Joint effects of neutralisation techniques and the dark triad of personality traits on gender: an insider threat perspective. In: 2021 Conference on Information Communications Technology and Society (ICTAS), pp. 40–45. IEEE, Durban (2021)

42. Simola, P., Virtanen, T., Sartonen, M.: Information security is more than just policy; it is in your personality. In: Cruz, T., Simoes, P. (eds.) ECCWS 2019 18th European Conference on Cyber Warfare and Security, pp. 459–465. Academic Conferences and publishing limited, UK (2019)

43. Payne, B.K.: White-collar cybercrime: white-collar crime, cybercrime, or both. Criminol. Crim. Just. Law Soc. **19**(3), 16–32 (2018)

44. Coles-Kemp, L., Theoharidou, M.: Insider threat and information security management. In: Probst, C.W., Hunker, J., Gollmann, D., Bishop, M. (eds.) Insider Threats in Cyber Security, pp. 45–71. Springer, Boston, MA (2010). https://doi.org/10.1007/978-1-4419-7133-3_3

45. Beebe, N.L., Roa, V.S.: Using situational crime prevention theory to explain the effectiveness of information systems security. In: 2005 SoftWars Conference, pp. 1–18. Las Vegas, Nevada (2005)

46. Willison, R.: Understanding the perpetration of employee computer crime in the organisational context. Inf. Organ. **16**(4), 304–324 (2006)

47. Hinduja, S., Kooi, B.: Curtailing cyber and information security vulnerabilities through situational crime prevention. Secur. J. **26**(4), 383–402 (2013)

48. Willison, R., Siponen, M.: Overcoming the insider: reducing employee computer crime through situational crime prevention. Commun. ACM **52**(9), 133–137 (2009)

49. Smith, T.R., Scott, J.: Policing and crime prevention. In: Mackey, D.A., Levan, K. (eds.) Crime prevention, pp. 6–88. Jones & Bartlett, Burlington, Massachusetts (2011)

50. Cornish, D.B., Clarke, R.V.: Opportunities, precipitators and criminal decisions: a reply to Wortley's critique of situational crime prevention. Crime Prev. Stud. **16**, 41–96 (2003)

51. Brown, C.R., Watkins, A., Greitzer, F.L.: Predicting insider threat risks through linguistic analysis of electronic communication. In: 46th Hawaii International Conference on System Sciences, pp. 1849–1858. IEEE, Wailea (2013)

52. Memory, A., Goldberg, H.G., Senator, T.E.: Context-aware insider threat detection. In: Twenty-Seventh AAAI Conference on Artificial Intelligence Workshop, pp. 44–47. Bellevue, Seattle (2013)

53. Sandhu, R.S., Coyne, E.J., Feinstein, H.L., Youman, C.E.: Role-based access control models. Computer **29**(2), 38–47 (1996)

54. Toscano, R., Price, G., Scheepers, C.: The impact of CEO arrogance on top management team attitudes. Eur. Bus. Rev. **30**(6), 630–644 (2018)

55. Lokanan, M.E.: Challenges to the fraud triangle: questions on its usefulness. Account. Forum **39**(3), 201–224 (2015)

56. Sorunke, O.A.: Personal ethics and fraudster motivation: the missing link in fraud triangle and fraud diamond theories. Int. J. Acad. Res. Bus. Social Sci. **6**(2), 159–165 (2016)

A Literature Review on Virtual Reality Authentication

John M. Jones[1]([⊠]), Reyhan Duezguen[2], Peter Mayer[2], Melanie Volkamer[2], and Sanchari Das[1]

[1] University of Denver, Denver, USA
{john.m.jones,sanchari.das}@du.edu
[2] Karlsruhe Institute of Technology, SECUSO - Security, Usability, Society, Karlsruhe, Germany
{reyhan.duezguen,peter.mayer,melanie.volkamer}@kit.edu

Abstract. As virtual reality (VR) sees an increase in use in several domains such as retail, education, military; a secure authentication scheme for VR devices is necessary to keep users' personal information safe. A smaller section of research focuses on the authentication schemes of VR devices. To further the understanding of this topic, we conducted a detailed literature review of VR authentication by exploring papers published till October 2020. A total of $N = 29$ papers were found. While many papers evaluate the accuracy of authentication methods, few conduct detailed user studies. In the user studies done, we found a lack of focus on diverse populations such as the elderly, with the mean age of the participants being 25.11. Our findings from the literature review give a detailed overview of VR-based authentication schemes and highlight trends as well as current research gaps. These findings drive future research direction to create robust and usable authentication strategies.

Keywords: Virtual reality · Authentication · Literature review · User studies

1 Introduction

Over the past five years Virtual Reality (VR) use has grown to encompass many new areas outside of recreation [1]. With the rise of VR technologies, a secure method of authenticating users has become a pressing issue [2]. Due to the nature of VR it leaves the user prone to observation attacks, in which a malicious user may observe them inputting a traditional password into their device [3,4]. As such, prior research shows that the solution exists in leveraging the unique benefits of the VR Head Mounted Device (HMD) by gathering biometric information from the user [5]. However, this collection of biometric data leaves the user at risk of exposure of biometric data attack vectors. Thus, we aim to analyze the current research on VR authentication through a detailed literature review.

© IFIP International Federation for Information Processing 2021
Published by Springer Nature Switzerland AG 2021
S. Furnell and N. Clarke (Eds.): HAISA 2021, IFIP AICT 613, pp. 189–198, 2021.
https://doi.org/10.1007/978-3-030-81111-2_16

In order to better understand the field of VR authentication, we conducted a literature review where the initial online database search yielded a total of $4,300,000$ publications focusing on VR, out of which only $N = 57$ were articles focused on the security aspects of VR devices. For an in-depth analysis we thereafter performed an analysis of the 29 articles among the 57 which detailed VR-based authentication. In this analysis we found that the papers primarily focused on two broad categories, including biometric-based authentication and knowledge-based authentication. While conducting our review, we recognized significant gaps in the research in the field of VR authentication including a lack of diverse population samples.

2   Methods

Our review is composed of three steps: (1) article collection from multiple digital libraries, (2) abstract and then full text screening, and finally (3) thematic analysis of the collected papers. Papers were included in our analysis corpus if they met the following criteria: (1) written in English; (2) provided some form of analysis or technique regarding VR authentication; (3) peer-reviewed workshop, conference, or journal papers, i.e., any work in progress papers or poster abstracts were excluded from our corpus.

Data Collection and Duplicate Removal: We collected the papers for our analysis using the research tool Publish or Perish[1]. We performed a keyword-based search on the platform to collect papers that were published in several digital libraries including, ACM, IEEE eXplore, SSRN, ScienceDirect, and Research-Gate. This initial search included the following keywords: "Authentication for VR", "Authentication VR", "Authentication in VR", "VR user authentication", "VR authentication". For each keyword the word VR was used both abbreviated and written out. We did not perform any time-based filtering on the article collection, however, we found that the earliest published paper was in 2008.

This initial search helped us to obtain a corpus of $N = 123$ articles which was further reduced to $N = 91$ by removing the duplicate articles that appeared in our keyword searches. Thereafter, we wanted to focus primarily on any published research, thus any patents were removed from the corpus; leaving us with a total of $N = 57$ articles on which we performed the abstract and full text screening for quality control.

Abstract and Full Text Screening: After the paper collection process was completed we read through the abstract of the articles. Thereafter, we continued with reading the full text of all 57 articles. We carefully assessed whether the published research met the criteria to be included in the final corpus. This process resulted in $N = 29$ articles on which our analysis was performed. We noticed that the other half of the articles talked about the technical details of the VR tools and devices, and mentioned authentication is needed for these devices.

---

[1] https://harzing.com/resources/publish-or-perish.

However, their research was not focused on VR-based authentication.

Analysis: We focused our analysis of VR authentication on the following aspects: (1) the types of authentication schemes applied or discussed by the researchers on VR tools and technologies; (2) any security evaluation of the proposed protocols they have done; (3) pros and cons of the authentication scheme the article was covering; (4) methods used by the researchers to look at any user studies done; and (5) the participant details of the user studies done to test the VR authentication scheme. Two researchers conducted thematic analysis on the work (inter-coder reliability score = 86.7%). Such techniques include collecting the pros and cons of each proposed VR authentication scheme, and collecting data that is relevant to the accuracy of the scheme.

3   Findings

We primarily evaluated the type of authentication, the security analyses of the proposals in the articles, and the user studies conducted to evaluate the properties of the proposals. Out of the overall 29 articles, $N = 26$ included at least one user study and seven of these conducted multiple user studies [2,4,6–10], leading to the analysis of 34 user studies across all articles. Therefore, in Sects. 3.1 and 3.2, the percentages are calculated off of $N = 29$ articles, while in Sect. 3.3 they are calculated off of $N = 34$ user studies.

3.1   Types of Authentication

In our analysis, we expanded on the authentication methodologies and found majorly three styles of authentication proposed by the researchers, including biometric, knowledge-based, and multi-modal authentication.

Knowledge-based Authentication: The most prevalent form of VR authentication implemented by the researchers has been the classical mode of password-based authentication. Overall, our corpus contains $N = 8$ (27.5%) [2,4,7,8,10–13] papers which covered knowledge-based authentication schemes. While using the knowledge-based authentication scheme, the commonly used technique implemented by the researchers has been to enter a PIN or an alphanumeric password before being allowed access to the VR device [2,4,8]. For example, Yu et al. [4] study the potential usability of PIN systems in VR, finding that they have an average entry time of 10.5 seconds, but leave the user prone to shoulder surfing attacks. Another article which covers PINs and patterns was written by George et al. [2], in which they find both PINs and patterns are well suited to VR, because of their high usability and security in authentication.

Biometric Authentication: Another form of authentication employed by the researchers uses biometric factors of the VR headset user. Our corpus contains $N = 15$ (51.7%) [3,14–26] papers that cover biometric authentication systems.

The types of biometric data utilized for the authentication varied between different studies, but the general principle of biometric authentication remains. Types of data collected in such schemes include, electroencephalogram (EEG) readings [17,27], body movements [3,14,16,18,20,21,23,24], and Electrooculography (EOG) readings [26]. A paper by Li et al. collects EEG signals in two ways, first subjects would view a video in VR and then on a laptop. They then extracted the EEG data from both the VR and non-VR sections and used it to later authenticate the users, achieving an accuracy of 80.91% [17]. An example of a study which authenticates based of off body movement data is the work by Kupin et al. In this paper they authenticate users based on how they complete the task of throwing a ball, as they throw the HMD measures the position of their dominant hand controller [23]. One of the key weaknesses of biometric authentication is that it requires users' personal biometric data increasing the susceptibility to security attacks increasing user privacy concerns.

Multi-model Authentication: Multi-model authentication schemes utilize two or more separate techniques in order to authenticate users. This helps improve the accuracy of the system as multiple things are being checked. It also improves the security of the system, as an attacker must bypass two systems instead of one. A prime example of this is RubikBiom, an authentication scheme designed by Mathis et al. which combines the knowledge-based system of entering a password on a Rubik's cube, with the gesture biometric data collected as you enter the password [3]. Thus, knowing the password is not enough to gain entry to the system, the password must also be entered in a way that matches the users biometric gesture data. These multi-model systems help to negate some of the downsides found in any of the individual type of authentication. However, they can also be plagued by similar weaknesses.

Gaze-based authentication: Another section of VR authentication research is found within systems that utilize the human gaze, known as gaze-based authentication methods. Gaze-based authentication can combine or use both biometric and knowledge based approaches given its implementation. Among our corpus, $N = 5$ (17.2%) [6,9,28–30] articles cover gaze-based schemes. Gaze-based schemes authenticate the user based off their eye gaze, such as measuring eye saccades as a user observes a video [22]. This can be combined with a knowledge-based system, where the user enters the password by looking at a PIN pad [9,28]. The concept revolves around your eye movements being tracked by the HMDs and then having the spot where you are looking at being displayed on the screen or tracked and analysed by the HMDs. This method helps to mitigate the possibility of observational attacks, as the user of the HMDs can authenticate without any outward body movements that could give away the password. George et al. [9] propose such a system in which the user selects a number of objects in a room by looking at them. Overall, this approach has a mean entry time of 5.94 seconds, with very few errors in entries.

3.2   Security Evaluation of Proposed Authentication Protocols

When evaluating the security of a given authentication scheme there are many different things to consider given the type of the system. In our corpus, $N = 12$ (41.38%) papers did the security evaluation of their protocol [2,4,7,9,10,14–16,24,26,27,31]. For biometric schemes, a clear indicator of security is a low equal error rate (EER). The biometric schemes in our corpus had an average EER of 8.67%, with the minimum being 1.4% from the study by Olade et al. [16]. The average accuracy amongst the biometric schemes was 92.34% with the highest being 99% accuracy obtained by Sivasamy et al. [20]. George et al. conducted and described two security studies in their paper which cover potential attacks on the system. Even when attackers were provided with video of the user entering their password, they were unable to guess the password indicating the schemes resilience to observational attacks [10]. Of the articles which covered knowledge-based schemes ($N = 8$ papers), $N = 5$ (62.5%) provided an additional study which analyzed potential attack threats and determined whether or not the system was resilient [2,4,7,9,10].

3.3   User Studies

The articles included in our further analysis had a resounding amount of user studies, with $N = 26$ (89.65%) of articles including some form of user study. Among these, seven articles included two or more user studies [2,4,6–10]. The articles which included multiple studies tended to work with knowledge-based authentication schemes [2,4,7,8,10–13], as multiple studies are needed to observe attacking patterns of the systems. Studies which covered biometric schemes had the highest average user study population size of 69.8 participants [3,5,14–22,24, 26,31], and gaze-based [6,9,28] as well as knowledge-based schemes had average sizes of 35 and 20 participants respectively. Across all user studies, the average sample size was 44.18.

Age: We noticed a significant gap in literature where the studies were mostly based of convenient samples, such as university students. For other populations, such as the elderly, their security perspective or VR usage was understudied. The mean age of participants in user studies was 25.11 years. Furthermore, the eldest participant amongst our the studies in our literature corpus was 57 [9].

Gender: In our literature corpus we found more male participants in the user studies (49%) than females (35.9%). 14.71% studies did not report the gender in their analysis [8,15,19,25,27]. This gap is most noticeable in articles which cover gaze-based schemes, with a 3 to 1 ratio [6,9,28]. Table 1 shows the gender distribution of the different types of studies analyzed in this paper.

Study duration: The majority ($N = 24$, 70.59%) of the studies were conducted in a single session [3,4,7,10,14,15,17,19–22,27,28,31]. However, some studies conducted multiple phase user studies [11,16,18,23–26]. While others implied both single session and multiple phase user studies [6,8,9]. There is a vast difference

Table 1. Showcases the Gender of Participants for Each Type of Authentication-based Studies on VR Devices

Gender			
Authentication method	Male	Female	Not eported
Biometric	467 (44.6%)	397 (37.9%)	183 (17.5%)
Multi-Modal (Gaze-based)	128 (74%)	45 (24%)	0 (0%)
Knowledge	149 (52.84%)	104 (36.88%)	29 (10.28%)
Total	744 (49.53%)	546 (36.4%)	212 (14.1%)

in the duration of studies, with the longest study taking 2 months to conclude while most are only single session.

Type of User Studies: We split the studies into four different categories that adequately describe the purpose of each study. Table 2 mentions the type of user studies we have found in our literature corpus. Dataset creation studies' primary goal was to build a dataset which they could then use to test out their authentication scheme, and tune their authentication mechanism [6,15,17–20, 22,23,25,31]. Authentication evaluation studies sought to test out the proposed authentication scheme and its working principle for VR devices [8,14,16,23,24, 26–28]. Usability studies are studies which tested the usability or memorability of their proposal [2–4,7,9–11]. Security studies measured the effective security of their proposed scheme using participants, whether they were able to hack the system [2,4,7,9,10]. There was one notable study conducted by George et al. which covered both security and usability domains [2]. So, this study appears in our table under both the usability and security evaluation sections.

Table 2. Showcases the Types of User Studies Done by Researchers, Along with the Number of Studies and Average Duration. The Percentages are Calculated on a Total of 34 User Studies in 26 Papers:

Type of study		
Type of study	Number of studies	Average study duration (days)
Dataset creation	10 (28.57%) [6,15,17–20,22,23,25,31]	1.1
Authentication evaluation	9 (25.71%) [8,14,16,21,23,24,26–28]	12.44
Usability	10 (28.57%) [2–4,7–11]	2.8
Security evaluation	6 (17.14%) [2,4,7,9,10]	1

4 Discussions and Implications

The various advantages and disadvantages of proposed authentication schemes vary greatly depending on many factors.

Knowledge-based: Knowledge-based authentication schemes offer an advantage by having arguably the greatest familiarity to users. Also, knowledge-based authentication does not require any personal data from the user to work (i.e. users might still choose secrets including their personal data, but in contrast to biometrics this is not required). However, the studies we found regarding such schemes point towards security problems, indicating e.g. a susceptibility to shoulder-surfing which is a bigger issue in VR as users don't see the real world when having their HMDs on.

Biometric: Biometric authentication schemes proposed for VR environments utilise a wide variety of user characteristics (e.g. EEG or body movements). These are less familiar to the users. Therefore, users might be reluctant to accept them as replacement alternative for the better-known schemes. Furthermore, authentication based on body movement might be challenging for elderly or people with handicaps. Thus, user groups with physical constraints need to be taken in consideration when investigating the usability of such schemes. Yet, biometric authentication offers in the proposed configurations a high level of security, in particular resilience to shoulder-surfing attacks. On the other hand, biometric authentication has the downside of needing to collect and store users' biometric data.

Multi-modal: Multi-modal authentication schemes offer the highest security. When combining knowledge-based schemes with gaze-based elements, the risk of shoulder-surfing attacks can be partly mitigated, as the attacker can not see what the user is inputting. For example, by combining a knowledge-based scheme with biometric readings, Mathis et al. created a secure authentication mechanism that negates the possibility of an observation attack [3]. On the other hand, low acceptance of one scheme might not be completely mitigated by combining it with a better-accepted one, but instead have the inverse effect.

Implications for future research: Firstly, we identified a potentially very low acceptance, which might hinder adoption of these schemes. In particular, since the VR market is currently still somewhat niche, this might have serious impacts. Yet, very few user studies actually explored this space and future studies should explore the acceptance of potentially more exotic schemes. Secondly, the long-term usability (in particular memorability) is a space mostly unexplored. Conducting these studies is of the essence to properly assess the real-world deployability of the schemes in the VR context. If using these schemes can aggravate issues which are specific to the VR context, such motion sickness or eye strain, otherwise suitable schemes might not be deployable in the VR context. Thirdly, the usability studies reported for the authentication schemes we found in our literature review mostly relied on convenience samples. While this problem is not specific to studies investigating authentication schemes for use with VR, this leads to a strong skew in the samples. Therefore, future studies must strive for more diverse samples. Especially elderly people are underrepresented in the user studies. Finally, multi-modal authentication seems to be under-researched in the VR context. Specifically, how multi-modal authentication can be best integrated into the VR context and work for users when wearing VR headsets is an open question. The few works done in this area (e.g., combining eye-gaze and a secret for knowledge-based authentication) seem promising, but alternatives and how easy proposals can be translated from a non-VR context should be investigated to harness the full potential of existing proposals and guide the design of new proposals specifically tailored to the VR context.

Limitations: This literature review reflects the current work in the field of VR authentication. It is possible that in gathering these articles some were missed. However, the corpus we gathered provides detailed representation of all major aspects of VR authentication.

5   Conclusion

This literature review reports on 29 papers within the field of VR authentication schemes. We found that certain gaps in literature exist, such as including elderly participants in user studies. We also provide in depth statistics on the current methods of authentication and the potential each system holds. We conclude that there should be more investigation into multi-model schemes, as they combine the advantages of both knowledge-based and biometric authentication and have been relatively unstudied yet.

Acknowledgement. This work was supported by the Helmholtz Association (HGF) through the subtopic Engineering Secure Systems (ESS) at Karlsruhe Institute of Technology. Furthermore, this research was supported through the Secure and Privacy Research in New-Age Technology (SPRINT) Lab, University of Denver. Any opinions, findings, and conclusions or recommendations expressed in this material are solely those of the author(s).

References

1. Lin, T.-J., Lan, Y.-J.: Language learning in virtual reality environments: past, present, and future. J. Educ. Technol. Soc. **18**(4), 486–497 (2015)
2. George, C., et al.: Seamless and secure vr: Adapting and evaluating established authentication systems for virtual reality. In: The 2017 Network and Distributed System Security Symposium (NDSS). NDSS (2017)
3. Mathis, F., Fawaz, H.I., Khamis, M.: Knowledge-driven biometric authentication in virtual reality. In: Extended Abstracts of the 2020 CHI Conference on Human Factors in Computing Systems, pp. 1–10 (2020)
4. Yu, Z., Liang, H.-N., Fleming, C., Man., K.L.: An exploration of usable authentication mechanisms for virtual reality systems. In: 2016 IEEE Asia Pacific Conference on Circuits and Systems (APCCAS), pp. 458–460. IEEE (2016)
5. Bowers, B., Rukangu, A., Johnsen, K.: Making it simple: expanding access and lowering barriers to novel interaction devices for virtual and augmented reality. In: 2020 IEEE Conference on Virtual Reality and 3D User Interfaces Abstracts and Workshops (VRW), pp. 1–6. IEEE (2020)

6. Ahuja, K., Islam, R., Parashar, V., Dey, K., Harrison, C., Goel, M.: Eyespyvr: interactive eye sensing using off-the-shelf, smartphone-based vr headsets. Proceedings of the ACM on Interactive, Mobile, Wearable and Ubiquitous Technologies **2**(2), 1–10 (2018)
7. Mathis, F., Williamson, J., Vaniea, K., Khamis, M.: Rubikauth: fast and secure authentication in virtual reality. In: Extended Abstracts of the 2020 CHI Conference on Human Factors in Computing Systems, pp. 1–9 (2020)
8. Olade, I., Liang, H.-N., Fleming, C., Champion, C.: Exploring the vulnerabilities and advantages of swipe or pattern authentication in virtual reality (vr). In Proceedings of the 2020 4th International Conference on Virtual and Augmented Reality Simulations, pp. 45–52 (2020)
9. George, C., Buschek, D., Ngao, A., Khamis, M.: GazeRoomLock: using gaze and head-pose to improve the usability and observation resistance of 3D passwords in virtual reality. In: De Paolis, L.T., Bourdot, P. (eds.) AVR 2020. LNCS, vol. 12242, pp. 61–81. Springer, Cham (2020). https://doi.org/10.1007/978-3-030-58465-8_5
10. George, C., Khamis, M., Buschek, D., Hussmann, H.: Investigating the third dimension for authentication in immersive virtual reality and in the real world. In: 2019 IEEE Conference on Virtual Reality and 3D User Interfaces (VR), pp. 277–285. IEEE (2019)
11. Gurary, J., et al.: Improving the Security of Mobile Devices Through Multi-Dimensional and Analog Authentication. Ph.D. thesis, Cleveland State University (2018)
12. Gurary, J., Zhu, Y., Huirong, F.: Leveraging 3d benefits for authentication. Int. J. Commun. Network Syst. Sci. **10**(8), 324–338 (2017)
13. Duezguen, R., Mayer, P., Das, S., Volkamer, M.: Towards secure and usable authentication for augmented and virtual reality head-mounted displays. arXiv preprint arXiv:2007.11663 (2020)
14. Morrison-Smith, S., et al.: Mmgatorauth: a novel multimodal dataset for authentication interactions in gesture and voice. In: Proceedings of the 2020 International Conference on Multimodal Interaction, pp. 370–377 (2020)
15. Griffith, H.K., Komogortsev, O.V.: Texture feature extraction from free-viewing scan paths using gabor filters with downsampling. In: ACM Symposium on Eye Tracking Research and Applications, pp. 1–3 (2020)
16. Olade, I., Fleming, C., Liang, H.-N.: Biomove: biometric user identification from human kinesiological movements for virtual reality systems. Sensors **20**(10), 2944 (2020)
17. Li, S., Savaliya, S., Marino, L., Leider, A.M., Tappert, C.C.: Brain signal authentication for human-computer interaction in virtual reality. In: 2019 IEEE International Conference on Computational Science and Engineering (CSE) and IEEE International Conference on Embedded and Ubiquitous Computing (EUC), pp. 115–120. IEEE (2019)
18. Ajit, A., Banerjee, N.K., Banerjee, S.: Combining pairwise feature matches from device trajectories for biometric authentication in virtual reality environments. In: 2019 IEEE International Conference on Artificial Intelligence and Virtual Reality (AIVR), pp. 9–97. IEEE Computer Society (2019)
19. Miller, R., Ajit, A., Banerjee, N.K., Banerjee, S.: Realtime behavior-based continual authentication of users in virtual reality environments. In: 2019 IEEE International Conference on Artificial Intelligence and Virtual Reality (AIVR), pp. 253–2531. IEEE (2019)

20. Sivasamy, M., Sastry, V.N., Gopalan, N.P.: Vrcauth: continuous authentication of users in virtual reality environment using head-movement. In: 2020 5th International Conference on Communication and Electronics Systems (ICCES), pp. 518–523. IEEE (2020)

21. Lu, Y., Gao, B., Long, J., Weng, J.: Hand motion with eyes-free interaction for authentication in virtual reality. In: 2020 IEEE Conference on Virtual Reality and 3D User Interfaces Abstracts and Workshops (VRW), pp. 715–716. IEEE (2020)

22. Iskander, J., et al.: A k-nn classification based vr user verification using eye movement and ocular biomechanics. In 2019 IEEE International Conference on Systems, Man and Cybernetics (SMC), pp. 1844–1848. IEEE (2019)

23. Kupin, A., Moeller, B., Jiang, Y., Banerjee, N.K., Banerjee, S.: Task-driven biometric authentication of users in virtual reality (VR) environments. In: Kompatsiaris, I., Huet, B., Mezaris, V., Gurrin, C., Cheng, W.-H., Vrochidis, S. (eds.) MMM 2019. LNCS, vol. 11295, pp. 55–67. Springer, Cham (2019). https://doi.org/10.1007/978-3-030-05710-7_5

24. Mustafa, T., Matovu, R., Serwadda, A., Muirhead, N.: Unsure how to authenticate on your vr headset? come on, use your head! In: Proceedings of the Fourth ACM International Workshop on Security and Privacy Analytics, pp. 23–30 (2018)

25. Miller, R., Banerjee, N.K., Banerjee, S.: Within-system and cross-system behavior-based biometric authentication in virtual reality. In: 2020 IEEE Conference on Virtual Reality and 3D User Interfaces Abstracts and Workshops (VRW), pp. 311–316. IEEE (2020)

26. Luo, S., Nguyen, A., Song, C., Lin, F., Xu, W., Yan, Z.: Oculock: exploring human visual system for authentication in virtual reality head-mounted display. In: 2020 Network and Distributed System Security Symposium (NDSS) (2020)

27. Krishna, V., Ding, Y., Xu, A., Höllerer, T.: Multimodal biometric authentication for vr/ar using eeg and eye tracking. In: Adjunct of the 2019 International Conference on Multimodal Interaction, pp. 1–5 (2019)

28. Khamis, M., Oechsner, C., Alt, F., Bulling, A.: Vrpursuits: interaction in virtual reality using smooth pursuit eye movements. In: Proceedings of the 2018 International Conference on Advanced Visual Interfaces, pp. 1–8 (2018)

29. Iglesias, R., Orozco, M., Alsulaiman, F.A., Valdes, J.J., El Saddik, A.: Characterizing biometric behavior through haptics and virtual reality. In: 2008 42nd Annual IEEE International Carnahan Conference on Security Technology, pp. 174–179. IEEE (2008)

30. Lohr, D., Berndt, S.-H., Komogortsev, O.: An implementation of eye movement-driven biometrics in virtual reality. In: Proceedings of the 2018 ACM Symposium on Eye Tracking Research & Applications, pp. 1–3 (2018)

31. Lohr, D.J., Aziz, S., Komogortsev, O.: Eye movement biometrics using a new dataset collected in virtual reality. In ACM Symposium on Eye Tracking Research and Applications, pp. 1–3 (2020)

Performance and Usability of Visual and Verbal Verification of Word-Based Key Fingerprints

Lee Livsey$^{(\boxtimes)}$ (ID), Helen Petrie (ID), Siamak F. Shahandashti (ID), and Aidan Fray

Department of Computer Science, University of York, York, UK
{lwl501,helen.petrie,siamak.shahandashti}@york.ac.uk

Abstract. The security of messaging applications against person-in-the-middle attacks relies on the authenticity of the exchanged keys. For users unable to meet in person, a manual key fingerprint verification is necessary to ascertain key authenticity. Such fingerprints can be exchanged visually or verbally, and it is not clear in which condition users perform best. This paper reports the results of a 62-participant study that investigated differences in performance and perceived usability of visual and verbal comparisons of word-based key fingerprints, and the influence of the individual's cognitive learning style. The results show visual comparisons to be more effective against non-security critical errors and are perceived to provide increased confidence, yet participants perceive verbal comparisons to be easier and require less mental effort. Besides, limited evidence was found on the influence of the individual's learning style on their performance.

Keywords: Key fingerprint verification · Verbal and visual comparisons · Usability evaluation · Index of learning styles (ILS)

1 Introduction

The use of secure messaging applications has grown rapidly over the last decade, as users seek to reclaim their privacy. An as yet unsolved problem, particularly when users are unable to meet in person, is a usable protocol for authenticated key exchange that eliminates the risk of person-in-the-middle attacks.

Current solutions begin with the exchange of a key-dependent verification message via an out-of-band channel (OOB), which assures the integrity of 'short' messages [7]. If users can meet in person, they may create an OOB channel between their devices and automatically verify the authenticity of each other's public key material (e.g. through NFC or scanning a QR code). This solves the problem for the in-person context, yet such applications are mainly intended for remote communication as it is not always feasible for users to meet in person.

In the remote setting, the OOB channel cannot be directly implemented between devices. The solution is to directly involve users in the comparison of

© IFIP International Federation for Information Processing 2021
Published by Springer Nature Switzerland AG 2021
S. Furnell and N. Clarke (Eds.): HAISA 2021, IFIP AICT 613, pp. 199–210, 2021.
https://doi.org/10.1007/978-3-030-81111-2_17

their *key fingerprints*, short strings usually computed through cryptographic hashing of key materials. If the received fingerprint from the manual OOB channel is identical to that from the communication channel, both users can be assured of the authenticity of the keys they hold and hence the security of their communication. Fingerprints are usually encoded into easy-to-use formats such as chunked numbers (e.g. in Signal/WhatsApp), or dictionary words (e.g. in Pretty Easy Privacy (PEP, www.pep.security)) for Pretty Good Privacy (PGP) keys.

Though comparison of fingerprints avoids the requirement to meet in person, it introduces significant potential for human error and opens an additional attack vector for adversaries. The adversary need only identify a near-collision fingerprint with sufficient similarity to the authentic fingerprint that it is likely to be accepted by an inattentive user. This is a considerably easier task than finding full collisions necessary for a successful attack in the in-person setting.

Historically users tended to compare fingerprints visually, but secure messaging applications increasingly encourage a verbal comparison, a substantially different task that places very different demands upon the user. As there has been no previous investigation of user performance and perceived usability between visual and verbal fingerprint comparisons, a within-participants study is designed to investigate such differences in the context of word-based fingerprints.

The study also investigates the influence of an individual's preferred method to receive and process information, known as *cognitive* or *learning style*, as measured by the Visual–Verbal subscale of the Index of Learning Styles (ILS) [4]. It may be that users have a preference for processing information either verbally or visually, which would affect the development of usable and secure fingerprint verification protocols and to our knowledge is yet to be investigated.

A within-participants study with 62 participants assessed the effectiveness, efficiency and perceived usability of each comparison mode. The results provide valuable insight and demonstrate a complex picture. The answer of which comparison mode is best remains unclear, with the more effective comparison mode also perceived to be less usable.

2   Background and Related Work

Usability issues in secure messaging applications have been extensively studied [12–14,20]. Recent work has identified usability issues specific to the authentication procedures of modern secure messaging applications. Schröder et al. investigated the usability of Signal and found that from a sample of 28 computer science students, 21 were unable to successfully verify their recipient's public key [15]. Related work identified similar issues with WhatsApp, Viber and Telegram, finding that participants were both unaware of the need to verify their recipient's key and unable to do so without additional instruction [6,19].

Dechand et al. performed a detailed investigation of textual fingerprint representations, finding that word-based formats led to higher usability scores and increased attack detection rates than the traditional hexadecimal format [3].

In a similar study, Tan et al. investigated a range of visual and textual fingerprint formats, finding that the performance of visual formats varied and that text-based formats achieved some of the lowest error rates [17]. Both studies simulated visual fingerprint comparisons, with the received fingerprint displayed on a business card. Though verbal comparisons were mentioned by Dechand et al., neither study performed a comparison between visual and verbal modes.

Studies investigating a range of existing device pairing methods identified interesting differences in usability between visual and verbal fingerprint comparisons, but they involve substantially shorter fingerprints that provide sufficient security only for short-range device pairing scenarios [8,9].

There has been considerable psychological and educational research into the concept of different cognitive or learning styles, with many different dimensions and models proposed. However, one of the more robust is visual-verbal processing. While the concept of learning style is controversial [21], and people are undoubtedly flexible in the ways they can process information, they may have preferences which would affect their perception of the usability of an authentication system. The Index of Learning Styles (ILS) was developed to gain insight into the preferred learning styles of engineering students and provide recommendations of how teaching can be adapted accordingly [4]. The ILS is a reliable and valid instrument to assess learning styles, and each of its four dimensions display high test-retest correlation coefficients after intervals of between four weeks and eight months [5,10,16,22]. The Visual–Verbal subscale of the ILS assesses individual preference to receive and process information visually (e.g., through pictures and diagrams) or verbally (e.g., through written or spoken-aloud text).

3   Method

3.1   Design

The study involved a within-participants design with two conditions, with each participant comparing 20 pairs of key fingerprints visually and 20 verbally. The order of taking conditions was counterbalanced. Two of the 20 comparisons were simulated attacks and the others were non-attack comparisons. A low attack rate was used to avoid raising participants' awareness of the possibility of attack and because attacks are uncommon in practice. Participants were asked to simulate an authentication task by matching a fingerprint of five words, either visually or verbally. The five words were selected from the Trustwords word base [11].

Performance was measured by time to make correct comparisons and errors, for both attack and non-attack comparisons. Usability was measured on a set of five-level rating items. Standard usability instruments such as the System Usability Scale (SUS) [1] do not capture all the aspects of the user experience of interest, e.g. trust that the comparison provides security and confidence in one's judgement. Therefore, a specific set of questions was developed (see Table 1).

The Hypotheses investigated were:

H_1 There is a significant difference in time to make the correct decision between the visual and verbal fingerprint comparisons.

Table 1. Dimensions of perceived usability and related concepts

Dimension	Rating items
Efficiency	I was able to do the comparisons very quickly with this method Comparisons using this method were unacceptably long
Ease of use	The method was easy to use The method was unnecessarily complex
Low mental workload	The comparisons did not need much mental effort I needed to concentrate a lot
Confidence	I would need a lot of technical support to be able to use this method I am confident that I can make comparisons using this method without making mistakes
Repeat use	Completing the comparisons using this method was annoying Using this method is worth it for the additional security it provides
Trust	Making comparisons using this method would keep my communications secure I would not trust this method when sending confidential information

H_2 There is a significant difference in the number of errors made using the visual and verbal fingerprint comparisons.

H_3 There is a significant difference in perceived usability ratings between the visual and verbal fingerprint comparisons.

H_4 Participants perform significantly better and report significantly greater perceived usability when the comparison mode aligns with their preferred method to receive and process information.

Ethical principles of no harm and informed consent were followed and formal ethical approval was obtained from the authors' departmental ethics committee.

Security Assumptions. The study assumed the adversary randomly generates a large set of public keys before implementing a person-in-the-middle attack. During the attack, they replace the authentic keys with ones from this set that display maximal similarity to the target fingerprint. This study simulated such an adversary using $2^{21.8}$ distinct PGP public keys scraped from PGP key servers, with optimal attacks found to possess fingerprints with three out of five identical words. The structure of the attacks remained consistent throughout, with all differences confined to the third and fourth words, which is consistent with previous studies [3,17]. The adversary was also assumed to be unable to manipulate any messages exchanged over the OOB channel.

Table 2. Age distribution.

Age	Count
18–24	2
25–34	22
35–44	22
45–64	14
65 and over	1
Prefer not to say	1

Table 3. Education background.

Highest education level	Count
High School education	9
Vocational training	4
Bachelors degree	32
Postgraduate degree	13
Other	3
Prefer not to say	1

3.2 Participants

Several methods of participant recruitment were used: through the University of York network, the authors' personal contacts, and through Amazon Mechanical Turk (MTurk). Participants recruited from local networks were entered into a prize draw, whilst participants from MTurk were paid USD 2.00. Some researchers have raised doubts about the care with which MTurk participants undertake tasks [2], but others have found that MTurk participants produce data of equal quality to those recruited in more traditional ways [18]. Therefore, it was decided to use both more traditional recruitment methods and MTurk and compare data from the two sources. No differences in responses were detected between the two groups (comparisons were made on times, errors and responses to rating questions), so results are presented for the whole sample.

In total, 75 people responded to the study, but data from 13 participants were eliminated: 2 experienced network errors, 8 provided a partial response, and 1 failed to identify a totally mismatching attention check. Data from 2 participants who are dyslexic was also eliminated. Both comparison modes involve reading words, including unusual words, which may be difficult for people with dyslexia. All participants whose data were excluded were still rewarded for their time.

Data from 62 participants were analysed, 25 men (40%), 36 women (58%) and one who identified as non-binary. Age ranged from 18–24 to over 65, with the majority being in the 25–44 years range (71%, see Table 2). Educational level ranged from high school education to postgraduate degree, with the majority having a bachelors or postgraduate degree (73%, see Table 3). As the experimental task involves reading and listening, participants were asked whether they had a visual or hearing impairment, none reported any. For the same reason, participants were asked about their proficiency in English; 98% (61/62) rated it as good or excellent, and one as average. There were 29 participants recruited via the local networks, all located in the UK except one from the USA. There were 33 participants recruited via MTurk, all in the USA. Participants responses showed 94% (58/62) use at least one secure messaging application, and 60% (37/62) do so every day. Furthermore, 87% (54/62) of participants agree that 'it is important to be able to have private conversations using secure

Fig. 1. Visual comparison task interface.

Fig. 2. Verbal comparison task interface.

messaging applications', yet 82% (51/62) of participants have never performed a fingerprint comparison.

3.3 Materials and Task

A web application was developed to enable participants to interact with mockups of two mobile devices and compare fingerprints, with PEP over PGP used as a template for the secure messaging application. PEP was chosen as it includes a word-based fingerprint representation which have been shown to provide high usability and low error rates. PEP uses a word list called Trustwords to replace every 16 bits of the hashed key with one word from Trustwords, hence resulting in five-word fingerprints to represent 80-bit hashes [11]. PEP is supported by popular email clients such as Mozilla Thunderbird.

The visual condition simulated a fingerprint exchange by text message (see Fig. 1). The verbal condition simulated an exchange by voice (e.g. by phone) by playing a recorded reading of the words (see Fig. 2). The web application did not allow study completion on small screens (e.g. smartphones) that could not display the two virtual devices side by side. The 11 forced-choice questions of the ILS Visual–Verbal subscale (see Sect. 2) were used to measure individuals' preferences for receiving and processing information. The subscale is scored from −11 (if all questions are answered with a verbal preference) to +11 (if all questions are answered with a visual preference).

A post-task questionnaire assessed the perceived usability of each condition. Six dimensions of usability and related concepts were identified as being of interest and two five-level rating scale items were used to measure each dimension (see Table 1). The scoring of items was reversed as appropriate so that a high number always indicates high usability. A post-study questionnaire asked participants which condition they preferred, their previous experiences using secure messaging applications and also collected demographic information.

3.4 Procedure

Before running the main study, a pilot study was conducted with four participants similar in characteristics to the target sample. This led to improvements in the explanation of the task (e.g. to clarify that participants were expected to make multiple comparisons in each condition). Several issues identified in the web application were also resolved. The main study procedure was as follows:

1. An information sheet explained the aims of the study, described the tasks participants would undertake and the data to be collected. Participants were asked to confirm that they were over 18 and to consent to participation.
2. Participants were asked two screening questions: if they could view an image displayed upon their device and if they could play and hear a sound clip. This ensured that participants' devices supported the experimental conditions.
3. Participants then completed the Visual–Verbal subscale of the ILS.
4. Participants were randomly assigned to complete either the visual or verbal condition, compared the 20 fingerprints in that condition, and answered a post-task questionnaire to assess the perceived usability of that condition.
5. The above step was then repeated for the other condition.
6. Participants then answered the post-study questionnaire.
7. Participants were then thanked and provided with the relevant reward.

4 Results

Data did not meet the requirements for parametric statistics (normality, homogeneity of variance), so non-parametric statistics were used, with medians and semi-interquartile range (SIQR) as measures of central tendency and spread. To compare between conditions, Wilcoxon related samples non-parametric tests were used. To compare participants with different information styles, Kruskal–Wallis tests were used.

4.1 Performance: Task Completion Time and Errors

The time to complete correct comparisons did not differ significantly between the visual and verbal modes for either the attack or non-attack trials, as tested by Wilcoxon signed-rank tests for related samples (see Table 4). Thus H_1, that there is a difference between the times on the two conditions, was not supported.

Table 4. Median times (seconds) and SIQR on correct comparisons for verbal and visual conditions with Wilcoxon signed rank tests of differences between conditions

	Verbal	Visual	Wilcoxon W	p-value
Attack comparisons	5.49 (0.75)	5.50 (1.04)	0.22	0.83
Non-attack comparisons	6.15 (0.55)	6.52 (1.96)	1.20	0.23

In general, participants did not make many errors (i.e. identifying a non-attack comparison as an attack or missing an attack comparison). There were only 2 attack comparisons in each condition, so errors could range from 0 to 2. There were 17 non-attack comparisons, so errors could range from 0 to 17. Figures 3 and 4 show the distribution of errors for the non-attack and attack comparisons. There was a difference in errors between the two conditions, with participants making significantly more errors in the verbal non-attack condition than in the visual non-attack condition (see Table 5). Thus H_2, that there will be a difference between the errors on the two conditions, was supported.

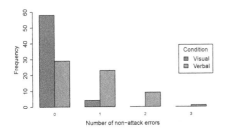
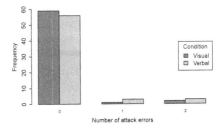

Fig. 3. Number of errors by each participant on 17 non-attack comparisons

Fig. 4. Number of errors by each participant on 2 attack comparisons

Table 5. Median errors on correct comparisons and SIQR for verbal and visual comparison conditions with Wilcoxon Signed Rank tests of differences between conditions

	Verbal	Visual	Wilcoxon W	p-value
Attack comparisons	0 (0.0)	0 (0.0)	1.19	0.23
Non-attack comparisons	1 (0.5)	0 (0.0)	4.84	< 0.01

4.2 Perceived Usability and Related Concepts

The ratings on the two items for all six dimensions of perceived usability and related concepts were all highly correlated (Spearman's ρ between 0.31 and 0.82, all $p < 0.01$), so median scores were calculated for each dimension and used in subsequent analyses. Table 6 shows participants' median ratings for the six dimensions for the visual and verbal conditions. There was a significant difference on the low mental workload dimension ($p < 0.01$), with the verbal condition perceived to require less mental workload than the visual condition. There was a strong trend towards a difference on the ease of use dimension ($p = 0.06$), with the verbal condition rated as easier than the visual condition. There was also a significant difference on the confidence dimension ($p = 0.02$). Although the median ratings were the same, inspection of the distributions showed that more participants had confidence in the visual condition than the verbal condition. These results show partial support for H_3, that there is a difference in the perceived usability of the two conditions, with the verbal condition being perceived as more usable on two out of six dimensions. In addition, at the end of the study, participants were asked which comparison mode they would prefer to use, verbal or visual. There was an almost even split between preferences for each system, with 53.2% choosing verbal and 46.8% choosing visual. This was not a significant difference ($\chi^2 = 0.26$, $p = 0.61$).

Table 6. Median ratings (with SIQR) of the perceived usability dimensions for verbal and visual conditions and Wilcoxon Signed Rank tests of differences between conditions

Dimension	Verbal	Visual	Wilcoxon W	p-value
Efficiency	4.00 (1.00)	4.00 (1.00)	0.22	0.83
Ease of use	4.50 (0.50)	4.25 (0.75)	1.84	0.06
Low mental workload	4.00 (0.82)	3.00 (1.00)	4.21	<0.01
Confidence	4.50 (0.50)	4.50 (0.75)	2.39	0.02
Repeat use	4.00 (0.75)	3.50 (1.00)	1.35	0.18
Trust	4.00 (0.82)	4.00 (1.00)	0.76	0.45

4.3 Effect of Preferred Information Style: Verbal Versus Visual

The participants' scores on the Visual–Verbal subscale of the ILS were skewed towards the visual end of the scale. To create groups of approximately equal size for analysis, participants were divided into three groups: Very Visual (scores 7 to 11, 23 participants); Moderately Visual (scores 1 to 5, 21 participants); and Verbal (scores −1 to −9, 18 participants).

There were no significant differences in time to complete correct comparisons in either the verbal or visual conditions between the three groups of participants. Nor were there any significant differences in the errors made on the attack comparisons. However, all three groups made significantly more errors in the verbal condition than in the visual condition (Wilcoxon related samples tests, Very Visual: $W = 2.95$, Moderately Visual: $W = 2.88$, Verbal: $W = 2.64$, all $p < 0.01$). This does not support H_4, which predicted verbal users make more errors on the visual condition and visual users make more errors on the verbal condition.

5   Discussion and Conclusions

This paper reported the results of the first investigation of differences in effectiveness, efficiency and perceived usability between visual and verbal comparisons of word-based key fingerprints.

Participants were found to make more non-attack errors when using a verbal comparison mode. One explanation for this result is that it is easier to mishear than misread a word. Without asking for the word to be spelt out, users are unable to check the spelling of any unfamiliar spoken words, and this uncertainty may cause users to reject fingerprints that they would otherwise accept if a visual comparison mode was used. This explanation gains further support since participants perceived that the visual condition provided increased confidence that they were getting the comparisons correct. In contrast, the verbal condition was perceived to require less mental effort and be easier to use. Since fingerprint comparisons are a secondary task to actual communication, these factors may motivate them to choose a verbal comparison mode even though visual comparisons would provide increased effectiveness and confidence.

Even though visual comparisons were shown to be effective and perceived to provide increased usability in two of the six dimensions assessed, practical examples of secure messaging applications largely encourage the use of a verbal comparison mode and tend not to support or encourage visual comparisons. Given these findings, it seems some users would benefit from applications adding increased support for both visual and verbal fingerprint comparisons.

A surprising result was the lack of effect between comparison mode and Visual–Verbal subscale score. One interpretation is that the main effect of comparison mode dominates, and visual comparisons are significantly more effective against non-attack errors for all users. However, care must be taken before reaching this conclusion given the sample's skew towards participants with a visual preference to receive and process information. Further research, that includes a greater proportion of participants with a verbal preference, is required to clarify this. Another explanation is that the Visual–Verbal subscale does not measure the intended phenomena and an alternative scale may be more appropriate. 7 of the 11 Visual–Verbal subscale questions actually provide 2 visual responses (e.g. written text or diagrams). Future work will attempt to identify a measure of difference between auditory and visual preferences to receive information.

All the fingerprints in this study were based on the Trustwords representation of PEP over PGP. The Trustwords word base contains many unusual and unfamiliar words which may have contributed to the increased number of non-attack errors in the verbal condition. Future research may include fingerprints in other representations (e.g. the numeric representation used by Signal/WhatsApp) to determine if the effects observed in this study are specific to the Trustwords representation or fundamental properties of a fingerprint verification.

A limitation of the study was that each condition included only two attacks. Though there were good reasons for the low attack rate, it made identification of a significant effect between conditions difficult. Furthermore, attacks lacked enough similarity and participants identified them with ease. Future work will include a greater number of attack trials that display greater similarity.

The answer to which comparison mode is best remains unclear. Visual comparisons were found to be more effective against non-security errors and perceived to provide increased confidence, yet verbal comparisons were perceived to be easier and require less mental effort. Though participants often displayed a preference for a particular comparison mode (based on measures of both performance and perceived usability), this did not correlate with their score on the Visual–Verbal subscale of the ILS. The results show that identification of the optimal comparison mode and the related influence of a user's cognitive learning style on key fingerprint comparisons remain unclear. These present complex and interesting research questions that require further investigation.

References

1. Brooke, J.: SUS: a quick and dirty usability scale. Usability Eval. Ind. **189**, 189–195 (1996)
2. Chandler, J., Mueller, P., Paolacci, G.: Nonnaïveté among amazon mechanical turk workers: consequences and solutions for behavioral researchers. Behav. Res. Methods **46**(1), 112–130 (2014)
3. Dechand, S., Schürmann, D., Busse, K., Acar, Y., Fahl, S., Smith, M.: An empirical study of textual key-fingerprint representations. In: USENIX Security, pp. 193–208 (2016)
4. Felder, R.M., Silverman, L.K., et al.: Learning and teaching styles in engineering education. Eng. Educ. **78**(7), 674–681 (1988)
5. Felder, R.M., Spurlin, J.: Applications, reliability and validity of the index of learning styles. Int. J. Eng. Educ. **21**(1), 103–112 (2005)
6. Herzberg, A., Leibowitz, H.: Can Johnny finally encrypt? evaluating E2E-encryption in popular IM applications. In: STAST 2016, pp. 17–28. ACM (2016)
7. Kainda, R., Flechais, I., Roscoe, A.W.: Usability and security of out-of-band channels in secure device pairing protocols. In: SOUPS, p. 11. ACM (July 2009)
8. Kobsa, A., Sonawalla, R., Tsudik, G., Uzun, E., Wang, Y.: Serial hook-ups: a comparative usability study of secure device pairing methods. In: SOUPS, pp. 1–12. ACM (2009)
9. Kumar, A., Saxena, N., Tsudik, G., Uzun, E.: Caveat eptor: a comparative study of secure device pairing methods. In: IEEE PerCom, pp. 1–10, (March 2009)
10. Livesay, G.A., Dee, K.C., Nauman, E.A., Hites, L.S. Jr.: Engineering student learning styles: a statistical analysis using felder's index of learning styles. In: Annual Conference of the American Society for Engineering Education (2002)
11. Marques, H., Hoeneisen, B.: pretty Easy privacy (pEp): Contact and Channel Authentication through Handshake. IETF Network Working Group, Draft (2020)
12. Orman, H.: Why won't Johnny encrypt? IEEE Internet Comput. **19**(1), 90–94 (2015)
13. Ruoti, S., Andersen, J., Zappala, D., Seamons, K.: Why Johnny still, still can't encrypt: Evaluating the usability of a modern PGP client. arXiv: 1510.08555 (2015)
14. Ruoti, S., Kim, N., Burgon, B., van der Horst, T., Seamons, K.: Confused Johnny: when automatic encryption leads to confusion and mistakes. In: SOUPS, pp. 1–12. ACM (2013)
15. Schröder, S., Huber, M., Wind, D., Rottermanner, C.: When SIGNAL hits the fan: On the usability and security of State-of-the-Art secure mobile messaging. In: 1st European Workshop on Usable Security. Internet Society (2016)
16. Seery, N., Gaughran, W.F., Waldmann, T.: Multi-modal learning in engineering education. In: ASEE Conference and Exposition. Society for Engineering Education (2003)

17. Tan, J., Bauer, L., Bonneau, J., Cranor, L.F., Thomas, J., Ur, B.: Can unicorns help users compare crypto key fingerprints? In: CHI 2017, pp. 3787–3798 (2017)
18. Thomas, K.A., Clifford, S.: Validity and mechanical turk: an assessment of exclusion methods and interactive experiments. Comput. Human Behav. **77**, 184–197 (2017)
19. Vaziripour, E., et al.: Is that you, Alice? a usability study of the authentication ceremony of secure messaging applications. SOUPS **2017**, 29–47 (2017)
20. Whitten, A. and Tygar, J.D.: Why Johnny can't encrypt: a usability evaluation of PGP 5.0. In USENIX Security, vol. 348. USENIX (1999)
21. Willingham, D.T., Hughes, E.M., Dobolyi, D.G.: The scientific status of learning styles theories. Teach. Psychol. **42**(3), 266–271 (2015)
22. Zywno, M.S.: A contribution to validation of score meaning for Felder-Soloman's index of learning styles. In: ASEE Annual Conference, vol. 119 (2003)

The One-Eyed Leading the Blind: Understanding Differences Between IT Professionals and Non-IT Staff When Creating and Managing Passwords

Paul Brockbanks and Martin J. Butler[✉] 🆔

Stellenbosch University, Stellenbosch, South Africa
martin.butler@usb.ac.za

Abstract. Passwords remains the standard mechanism by which organisations protect their data from unauthorised entities accessing, changing or misusing their information. Organisations go to great lengths to educate their workers on the importance of creating and maintaining secure passwords.

Extensive research has been conducted on how users create and manage their passwords. To date, there is limited insight on how the behaviour of IT workers may differ from that of non-IT workers. It is generally assumed that IT workers have a greater understanding of what a secure password entails and how insecure password behaviour may put an organisation's resources at risk by the nature of their roles. Consequently, they are expected to have a positive influence on non-IT workers' password behaviour.

This research sets out to test this assumption. The findings suggest significant differences between the password practices applied when IT and non-IT workers create and manage their passwords. However, poor security behaviour by both IT and non-IT workers was evident.

Keywords: Human behaviour · IT · Non-IT · Passwords · Security · Password-fatigue · Users

1 Introduction

Passwords remain the most common control mechanism for authenticating a user's identity when accessing a system [1]. It serves as the first line of defence against unauthorised access [2]. Passwords are generally governed by specific criteria that should be used to secure passwords and improve security [3].

Employees working outside the IT function often turn to their colleagues in the IT department to create strong passwords and help manage them [4]. The different roles of non-IT and IT workers may contribute to differences in their understanding of security issues [5]. It was suggested that IT workers better understand access rules' value and purpose than other users [6]. By the nature of their role, IT workers may have had more

© IFIP International Federation for Information Processing 2021
Published by Springer Nature Switzerland AG 2021
S. Furnell and N. Clarke (Eds.): HAISA 2021, IFIP AICT 613, pp. 211–222, 2021.
https://doi.org/10.1007/978-3-030-81111-2_18

exposure to password security best practices than non-IT workers. IT workers implement and monitor the security policies and have extensive system access, and should have increased awareness of what constitutes a safe password and how to secure it properly [7].

However, IT workers may not be as security-conscious as expected. Despite their assumed additional password security awareness, it may be possible that IT workers are a 'weak link in the chain'. This study aimed to investigate whether IT workers applied more secure password practices than non-IT workers.

2 Prior Research

2.1 User Generated Passwords

The growing dependence on systems that contains sensitive data has given rise to individuals or groups that seek to access this information with malicious intent [8]. Although user passwords have been the cornerstone of authentication for over 50 years, very little has changed regarding the user experience [9]. A user typically logs onto a system by providing a unique identifier and password. The security mechanism then verifies the match between the user identifier and the password; if both are correct and valid, the user is granted access to the system [10].

The strength of a password lies in its resistance to malicious activities [11]. A password is only useful to the extent that it denies access to organisation assets to adversaries [12]. For example, the greater the length and the larger number of different characters, the more resistant the password will be [3].

The composition of passwords also contributes to their strength. Passwords based on dictionary membership or containing repeated characters or consecutive sequences, are weaker and may be easily guessed [13]. There are nearly three trillion possible eight-character password combinations using the 26 letters of the alphabet and the numerals 0 to 9 [14]. Despite this large pool of possibilities, users prefer to create easy to remember passwords [15].

Kaplan-Leiserson [16] suggested that 70% of security breaches were indirectly or directly due to staff's actions within companies. The 2020 Data Breach Investigations report [17] clarifies that although most threat actors are external to the organisation, they often exploit internal staff vulnerabilities.

These vulnerabilities could include poor password creation practices (e.g. creating passwords that are easy to guess), poor password management practices (e.g. reusing passwords), or falling victims to social phishing. Although the threat actors may be external, they exploit employees insecure practices, damaging consequences for organisations [18].

2.2 Defining and Categorizing Password Practices

Butler and Butler [19] separated password activities into creation and management practices (Fig. 1). Although this presents a valuable lens to analyse the different practices, not all user actions fall distinctly into either creation or management activities. For example, the practice of reusing passwords does not fit uniquely into these categories since it is a password management practice, but the application manifests during passwords creation. As such, password reuse measures are defined as creation and management activities (refer to Fig. 1 and Table 1).

Password policy restrictions may include users having to choose passwords that contain characters outside of the 26-letter alphabet, uppercase characters, lowercase characters, digits and symbols. When users create passwords, dictionary membership may also be automatically checked by the system to ensure that no common passwords are created [20]. Policy restrictions often enforce more secure creation practices. Password management rules guide users to manage their passwords securely, once created. It is more difficult, if not impossible, to measure the level of compliance with management practices [12].

Florêncio et al. [11] observed that usability imperatives played a role in implementing an organisation's password policies. Kelley et al. [21] questioned the use of strict policies by suggesting that administrators have steadily increased the requirement for more complex passwords, even when the value thereof is poorly understood. Password policies may have been created decades ago when it was assumed that minimum length and complex character sets made it more difficult for passwords to be guessed [22].

Hicock [23] challenged some conventional beliefs and indicated that several policies might be unnecessary or too onerous for the user. The term 'anti-patterns' was adopted to describe these common but questionable security practices [24]. Examples of anti-patterns include the belief that passwords should contain multiple character sets, including the need for passwords to consist of a combination of uppercase, lowercase and numeric characters. It is suggested that this approach is not practical as threat actors looking to guess passwords have already included substitutions in the standard dictionary. Toulouse [25] supports Hicock's view by highlighting, in his view, the much-needed shift from a purist approach that relies exclusively on complex and strict rules to an approach that recognises the challenges that users face when trying to manage passwords more efficiently while keeping them safe.

The challenge of conventional views on security practices extends to the management practices as well. For example, Herley [26] argues that preventing users from writing down passwords increases the user's burden, whilst offering marginal security gain in return. Zhang-Kennedy [12] support this view by suggesting a significant usability gain by allowing a practice that presents a slight security risk. Examples of this gain include the increased ability of users to create multiple passwords across different systems and provide a mechanism to allow users to compose more complicated passwords [27].

Despite these valid questions about common passwords security believes, in this article, and aligned with the data available for analysis, the conventional beliefs about stronger passwords and more desirable management practices are used to analyse the difference between the practices applied by IT and non-IT users.

2.3 Unsafe Passwords Creation and Management Practices

Users continue to adopt methods that may not be secure, despite being provided with security guidelines and policies [28]. Undesirable password creation practices include more complex and longer passwords and not using common words or numbers that can be easily recognized [29]. The management practices that are not desirable includes writing down and sharing passwords.

According to Adams, Sasse and Lunt [30], writing down passwords started when it became customary for users to receive a system-generated password that was difficult to remember. Adams and Sasse [31] suggested that whilst system-generated passwords provided the optimal security approach, user-generated passwords were potentially more memorable and less likely to be written down. The writing down of passwords has conventionally been seen as an insecure practice [32]. It is one of the many risky behaviours that undermine system security [33]. Nearly four decades ago, Porter [34] suggested that once one has written down a password, it is no longer a password.

However, recording passwords as a security practice is not as generalizable as it would seem at first glance. Although users may think that password rules are complex and write down passwords to remember them, there are secure ways to achieve this without compromising security [35]. For example, using a password manager or keeping a written down password in safekeeping could be desirable if correctly applied by users [36].

As with the reuse and writing down of passwords, sharing passwords has conventionally been seen as a risk to system security [31]. Sharing of passwords defeats the underlying purpose of the identification process [12]. Adams and Sasse [31] dams and Sasse (1999) noted that passwords were often shared among work colleagues and friends due to practical and convenience reasons. Weirich and Sasse [33] suggested multiple reasons why users may feel compelled to share passwords, such as circumstances at work necessitating sharing a password to enable a colleague to access the system on their behalf or being pressured to share their passwords by a superior. Users may also feel safe providing passwords to those more technically capable than themselves when seeking support with a task or needing technical assistance. The inability to memorize the increasing number of passwords is no doubt a contributing factor to sharing passwords [37].

Although the reuse of passwords is common among users, it may allow a threat actor to access many systems with one password [32]. A password initially created on a low-security system may ultimately be used on a secure system that contains confidential information [38]. Ives and Walsh [39] refer to this as the 'Domino Effect', highlighting that once the weakest password has failed, other systems accessed may provide more password information that, in turn, may cause more systems to be compromised.

3 Research Problem and Objectives

Business managers find the impact of security policies on productivity more important than IT professionals, whose primary concern appears to be the system's security [40]. However, Shay et al. [41] suggest that IT users are less likely to share their passwords than non-IT users and prefer security policies that are more stringent than more user-friendly policies that may have fewer security attributes.

Both IT and non-IT users expressed overall dissatisfaction with the state of current password rules but differed on the reasons for this dissatisfaction. IT users were more likely to indicate that IT policies were thought through and sensible [42]. However, both sets of users suggested that they could envisage scenarios where they would circumvent security rules.

Loutfi and Jøsang [7] suggest that IT professionals' tacit knowledge of safe passwords practices does not always translate into safe practices. IT professionals used unsafe methods to store passwords and did not create complex passwords unless forced to do so [7]. One area that IT users appeared to perform well in was memorising longer passwords (more than eight characters). The authors concluded by suggesting that whilst IT users were aware of what constituted correct password behaviour, in many instances, they failed to translate this awareness into practice.

Although numerous studies have been conducted to understand users' behaviour and their motivation when creating or safeguarding their passwords [43], it is unclear whether IT workers, who may be seen as setting the standard, really possess greater knowledge or behave more securely than non-IT workers. This study's primary objective was to compare how IT and non-IT workers create and manage their user-generated passwords.

4   Research Methods

The focus on security awareness within financial services institutions made it an ideal environment for research focusing on how IT and non-IT workers secured their user-generated passwords. IT workers were defined as those with a direct technical executions responsibility, that forms part of the organisation's IT department. The grouping of IT users includes all the different IT roles and is not limited to security professionals. Respondents not within the IT services organisations were classified as non-IT users.

The financial institution selected for this research conducts regular IT security awareness campaigns and surveys. The data collected through surveys is used to ascertain IT security awareness amongst the staff and determine the need for awareness campaigns. The organisation surveyed employees to understand how they secured their user-generated passwords. Confidentiality is ensured by restricting responses to predefined options and not collecting any information that may be linked back to an employee. Data collected as part of the original survey was made available to the researchers after obtaining ethical clearance.

An inferential analysis follows a descriptive study to test for a significant difference between IT and non-IT workers in securing their passwords. The data contained responses from 182 employees, of which 118 (65%) were classified as non-IT users and 64 (35%) as IT users. The data were analysed through t-tests that checked for significant difference (p-value < 0.05) between IT and non-IT users' responses.

5   Research Results

5.1   Descriptive Analysis

Figure 1 depicts the descriptive data indicating poor password practices among IT and non-IT users. The data (that is more granular than presented) contained responses both in the negative (non-desirable action or lack of action), and the positive (desirable action or absence of non-desirable action). The detailed data was summarised to provide a single measure in the negative (higher result is less desirable) for descriptive purposes. Only 19% of the IT user group reported *using random characters* in their passwords. Within the non-IT user group, 11% of the users reported using random characters in their passwords. Both IT (49%) and non-IT (52%) users *included descriptive names* when creating their passwords.

Within the IT user group, 39% of the users reported *using sequential numbers or dates* in passwords. Whilst there is a significant difference with 57% of non-IT users engaging in this insecure practice, any use of sequential numbers is a security risk. Patterns in passwords created using recognisable number combinations may enable language-independent password guessing algorithms to exploit passwords that can be used to gain successful entry into systems [29].

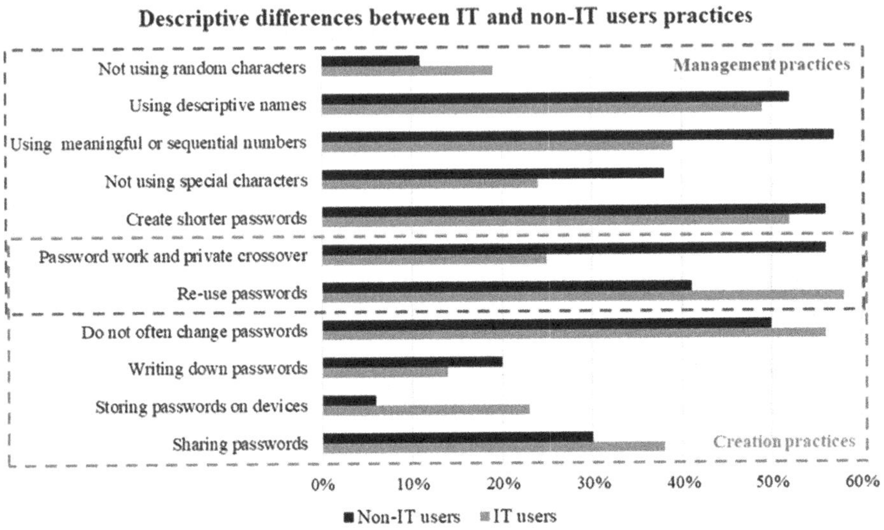

Descriptive differences between IT and non-IT users practices

Fig. 1. Descriptive difference between IT and non-IT users (n = 182)

A total of 76% of IT users reported *using special characters* (i.e. %$_*#) compared to 62% of the non-IT user group. In terms of *password length*, IT-users outperformed non-IT-users significantly with 44% versus 20%, respectively creating passwords of nine characters or longer. It is plausible that IT-users may have developed methods like passwords phrases to remember long passwords.

One significant difference is using passwords for *both private purposes and access to work systems*. Within the IT user group, 25% of the users used the same or a similar password in the workplace as they did in their private capacity, compared to 56% in the non-IT user group. Similarly, both IT (69%) and non-IT (62%) users *reused passwords* across some or all of their applications. Once one particular password has been breached, other applications that use the same password become vulnerable.

Both IT (58%) and non-IT (41%) users indicated that they reused the same or similar passwords when creating new passwords. Password reuse may be caused by the number of different passwords that users must create and the challenge to remember them

[31]. Password expiration policies may also contribute to password reuse. Hicock [23] challenged the use of password expiration policies since they may force users to create more predictable passwords that include sequential words.

IT-users *change their passwords* more frequently than non-IT users and are less likely to write them down. Within the IT user group, 14% of the users reported *writing down their passwords*, and 20% of the non-IT user groups did. Both IT (23%) and non-IT (6%) users indicated that they *stored their passwords* on devices. Storing passwords on other devices is a common practice amongst users and may be a safe way of keeping track of passwords, as long as these devices cannot be accessed by another user [12]. Given that no further data about these devices being available, this study defines it as an unsafe practice.

Both IT (38%) and non-IT (30%) users indicated that they *shared their passwords* with other users. Zhang-Kennedy et al. [12] suggest that the sharing of passwords defeats the underlying purpose of the identification process, maintaining a one-to-one mapping of the users' identification and the data that they are authorised to access.

5.2 Inferential Analysis

The primary objective of this study was to compare how IT and non-IT workers secured their passwords. It is evident from Table 1 that there is no significant difference between IT and non-IT users' behaviour in five of the eleven data points measured, whilst six indicate a significant difference between IT and non-IT users.

A trend is evident once the practices are categorized as creation and management practices. In all instances of significant differences in creation practices, IT users displayed more desirable practices and could provide more secure examples and guidance. However, when investigating the two management practices where a statistical difference exists, non-IT users display the more desirable behaviour.

IT-users thus do not practice examples to follow, or may not be able to provide correct guidance, unless other factors lead to their less secure behaviour, for example, the burden to have more passwords. However, it is concerning that IT users' passwords with system-level access may conceivably provide access to more valuable information resources.

Table 1. Inferential differences between IT and non-IT users (n = 182)

Practice group	Criteria tested	Statistically significant	P value	More desirable behavior group
Creation	Password length	Yes	0.00003	IT users
Creation	Using descriptive names	No	0.75618	-
Creation	Using meaningful or sequential numbers	Yes	0.01938	IT users

(continued)

Table 1. (*continued*)

Practice group	Criteria tested	Statistically significant	P value	More desirable behavior group
Creation	Not using special characters	Yes	0.04412	IT users
Creation	Using random characters	No	0.13797	-
Creation & Management	Password work and personal cross-over	Yes	0.00002	IT users
Creation & Management	Reuse passwords	Yes	0.02810	Non-IT users
Management	Not regularity changing passwords	No	0.30239	-
Management	Writing down passwords	No	0.31091	-
Management	Storing passwords on devices	Yes	0.00232	Non-IT users
Management	Sharing passwords	No	0.25127	-

One plausible cause for poor password practices is password fatigue, measured by questions on the number of passwords to be remembered. Within the IT user group, 18% needed to remember more than ten passwords, compared to only 2% in the non-IT group. When analysing the detailed data, there was a statistically significant difference ($p > 0.001$) in the number of workplace passwords used between IT and non-IT users, indicating that IT users may be under more pressure to use less secure coping mechanisms.

6   Managerial Implications and Recommendations

Prior research suggests that IT workers' assumed knowledge of safe password practices does not always translate into safe practices [7]. This research supports this suggestion and advises that both IT and non-IT workers engage in insecure password creation and management practices.

Organisations need to continue focusing on external security threats exploiting internal weaknesses that expose their assets to potential security breaches. Organisations should acknowledge and correct perceptions that differences in roles between IT and non-IT workers may contribute to differences in their security knowledge and practices. Therefore, we recommend that managers ensure that sufficient and equal attention is paid to IT and non-IT workers whilst educating them on the importance of password security. Organisations should not blindly rely on IT workers to educate non-IT workers on safe password practices.

The research highlights a potential link between the number of passwords that a user must remember and users' coping mechanisms. In the omnipresence of online systems requiring authentication credentials, IT-users' insecure behaviour could be linked to password fatigue. It should serve as a warning for organisations exposing non-IT employees to an increasing number of systems. The findings suggest that using coping mechanisms, such as password reuse and storing passwords on devices, may be avoided if employers limit the number of passwords they require their workers to use.

The general assumption that IT workers apply more secure password behaviours than non-IT workers may be incorrect. This assumption may be placing organisations at financial and reputational risk, warranting further research.

7   Limitations and Future Research

The research is limited by the validity of the measures that define poor password practices. It is acknowledged that specific policies traditionally seen as desirable (e.g. longer passwords or regularly changing passwords) are no longer above approach in the current academic discourse.

Some practices like recording passwords need to be defined and measured at a more granular level to improve the robustness of the research. The recording of passwords once for safe storing or in a secure online password manager should instead be viewed as desirable practice and recorded distinct from recording in a non-secure manner. More attention should be given to the constructs that typically define desirable and not desirable behaviours.

In addition, the research does not take into account practices that may vary due to the nature of the information assets being protected. It is also acknowledged that the study was performed in a single company within financial services in South Africa. Since it is plausible that there may be a difference between industries and cultural differences between countries, it is recommended that future sampling to validate the findings use samples covering multiple industries and, if possible, geographic locations.

The research is also limited by not checking for cross-loadings and relationships between specific practices. Additional insight may be gained from different clusters and associations that could explain more behavioural differences.

Given the findings of this research that suggest that IT workers do not generally display more secure passwords practices than non-IT workers, future research focusing specifically on IT workers' behaviours and coping strategies is required. Further analysis of the data may indicate if IT workers are indeed the 'weak link in the chain' or if the increased number of passwords are the drivers of non-secure behaviour.

References

1. Kävrestad, J., Lennartsson, M., Birath, M., Nohlberg, M.: Constructing secure and memorable passwords. Inf. Comput. Secur. **28**(5), 701–717 (2020). https://doi.org/10.1108/ICS-07-2019-0077

2. Gehringer, E.F.: Choosing passwords: security and human factors. In: IEEE 2002 International Symposium on Technology and Society (ISTAS'02). Social Implications of Information and Communication Technology. Proceedings (Cat. No.02CH37293), pp. 369–373 (2002). https://doi.org/10.1109/ISTAS.2002.1013839

3. Butler, R., Butler, M.: Some password users are more equal than others: towards customisation of online security initiatives. SA J. Inf. Manag. **20**(1), 1 (2018). https://doi.org/10.4102/sajim.v20i1.920

4. Al Awawdeh, S., Tubaishat, A.: An information security awareness program to address common security concerns in IT unit. In: Proceedings of 11th International Conference on Information Technology: New Generation – ITNG 2014, pp. 273–278 (2014). https://doi.org/10.1109/ITNG.2014.67

5. Guo, K.H.: Security-related behavior in using information systems in the workplace: a review and synthesis. Comput. Secur. **32**(1), 242–251 (2013). https://doi.org/10.1016/j.cose.2012.10.003

6. Kothari, V., Blythe, J., Smith, S.W., Koppel, R.: Measuring the security impacts of password policies using cognitive behavioral agent-based modeling. In: ACM International Conference Proceedings, pp. 1–9, 21–22 April 2015. https://doi.org/10.1145/2746194.2746207

7. Loutfi, I., Jøsang, A.: Passwords are not always stronger on the other side of the fence. In: Proceedings Networks and Distributed Systems Security Conference USEC Work, no. February, pp. 1–10 (2015). https://doi.org/10.14722/usec.2015.23005

8. Kumar, A., Singh, P.: Information technology as facilitator of workforce. Bus. Manag. Dyn. **3**(12), 15–20 (2014)

9. Bonneau, J., Herley, C., van Oorschot, P.C., Stajano, F.: Passwords and the evolution of imperfect authentication. Commun. ACM **58**(7), 78–87 (2015)

10. Bishop, M., Klein, D.V.: Improving system security via proactive password checking. Comput. Secur. **14**(3), 233–249 (1995). https://doi.org/10.1016/0167-4048(95)00003-Q

11. Florêncio, D., Herley, C.: Where do security policies come from? In: Proceedings of the Sixth Symposium on Usable Privacy and Security – SOUPS 2010, p. 1 (2010). https://doi.org/10.1145/1837110.1837124

12. Zhang-Kennedy, L., Chiasson, S., Van Oorschot, P.: Revisiting password rules: facilitating human management of passwords. In: eCrime Researchers Summit, eCrime 2016, vol. 2016-June, pp. 81–90 (2016). https://doi.org/10.1109/ECRIME.2016.7487945

13. Hussain, T.: Passwords and user behavior. J. Comput. **13**(6), 692–704 (2018). https://doi.org/10.17706/jcp.13.6.692-704

14. Kevin, B.: Hacking For Dummies, 4th edn (2013)

15. Obedur, S.R.: Strategies for password management Master thesis Shazia Rahman Obedur. University of Oslo (2013)

16. Kaplan-Leiserson, E.: People and plans: training's role in homeland security. T+D **57**(9), 66–74 (2003)

17. Nathan, A.J., Scobell, A.: 2020 Data Breach Investigations Report (2020). https://enterprise.verizon.com/resources/reports/2020-data-breach-investigations-report.pdf, https://bfy.tw/HJvH

18. Davidson, A., King, S.: Data breaches continue to rise: how financial institutions can prepare & respond. In: Risk Webinar, pp. 2–3 (2016)

19. Butler, R., Butler, M.: The password practices applied by South African online consumers: perception versus reality. SA J. Inf. Manag. **17**(1), 1–11 (2015). https://doi.org/10.4102/sajim.v17i1.638

20. Florêncio, D., Herley, C., Van Oorschot, P.: An administrator's guide to internet password research. In: 28th Large Installation System Administration Conference (LISA 2014), pp. 35–52 (2014)

21. Kelley, P.G., et al.: Guess again (and again and again): measuring password strength by simulating password-cracking algorithms. In: Proceedings - IEEE Symposium on Security and Privacy, pp. 523–537 (2012). https://doi.org/10.1109/SP.2012.38
22. Komanduri, S., Shay, R., Cranor, L.F., Herley, C., Schechter, S.: Telepathwords: preventing weak passwords by reading users' minds. In: Proceedings of 23rd USENIX Security Symposium, pp. 591–606 (2014)
23. Hicock, R.: Microsoft Password Guidance (2016)
24. Julisch, K.: Understanding and overcoming cyber security anti-patterns. Comput. Net. **57**(10), 2206–2211 (2013). https://doi.org/10.1016/j.comnet.2012.11.023
25. Toulouse, S.: On changing password guidance: a good first step from Microsoft. Leviathan Security Group (2017)
26. Herley, C.: So long, and no thanks for the externalities: the rational rejection of security advice by users (2009)
27. Stajano, F., Mjølsnes, S.F., Jenkinson, G., Thorsheim, P. (eds.): PASSWORDS 2015. LNCS, vol. 9551. Springer, Cham (2016). https://doi.org/10.1007/978-3-319-29938-9
28. Tam, L., Glassman, M., Vandenwauver, M.: The psychology of password management: a tradeoff between security and convenience. Behav. Inf. Technol. **29**(3), 233–244 (2010). https://doi.org/10.1080/01449290903121386
29. Veras, R., Collins, C., Veras, R., Thorpe, J., Collins, C.: Visualizing semantics in passwords : the role of dates. In: Proceedings of 9th International Symposium on Visualization for Cyber Security, pp. 88–95 (2012). https://doi.org/10.1145/2379690.2379702
30. Adams, A., Sasse, M.A., Lunt, P.: Making passwords secure and usable. People Comput. **34**(1), 1–15 (1997). https://doi.org/10.1145/99977.99993
31. Adams, A., Sasse, M.A.: Users are not the enemy. Commun. ACM **42**(12), 40–46 (1999). https://doi.org/10.1145/322796.322806
32. Stobertm E., Biddle, R.: The password life cycle: user behaviour in managing passwords. In: Proceedings of 10th Symposium on Usable Privacy and Security – (SOUPS 2014), pp. 243–255 (2014)
33. Weirich, D., Sasse, M.A.: Pretty good persuasion: a first step towards effective password security in the real world. In: Proceedings of the New Security Paradigms Workshops – NSPW 2001, pp. 137–143 (2001). https://doi.org/10.1145/508171.508195
34. Porter, S.N.: A password extension for improved human factors. Comput. Secur. **1**(1), 54–56 (1982)
35. Khatib, R., Barki, H.: An activity theory approach to information security non-compliance. Inf. Comput. Secur. **28**(4), 485–501 (2020). https://doi.org/10.1108/ICS-11-2018-0128
36. Joudaki, Z., Thorpe, J., Vargas Martin, M.: Enhanced tacit secrets: system-assigned passwords you can't write down, but don't need to. Int. J. Inf. Secur. **18**(2), 239–255 (2019). https://doi.org/10.1007/s10207-018-0408-2
37. Grawemeyer, B., Johnson, H.: Using and managing multiple passwords: a week to a view. Interact. Comput. **23**(3), 256–267 (2011). https://doi.org/10.1016/j.intcom.2011.03.007
38. Notoatmodjo, G., Thomborson, C.: Passwords and perceptions. Conf. Res. Pract. Inf. Technol. Ser. **98**, 71–78 (2009)
39. Ives, B.B., Walsh, K.R.: The domino effect of password reuse. Commun. ACM **47**(4), 75–78 (2004)
40. Rainer, R.K., Jr., Marshall, T.E., Knapp, K.J., Montgomery, G.H.: Do information security professionals and business managers view information security issues differently? Inf. Syst. Secur. **16**, 100–108 (2007). https://doi.org/10.1080/10658980701260579
41. Shay, R., et al.: Encountering stronger password requirements: user attitudes and behaviors. In: Proceedings of the Sixth Symposium on Usable Privacy and Security, 1–20 July 2010. https://doi.org/10.1145/1837110.1837113

42. Koppell, R., Blythe, J., Kothari, V., Smith, S.: Beliefs about cybersecurity rules and passwords: a comparison of two survey samples of cybersecurity professionals versus regular users. In: Proceedings of 12th Symposium on Usable Privacy and Security (SOUPS 2016) (2016). https://www.usenix.org/conference/soups2016/workshop-program/wsf/presentation/koppel
43. Kothari, V., Blythe, J., Smith, S., Koppell, R.: Measuring the security impacts of password policies using cognitive behavioral agent-based modeling. In: Proceedings of the 2015 Symposium and Bootcamp on the Science of Security, pp. 1–9 (2015)

Author Index

Printed in the United States
by Baker & Taylor Publisher Services